MEMORY OF FIRE

By the same author:

Memory of Fire: I. Genesis

Memory of Fire: II. Faces and Masks

Eduardo Galeano

MEMORY OF FIRE

III. CENTURY OF THE WIND

Part Three of a Trilogy

Translated
by Cedric Belfrage

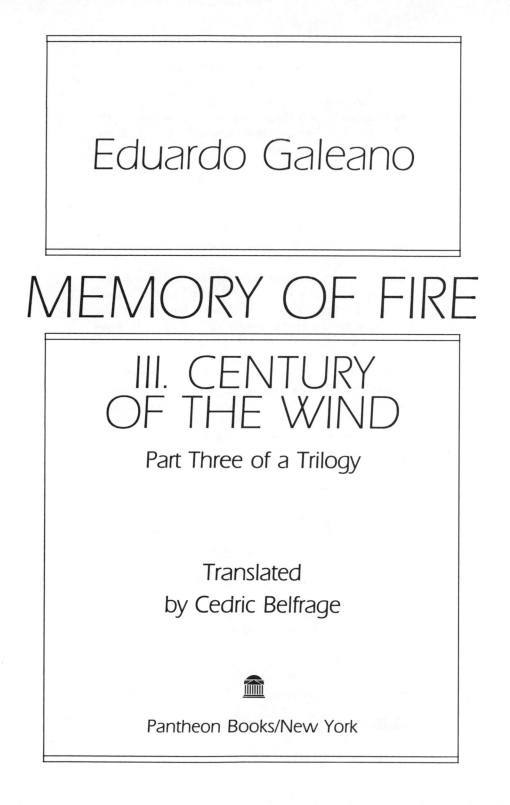

Pantheon Books/New York

Translator's Acknowledgments

To Monica Weiss, and all the wonderful young people who formed a human word-processor to get this on paper; and above all to Fernando Molina, who back-stopped the work of all three volumes.

First American Edition
Translation copyright © 1988 by Cedric Belfrage

Originally published in 1986 in Spain as *Memoria del fuego III: El siglo del viento* by Siglo Veintiuno de España Editores, S.A. Copyright © 1986 by Siglo XXI de España Editores, S.A.; copyright © 1986 by Siglo XXI Editores, S.A.; copyright © 1986 by Catálogos, S.R.L.; copyright © 1986 by Eduardo Galeano.

Library of Congress Cataloging-in-Publication Data

Galeano, Eduardo H., 1940–
  Memory of fire.
  Translation of: Memoria del fuego.
  Includes bibliographies.
  Contents: 1. Genesis—2. Faces and masks—
3. Century of the wind.
  1. Latin America—History—Anecdotes, facetiae,
satire, etc. 2. America—History—Anecdotes, facetiae,
satire, etc. I. Title.
F1408.27.G3413   1985   85-42866
ISBN 0-394-55361-6 (v. 3)
ISBN 0-394-75726-2 (pbk. : v. 3)

Manufactured in the United States of America

Text design by Marsha Cohen

Contents

Preface

This Book

is the last volume of the trilogy *Memory of Fire*. It is not an anthology but a literary creation, based on solid documentation but moving with complete freedom. The author does not know to what literary form the book belongs: narrative, essay, epic poem, chronicle, testimony . . . Perhaps it belongs to all or to none. The author relates what has happened, the history of America, and above all, the history of Latin America; and he has sought to do it in such a way that the reader should feel that what has happened happens again when the author tells it.

At the head of each text is given the year and place of each episode, except in certain texts which cannot be situated in any specific moment or place. At the foot, the numbers show the chief works the author has consulted in search of information and reference points. The absence of numbers shows that in that particular case the author has consulted no written source, or that he obtained his raw material from general information in periodicals or from the mouths of protagonists or witnesses. The sources consulted are listed at the end of the book.

Literal transcriptions are italicized.

Acknowledgments

To Helena Villagra, who helped so much at each stage of the work. Without her, *Memory of Fire* would not have been possible;

To the friends whose contributions were gratefully acknowledged in the previous volumes, and who also helped here with sources, trails, and suggestions;

To Alfredo Ahuerma, Susan Bergholz, Leonardo Cáceres, Rafael Cartay, Alfredo Cedeño, Rosa del Olmo, Enrique Fierro, César Galeano, Horacio García, Sergius Gonzaga, Berta and Fernanda Navarro, Eric Nepomuceno, David Sánchez-Juliao, Andrés Soliz Rada, and Julio Valle-Castillo, who provided access to the necessary bibliography;

To Jorge Enrique Adoum, Pepe Barrientos, Álvaro Barros-Lémez, Jean-

Paul Borel, Rogelio García Lupo, Mauricio Gatti, Juan Gelman, Santiago Kovadloff, Ole Østergaard, Rami Rodríguez, Miguel Rojas-Mix, Nicole Rouan, Pilar Royo, José María Valverde, and Daniel Vidart, who read the drafts with Chinese patience.

This book

is dedicated to Mariana, the Little Flea.

and clawing ourselves out of the wind with our fingernails

—Juan Rulfo

1900: San José de Gracia
The World Goes On

There were some who spent the savings of several generations on one last spree. Many insulted those they couldn't afford to insult and kissed those they shouldn't have kissed. No one wanted to end up without confession. The parish priest gave preference to the pregnant and to new mothers. This self-denying cleric lasted three days and three nights in the confessional before fainting from an indigestion of sins.

When midnight came on the last day of the century, all the inhabitants of San José de Gracia prepared to die clean. God had accumulated much wrath since the creation of the world, and no one doubted that the time had come for the final blowout. Breath held, eyes closed, teeth clenched, the people listened to the twelve chimes of the church clock, one after the other, deeply convinced that there would be no afterwards.

But there was. For quite a while the twentieth century has been on its way; it forges ahead as if nothing had happened. The inhabitants of San José de Gracia continue in the same houses, living and surviving among the same mountains of central Mexico—to the disenchantment of the devout who were expecting Paradise, and to the relief of sinners, who find that this little village isn't so bad after all, if one makes comparisons.

(200)*

1900: West Orange, New Jersey
Edison

Through his inventions the new century receives light and music.

Everyday life bears the seal of Thomas Alva Edison. His electric lamp illumines the nights and his phonograph preserves and diffuses the voices of the world, no longer to be lost. People talk by telephone thanks to the microphone he has added to Bell's invention, and pictures move by virtue of the projecting apparatus with which he completed the work of the Lumière brothers.

* The numbers at the foot of each item refer to the documentary sources consulted by the author, listed on pages 281–301.

In the patent office they clutch their heads when they see him coming. Not for a single moment has this multiplier of human powers stopped inventing, a tireless creator ever since that distant time when he sold newspapers on trains, and one fine day decided he could make them as well as sell them—then set his hand to the task.

(99 and 148)

1900: Montevideo
Rodó

The Master, the talking statue, sends forth his sermon to the youth of America.

José Enrique Rodó vindicates ethereal Ariel, the pure spirit against savage Caliban, the brute who wants to eat. The century being born is the time of anybodies. The people want democracy and trade unions; and Rodó warns that the barbarous multitude can scale the heights of the kingdom of the spirit where superior beings dwell. The intellectual chosen by the gods, the great immortal man, fights in defense of private property in culture.

Rodó also attacks North American civilization, rooted in vulgarity and utilitarianism. To it he opposes the Spanish aristocratic tradition which scorns practical sense, manual labor, technology, and other mediocrities.

(273, 360, and 386)

1901: New York
This is America,
to the South There's Nothing

For 250 million dollars Andrew Carnegie sells the steel monopoly to banker John Pierpont Morgan, master of General Electric, who thereupon founds the United States Steel Corporation. A fever of consumption, a vertigo of money cascading from the tops of skyscrapers: the United States belongs to the monopolies, and the monopolies to a handful of men; but multitudes of workers flock here from Europe, year after year, lured by the factory sirens, and sleeping on deck they dream of becoming millionaires as soon as they jump onto the New

York piers. In the industrial era, El Dorado is the United States; and the United States is America.

To the south, the other America hasn't yet managed to mumble its own name. A recently published report states that *all* the countries of this sub-America have commercial treaties with the United States, England, France, and Germany—but *none* has any with its neighbors. Latin America is an archipelago of idiot countries, organized for separation, and trained to dislike each other.

(113 and 289)

1901: In All Latin America
Processions Greet the Birth of the Century

In the villages and cities south of the Rio Grande, Jesus Christ marches to the cemeteries, a dying beast lustrous with blood, and behind him with torches and hymns comes the crowd, tattered, battered people afflicted with a thousand ills that no doctor or faith-healer would know how to cure, but deserving a fate that no prophet or fortuneteller could possibly divine.

1901: Amiens
Verne

Twenty years ago Alberto Santos Dumont read Jules Verne. Reading him, he had fled from his house, from Brazil, and from the world, until, sailing through the sky from cloud to cloud, he decided to live entirely on air.

Now Santos Dumont defies wind and the law of gravity. The Brazilian aeronaut invents a dirigible balloon, master of its own course, that does not drift, that will not get lost in the high seas or over the Russian Steppe or at the North Pole. Equipped with motor, propeller, and rudder, Santos Dumont rises into the air, makes a complete circuit of the Eiffel Tower, and lands at the announced spot, against the wind, before an applauding crowd.

Then he journeys to Amiens, to shake the hand of the man who taught him to fly.

Settled in his rocking chair, Jules Verne smooths his big white beard. He takes a shine to this child badly disguised as a gentleman, who calls him *my Captain* and looks at him without blinking.

(144 and 424)

1902: Quetzaltenango
The Government Decides That Reality Doesn't Exist

Drums and trumpets blast in the main plaza of Quetzaltenango, calling the citizenry; but all anyone can hear is the terrifying thunder of the Santa María volcano in full eruption.

At the top of his voice the town crier reads the proclamation of the sovereign government. More than a hundred towns in this section of Guatemala are being destroyed by avalanches of lava and mud and an endless rain of ashes while the town crier, protecting himself as best he can, performs his duty. The Santa María volcano shakes the ground beneath his feet and bombards his head with stones. At noon there is total night. In the blackout nothing can be seen but the volcano's vomit of fire. The town crier yells desperately, reading the proclamation by the shaky light of a lantern.

The proclamation, signed by President Manuel Estrada Cabrera, informs the populace that the Santa María volcano is quiet, that all of Guatemala's volcanos are quiet, that the earthquake is occurring far from here in some part of Mexico, and that, the situation being normal, there is no reason not to celebrate the feast of the goddess Minerva, which will take place today in the capital despite the nasty rumors being spread by the enemies of order.

(28)

1902: Guatemala City
Estrada Cabrera

In the city of Quetzaltenango, Manuel Estrada Cabrera had for many years exercised *the august priesthood of the Law in the majestic temple of Justice upon the immovable rock of Truth.* When he got through stripping the province, the doctor came to the capital, where he brought his political career to a happy culmination, pistol in hand, assaulting the presidency of Guatemala.

Since then he has reestablished throughout the country the use of stocks, whips, and gallows. Now Indians pick plantations' coffee for nothing, and for nothing bricklayers build jails and barracks.

Almost daily, in a solemn ceremony, President Estrada Cabrera lays the foundation stone of a new school that will never be built. He has conferred on himself the title Educator of Peoples and Protector of Studious Youth, and in homage to himself celebrates each year the colossal feast of the goddess Minerva. In his Parthenon here, a full-scale replica of the Greek original, poets pluck their lyres as they announce that Guatemala City, the Athens of the New World, has a Pericles.

(28)

1902: Saint Pierre

Only the Condemned Is Saved

On the island of Martinique, too, a volcano explodes. As if splitting the world in two, the mountain Pelée coughs up a huge red cloud that covers the sky and falls, glowing, over the earth. In a wink the city of Saint Pierre is annihilated. Its thirty-four thousand inhabitants disappear—except one.

The survivor is Ludger Sylbaris, the only prisoner in the city. The walls of the jail had been made escape-proof.

(188)

1903: Panama City

The Panama Canal

The passage between the oceans had obsessed the conquistadors. Furiously they sought and finally found it, too far south, down by remote, glacial Tierra del Fuego. But when someone suggested opening the narrow waist of Central America, King Philip II quickly squelched it: he forbade excavation of a canal on pain of death, because *what God hath joined let no man put asunder.*

Three centuries later a French concern, the Universal Inter-Oceanic Canal Company, began the work in Panama, but after thirty-three kilometers crashed noisily into bankruptcy.

Now the United States has decided to complete the canal, and hang on to it, too. There is one hitch: Colombia doesn't agree, and Panama is a province of Colombia. In Washington, Senator Hanna advises waiting it out, *due to the nature of the beast we are dealing with*, but President Teddy Roosevelt doesn't believe in patience. He sends in the Marines. And so, by grace of the United States and its warships, the province becomes an independent state.

(240 and 423)

1903: Panama City
Casualties of This War:
One Chinese, One Burro,

victims of the broadsides of a Colombian gunboat. There are no further misfortunes to lament. Manuel Amador, Panama's brand-new president, parades between U.S. flags, seated in an armchair that the crowd carries on a platform. As he passes, Amador shouts vivas for his colleague Roosevelt.

Two weeks later, in Washington, in the Blue Room of the White House, a treaty is signed granting the United States in perpetuity the half-finished canal and more than fourteen hundred square kilometers of Panamanian territory. Representing the newborn republic is Philippe Bunau-Varilla, commercial magician, political acrobat, French citizen.

(240 and 423)

1903: La Paz
Huilka

The Bolivian liberals have won the war against the conservatives. More accurately, it has been won for them by the Indian army of Pablo Zárate Huilka. The feats claimed by the mustachioed generals were performed by Indians.

Colonel José Manuel Pando, leader of the liberals, had promised Huilka's soldiers freedom from serfdom and recovery of their lands. From battle to battle, as he passed through the villages, Huilka returned stolen lands to the communities and cut the throat of anyone wearing trousers.

With the conservatives defeated, Colonel Pando appoints himself general and president, and, dotting all the *i*'s, proclaims: *"The Indians are inferior beings. Their elimination is not a crime."*

Then he gets on with it. Many are shot. Huilka, yesterday's indispensable ally, he kills several times, by bullet, blade, and rope. Still, on rainy nights, Huilka awaits the president at the gate of the government palace and stares at him, saying nothing, until Pando turns away.

(110 and 475)

1904: Rio de Janeiro
Vaccine

With the slaughter of rats and mosquitos, bubonic plague and yellow fever have been vanquished. Now Oswaldo Cruz declares war on smallpox.

By the thousands Brazilians die of the disease, while doctors bleed the moribund and healers scare off the plague with the smoke of smoldering cowshit. Oswaldo Cruz, in charge of public health, makes vaccination obligatory.

Senator Rui Barbosa, pigeon-chested and smooth-tongued orator, attacks vaccination using juridical weapons flowery with adjectives. In the name of liberty Rui Barbosa defends the right of every individual to be contaminated if he so desires. Torrential applause, thunderous ovations interrupt him from phrase to phrase.

The politicians oppose vaccination. And the doctors. And the journalists. Every newspaper carries choleric editorials and cruel caricatures victimizing Oswaldo Cruz. He cannot show his face on any street without drawing insults and stones.

The whole country closes ranks against vaccination. On all sides, "Down with vaccination!" is heard. Against vaccination the cadets of the military school rise in arms, and just miss overthrowing the president.

(158, 272, 378, and 425)

1905: Montevideo
The Automobile,

that roaring beast, makes its first kill in Montevideo. An innocent pedestrian crossing a downtown street falls and is crushed.

Few automobiles have reached these streets, but as they pass, old ladies cross themselves and people scamper into doorways for protection.

Until not very long ago, the man who thought he was a streetcar still trotted through this motorless city. Going uphill, he would crack his invisible whip, and downhill pull reins that no one could see. At intersections he tooted a horn as imaginary as his horses, as imaginary as his passengers climbing aboard at each stop, as imaginary as the tickets he sold them and the change he received. When the man-streetcar stopped coming, never to pass again, the city found that it missed this endearing lunatic.

(413)

1905: Montevideo
The Decadent Poets

Roberto de las Carreras climbs to the balcony. Pressed to his breast, a bouquet of roses and an incandescent sonnet; awaiting him, not a lovely odalisque, but a gentleman of evil character who fires five shots. Two hit the target. Roberto closes his eyes and muses: *"Tonight I'll sup with the gods."*

He sups not with the gods but with the nurses in the hospital. And a few days later this handsome Satan reappears perfidiously strolling down Sarandí Street, he who has vowed to corrupt all the married and engaged women in Montevideo. His red vest looks very chic decorated with two bulletholes. And on the title page of his latest book, *Funereal Diadem*, appears a drop of blood.

Another son of Byron and Aphrodite is Julio Herrera y Reissig, who calls the foul attic in which he writes and recites the Tower of Panoramas. The two have long been at odds over the theft of a metaphor, but both fight the same war against hypocritical, pre-Colum-bian Monte-idioto, which in the department of aphrodisiacs has progressed no further than egg yolks mixed with grape wine, and in the department of literature—the less said the better.

(284 and 389)

1905: Ilopango
Miguel at One Week

Señorita Santos Mármol, unrespectably pregnant, refuses to name the author of her dishonor. Her mother, Doña Tomasa, beats her out of the house. Doña Tomasa, widow of a man who was poor but white, suspects the worst.

When the baby is born, the spurned señorita brings it in her arms: *"This is your grandson, Mama."*

Doña Tomasa lets out a fearful scream at the sight of the baby, a blue spider, a thick-lipped Indian, such an ugly little thing as to arouse anger more than pity, and slams the door, boom, in her daughter's face.

On the doorstep Señorita Santos falls in a heap. Beneath his unconscious mother the baby seems dead. But when the neighbors haul him out, the squashed newcomer raises a tremendous howl.

And so occurs the second birth of Miguel Mármol, age one week.

(126)

1906: Paris
Santos Dumont

Five years after creating his dirigible balloon, the Brazilian Santos Dumont invents the airplane.

He has spent these five years shut up in hangars, assembling and dismantling enormous iron and bamboo Things which are born and unborn at top speed around the clock: at night they go to bed equipped with seagull wings and fish fins, and wake up transformed into dragonflies or wild ducks. On these Things Santos Dumont wants to get off the earth, which tenaciously holds him back; he collides and crashes; he has fires, tailspins, and shipwrecks; he survives by sheer stubbornness. But he fights and fights until at last he makes one of the Things into an airplane or magic carpet that soars high into the sky.

The whole world wants to meet the hero of this immense feat, king of the air, master of the winds, who is four feet tall, talks in a whisper, and weighs no more than a fly.

(144 and 424)

1907: Sagua la Grande
Lam

In the first heat of this warm morning, the little boy wakes and sees. The world is on its back and whirling; and in that vertigo a desperate bat circles, chasing its own shadow. The black shadow retreats to the wall as the bat approaches, beating at it with a wing.

The little boy jumps up, covering his head with his hands, and collides with a big mirror. In the mirror he sees nobody, or someone else. Turning, he recognizes in the open closet the decapitated clothes of his Chinese father and his black grandfather.

Somewhere in the morning a blank sheet of paper awaits him. But this Cuban boy, this frenzy called Wilfredo Lam, still cannot draw his own lost shadow, which revolves crazily in the hallucinating world above him, having not yet discovered his dazzling way of exorcising fear.

(319)

1907: Iquique
The Flags of Many Countries

head the march of the striking nitrate workers across the gravelly desert of northern Chile—thousands of them and their thousands of women and children—marching on the port of Iquique, chanting slogans and songs. When the workers occupy Iquique the Interior Minister sends an order to kill. The workers decide to stick it out. Not a stone is to be thrown.

José Briggs, leader of the strike, is the son of a North American, but refuses to seek protection from the U.S. consul. The consul of Peru tries to save the Peruvian workers, but they won't abandon their Chilean comrades. The consul of Bolivia tries to lure away the Bolivian workers. The Bolivian workers say: *"With the Chileans we live, and with the Chileans we die."*

General Roberto Silva Renard's machineguns and rifles cut down the unarmed strikers and leave a blanket of bodies. Interior Minister Rafael Sotomayor justifies the carnage in the name of *the most sacred things*, which are, in order of importance, *property, public order, and life.*

(64 and 326)

1907: Rio Batalha

Nimuendajú

Curt Unkel was not born Indian, he became one, or discovered that he was one. Years ago he left Germany for Brazil, and in Brazil, in the deepest depths of Brazil, he recognized his people. Now he accompanies the Guaraní Indians as they wander the jungle as pilgrims seeking paradise. He shares their food and shares the joy of sharing food.

High aloft rise their chants. In the dead of night a sacred ceremony is performed. They perforate the lower lip of Curt Unkel, who comes to be known as Nimuendajú: *He who creates his house.*

(316, 374, and 411)

1908: Asunción

Barrett

Perhaps he once lived in Paraguay, centuries or millennia ago—who knows when—and has forgotten it. Certainly four years ago, when by chance or curiosity Rafael Barrett landed here, he felt he had finally reached the place that was waiting for him: this godforsaken place was his place in the world.

Ever since then, on street corners, mounted on a soapbox, he has harangued the people, while publishing articles of revelation and denunciation. In response, the government throws him out. Bayonets shove the young anarchist to the border—deported as a *foreign agitator.*

Most Paraguayan of all Paraguayans, true weed of this soil, true saliva of this mouth, he was born in Asturias, of a Spanish mother and English father, and was educated in Paris.

Barrett's gravest sin, unforgivable violation of a taboo, is to denounce slavery on the maté plantations.

Forty years ago, when the war of extermination against Paraguay ended, the victorious countries in the name of Civilization and Liberty legalized the enslavement of the survivors and the children of the survivors. Since then Argentine and Brazilian landowners count their Paraguayan peons by the head as if they were cows.

(37)

1908: San Andrés de Sotavento

The Government Decides That Indians Don't Exist

The governor, General Miguel Marino Torralvo, issues the order for the oil companies operating on the Colombian coast. *The Indians do not exist*, the governor certifies before a notary and witnesses. Three years ago, Law No. 1905/55, approved in Bogotá by the National Congress, established that Indians did not exist in San Andrés de Sotavento and other Indian communities where oil had suddenly spurted from the ground. Now the governor merely confirms the law. If the Indians existed, they would be illegal. Thus they are consigned to the cemetery or exile.

(160)

1908: San Andrés de Sotavento

Portrait of a Master of Lives and Estates

General Miguel Marino Torralvo, glutton of lands, who tramples on Indians and women, governs these Colombian coastal regions from the back of a horse. With the butt of his whip he strikes faces and doors, and shapes destinies. Those who cross his path kiss his hand. In an impeccable white habit he canters along the roads, always followed by a page on a burro. The page carries his brandy, his boiled water, his shaving kit, and the book in which the general notes the names of the girls he devours.

His properties increase as he rides by. He started out with one cattle farm and now has six. A believer in progress, but not to the exclusion of tradition, he uses barbed wire to set limits to his lands, the stocks to set limits for his people.

(160)

1908: Guanape
Portrait of Another Master of Lives and Estates

He orders: *"Tell him he'd better carry his shroud on the back of his horse."*

He punishes with five shots, for nonperformance of duty, the serf who is late with the bushels of corn he owes, or who makes trouble about delivering a daughter or a plot of land.

"Don't hurry it," he orders. *"Only the last shot should kill."*

Not even his family is spared the wrath of Deogracias Itriago, supreme boss of the Venezuelan valley of Guanape. One night a relative borrows his best horse to go to a dance in style. The next morning Don Deogracias has him tied face down to four stakes, and skins the soles of his feet and his buttocks with a cassava grater to cure him of the urge to dance and show off on someone else's horse.

When in an unguarded moment he is finally killed by some peons he himself had condemned to death, for nine nights the family chants the novena for the dead, and for nine nights the people of Guanape go wild celebrating. No one tires of making merry and no musician wants payment for the marathon.

(410)

1908: Mérida, Yucatán
Curtain Time and After

The train is already disappearing, and the president of Mexico with it. Porfirio Díaz has examined the henequén plantations in Yucatán and is taking away a most favorable impression.

"A beautiful spectacle," he said, as he supped with the bishop and the owners of millions of hectares and thousands of Indians who produce cheap fibers for the International Harvester Company. *"Here one breathes an atmosphere of general happiness."*

The locomotive smoke is scarcely dissipated when the houses of painted cardboard, with their elegant windows, collapse with the slap of a hand. Garlands and pennants become litter, swept up and burned, and the wind undoes with a puff the arches of flowers that spanned the roads. The lightning visit over, the merchants of Mérida repossess the sewing machines, the North American furniture, and the brand-new clothes the slaves have worn while the show lasted.

The slaves are Mayan Indians who until recently lived free in the kingdom of the little talking cross, and Yaqui Indians from the plains of the north, purchased for four hundred pesos a head. They sleep piled up in fortresses of stone and work to the rhythm of a moistened whip. When one of them gets surly, they bury him up to his ears and turn the horses loose on him.

(40, 44, 245, and 451)

1908: Ciudad Juárez
Wanted

A few years ago, at the request of Porfirio Díaz, North American Rangers crossed the border here to crush the striking copper miners of Sonora. Later, the strike in the Veracruz textile plants ended in arrests and executions. Still, strikes have broken out again this year in Coahuila, Chihuahua, and Yucatán.

Striking, which disturbs order, is a crime. Whoever does it commits a crime. The Flores Magón brothers, agitators of the working class, are criminals of the highest order. Their faces are plastered on the wall of the railroad station in Ciudad Juárez as in all stations on both sides of the border. The Furlong detective agency offers a forty-thousand-dollar reward for each of them.

For years, the Flores Magón brothers have flouted the authority of eternal president Porfirio Díaz. In journals and pamphlets they have taught the people to lose respect for him. With respect once lost, the people begin to lose their fear.

(40, 44, and 245)

1908: Caracas

Castro

He shakes hands with just the index finger, because no one is worthy of the other four. Cipriano Castro reigns in Venezuela, his crown a cap with hanging tassel. A fanfare of trumpets, a thunder of applause, and a rustle of bowing shoulders announce his appearance, followed by his retinue of bullies and court jesters. Like Bolívar, Castro is short, quick-tempered, and addicted to dancing and women; and he plays Bolívar when posing for immortality; but Bolívar lost some battles and Castro, Semper Victorious, never.

His dungeons are crammed. He trusts no one, with the exception of Juan Vicente Gómez, his right hand in war and government, who calls him the Greatest Man of Modern Times. Least of all does Castro trust the local medics, who cure leprosy and insanity with a broth of boiled buzzard. Instead he decides to put his ailments in the hands of learned German physicians.

At the port of La Guaira he embarks for Europe. Hardly has the ship cast off when Gómez seizes power.

(193 and 344)

1908: Caracas

Dolls

Every Venezuelan male is a Cipriano Castro to the women who come his way.

A proper señorita serves her father and her brothers as she will serve her husband, and neither does nor says anything without asking permission. If she has money or comes from a good family, she attends early morning Mass, then spends the day learning to give orders to the black staff—cooks, maids, wet nurses, nannies, laundrywomen—and working with needle or bobbin. At times she receives friends, and even goes so far as to recommend some outrageous novel, whispering: "You should have seen how I cried . . ."

Twice a week, in the early evening, seated on a sofa under an aunt's attentive gaze, she spends a few hours listening to her fiancé without looking at him or letting him near. Every night, before bed, she repeats her Ave Marias and, by moonlight, applies to her skin an infusion of jasmine petals steeped in rainwater.

If her fiancé deserts her, she becomes an aunt, condemned forever to clothe saints, corpses, and new babies, watch engaged couples, tend the sick, teach catechism, and spend the night in her solitary bed, sighing over the portrait of her disdainful lover.

(117)

1909: Paris

A Theory of National Impotence

The Bolivian Alcides Arguedas, sent to Paris on a scholarship by Simón Patiño, publishes a new book entitled *Sick People*. The tin king feeds Arguedas so that Arguedas may reveal that the Bolivian people are not just ailing, but incurable.

A while ago another Bolivian thinker, Gabriel René Moreno, discovered that the native and mestizo brains are *cellularly incapable*, and that they weigh from five to seven or even ten ounces less than the brain of the white man. Now Arguedas proclaims that mestizos inherit the worst characteristics of their forebears and this is why the Bolivian people do not want to wash or learn, can't read, only drink, are two-faced, egoistic, lazy, and altogether deplorable. Their thousand and one miseries thus spring from their own nature, not the voracity of their masters. Here is a people condemned by biology and reduced to zoology. Theirs is the bestial fate of the ox: incapable of making his own history, he can only fulfill his destiny. And that destiny, that hopeless disaster, is written not in the stars, but in the blood.

(29 and 473)

1909: New York

Charlotte

What would happen if a woman woke up one morning changed into a man? What if the family were not a training camp where boys learn to command and girls to obey? What if there were daycare for babies, and husbands shared the cleaning and cooking? What if innocence turned into dignity and reason and emotion went arm in arm? What if preachers and newspapers told the truth? And if no one were anyone's property?

So Charlotte Perkins Gilman raves, while the press attacks her, calling her an *unnatural mother*. Yet the fantasies that inhabit her soul and bite at her guts attack her far more fiercely. It is they, those terrible enemies inside, that sometimes bring her down. She falls but recovers, falls and recovers again, some impulse to go forward never abandoning her entirely. This stubborn wayfarer travels tirelessly around the United States, announcing a world upside down.

(195 and 196)

1909: Managua
Inter-American Relations at Work

Philander Knox is a lawyer and a shareholder in the Rosario and Light Mines Company. He is also secretary of state of the United States. The president of Nicaragua, José Santos Zelaya, does not treat the company with due respect. He wants Rosario and Light to pay taxes. Nor does he respect the Church enough. The Holy Mother has judged him to be in sin ever since he expropriated her lands and suppressed tithes and first-fruits and profaned the sacrament of matrimony with a divorce law. So the Church applauds when the United States breaks relations with Nicaragua and Secretary of State Knox sends down some Marines who overthrow President Zelaya and put in his place the accountant of the Rosario and Light Mines Company.

(10 and 56)

1910: Amazon Jungle
The People Eaters

Overnight the price of rubber collapses, and the Amazonian dream of prosperity comes to nothing. With a rude slap the world market abruptly awakens Belém do Pará, Manaos, Iquitos, all the sleeping beauties who lie in the jungle in the shade of the rubber tree. From one day to the next the so-called Land of Tomorrow turns into Never-Never Land, or the Land of Yesterday, abandoned by the merchants who have extracted its sap. The big rubber money flees the Amazon jungle for new Asian plantations which produce better rubber at cheaper prices.

This has been a cannibalistic business. *People eaters* the Indians called the slave hunters who cruised the rivers in search of labor. All that is left of substantial villages is the scraps. The people eaters sent the Indians, bound, to the rubber companies. They sent them in the holds of ships along with other merchandise, appropriately invoiced for sales commissions and freight charges.

(92, 119, and 462)

1910: Rio de Janeiro

The Black Admiral

On board, the order for silence. An officer reads out the sentence. Drums beat furiously as a sailor is flogged for a breach of discipline. On his knees, bound to the deck balustrade, the condemned man receives his punishment before the whole crew. The last of the lashes—two hundred and forty-eight, two hundred and forty-nine, two hundred and fifty—fall upon a flayed body, bathed in blood, unconscious or dead.

Then the mutiny breaks out. In the waters of Guanabara Bay, the sailors rise up. Three officers fall, knifed to death. The warships fly the red ensign. An ordinary seaman is the squadron's new commander. João Cándido, the Black Admiral, leans into the wind on the command tower of his flagship, and the rebel pariahs present arms to him.

At dawn two booming guns wake Rio de Janeiro. The Black Admiral issues a warning: the city is at his mercy. Unless flogging—the custom of the Brazilian fleet—is prohibited and an amnesty granted, he will bombard Rio, leaving no stone upon stone. The mouths of the warships' cannons are pointed at Rio's most important buildings.

"We want an answer now, right now."

The city, in panic, obeys. The government declares the abolition of corporal punishment in the fleet and an amnesty for the rebels. João Cándido removes the red kerchief from his neck and surrenders his sword. The admiral transforms himself back into a sailor.

(303)

1910: Rio de Janeiro

Portrait of Brazil's Most Expensive Lawyer

Six years ago he opposed smallpox vaccination in the name of Liberty. An individual's skin is as inviolable as his conscience, said Rui Barbosa. The State has no right to violate thought or body, not even in the name of public hygiene. Now, he condemns *with all severity the violence and barbarity* of the sailors' rebellion. This illustrious jurist and preeminent legislator opposes flogging but denounces the methods of the flogged. The sailors, he says, did not make their just demand in a civilized way, *by constitutional means, using the proper channels within the framework of prevailing juridical norms.*

Rui Barbosa believes in the law, and bases his belief on erudite quotations from imperial Romans and English liberals. But he doesn't believe in reality. The doctor shows a certain realism only when, at the end of the month, he collects his salary as lawyer for Light and Power, that foreign enterprise which in Brazil exercises more power than God.

(272 and 303)

1910: Rio de Janeiro

Reality and the Law Seldom Meet

in this country of legally free slaves, and when they do they don't shake hands. The ink is still fresh on the laws that put an end to the sailors' revolt when the officers resume flogging and kill the recently amnestied rebels. Many sailors are shot on the high seas; others are buried alive in the catacombs of Cobra Island, called the Isle of Despair, where they are thrown quicklimed water when they complain of thirst.

The Black Admiral ends up in a lunatic asylum.

(303)

1910: Mauricio Colony
Tolstoy

Exiled for being poor and a Jew, Isaac Zimmerman ends up in Argentina. The first time he sees a maté cup he takes it for an inkpot, the straw for a pen, and that pen burns his hand. On this pampa he built his hut, not far from the huts of other pilgrims, exiles like him from the valleys of the Dniester River; and here he produces children and crops.

Isaac and his wife have very little, almost nothing, and the little they have they possess graciously. Some vegetable crates serve as a table, but the tablecloth is always starched and very white, and on it flowers lend color, and apples perfume.

One night the children come upon Isaac collapsed at this table, his head buried in his hands. By the candle's light they see his face glistening with tears. And he tells them. By sheer accident, he says, he has just learned that over there, on the far side of the world, Leo Tolstoy has died. And he explains who this old friend of the peasants was, this man who knew how to portray his time so grandly and to foretell another.

(155)

1910: Havana
The Cinema

Ladder on shoulder, the lamplighter goes on his way. With his long pole he lights the wicks, so that people can walk without tripping through the streets of Havana.

The messenger goes by bicycle. Under his arm he carries rolls of film from one cinema to another, so that people may walk without tripping through other worlds and other times and float high in the sky with a girl seated on a star.

This city has two halls consecrated to the greatest marvel of modern life. Both offer the same films. When the messenger dawdles with the rolls, the pianist will entertain the audience with waltzes and dance tunes, or the usher will recite selected fragments from *Don Juan Tenorio*. But the audience bites its nails waiting for the femme fatale with the bedroom circles under her eyes to dazzle in the darkness, or for the knights in coats of mail to gallop at epileptic speed toward the castle wreathed in mist.

The cinema robs the public of the circus. No longer does the crowd queue up to see the mustachioed lion-tamer or Lovely Geraldine, sheathed in sequins, glittering erect on the horse with enormous haunches. The puppeteers, too, abandon Havana to wander the beaches and villages, and the gypsies who read fortunes depart along with the sad bear that dances to the rhythm of the tambourine, with the goat that gyrates on a stool, with the gaunt acrobats in their checkered costumes. All quit Havana because people no longer throw them pennies of admiration, but only of pity.

No one can compete with the cinema. The cinema is more miraculous than the water of Lourdes. Stomach chills are cured by Ceylon cinnamon; colds by parsley; everything else by the cinema.

(292)

1910: Mexico City
The Centennial and Love

Celebrating a hundred years of Mexico's independence, all of the capital's whorehouses display the portrait of President Porfirio Díaz.

In Mexico City, out of every ten young women, two engage in prostitution. Peace and Order, Order and Progress: the law regulates the practice of this crowded profession. The brothel law, promulgated by Don Porfirio himself, prohibits carnal commerce without the proper façade, or in the proximity of schools and churches. It also prohibits the mixing of social classes—*In the brothels there shall only be women of the class to which the customers belong*—while it imposes all sorts of sanitary controls and penalties, and even obliges the madams *to prevent their pupils from going into the streets in groups that might attract attention.* They are allowed to go out singly: condemned to exist between bed, hospital, and jail, the whores at least have the right to an occasional stroll through the city. In this sense, they are better off than the Indians. By order of the almost pure Mixtec Indian president, Indians may not walk on the principal avenues or sit in public plazas.

(300)

1910: Mexico City

The Centennial and Food

The Centennial is inaugurated with a banquet of French *haute cuisine* in the salons of the National Palace. Three hundred and fifty waiters serve dishes prepared by forty chefs and sixty assistants under the direction of the renowned Sylvain Daumont.

Elegant Mexicans eat in French. They prefer the *crêpe* to its poor relation of native birth, the corn tortilla; *oeufs en cocotte* to the humble rancheros. They find *béchamel* sauce more worthy than guacamole, that delicious but excessively indigenous mixture of avocados, tomatoes, and chili. Faced with foreign peppers or Mexican chilies, the gentry reject the chili, although later they sneak back to the family kitchen and devour it secretly, ground or whole, side dish or main dish, stuffed or plain, unpeeled or naked.

(318)

1910: Mexico City

The Centennial and Art

Mexico celebrates its national fiesta with a great exhibition of Spanish art, brought from Madrid. To give these Spanish artists the presentation they deserve, Don Porfirio has built a special pavilion for them in the city center.

In Mexico, even the stones for building the post office come from Europe, like all that is considered worthwhile. From Italy, France, Spain, or England come construction materials and architects, or when money is lacking for imported architects, native architects undertake to put up houses just like those of Rome, Paris, Madrid, or London. Meanwhile, Mexican artists paint ecstatic Virgins, plump Cupids, and high-society ladies in the European mode of half a century ago, and sculptors entitle their monumental marbles and bronzes *Malgré Tout, Désespoir, Après l'Orgie*.

Beyond the boundaries of official art, far removed from its star performers, the genius engraver José Guadalupe Posada strips naked his country and his time. No critic takes him seriously. He has no pupils, although two young artists have been following him since they were children. José Clemente Orozco and Diego Rivera haunt Po-

sada's little workshop and watch him labor, with devotion as if at a
Mass, as the metal shavings fall to the floor at the passage of the burin
over the plates.

(44 and 47)

1910: Mexico City
The Centennial and the Dictator

At the height of the Centennial celebrations, Don Porfirio opens a
mental asylum. Soon afterward he lays the foundation stone for a new
jail.

Don Porfirio is decorated from his paunch up to his plumed head,
which reigns above a cloud of top-hats and imperial helmets. His
courtiers, rheumatic antiques in frock coats and gaiters, with flowers
in their buttonholes, dance to the strains of "Long Live My Misery,"
the latest hit waltz. An orchestra of a hundred and fifty musicians
plays beneath thirty thousand electric stars in the National Palace's
grand ballroom.

The festivities last a whole month. Don Porfirio, eight times
reelected by himself, makes one of these balls the occasion for
announcing the imminence of his ninth term, while conferring ninety-
nine-year concessions of copper, oil, and land on Morgan, Guggen-
heim, Rockefeller, and Hearst. For more than thirty years the deaf,
rigid dictator has administered the largest tropical territory of the
United States.

On one of these nights, at the peak of this patriotic binge, Halley's
Comet bursts into the sky. Panic spreads. The press announces that
the comet will stick its tail into Mexico and set everything on fire.

(40, 44, and 391)

1911: Anenecuilco
Zapata

He was born in the saddle, a rider and breaker-in of horses. He
navigates the countryside on horseback, careful not to disturb the
deep sleep of the earth. Emiliano Zapata is a man of silences, someone
who talks by keeping quiet.

The campesinos of his village Anenecuilco, little palm-thatched adobe houses peppered over a hill, have made Zapata their leader, entrusting him with papers from the time of the viceroys. The bundle of documents proves that this community, rooted here from the beginning, is no intruder on its own land.

Anenecuilco is being strangled, like all the other communities in the Mexican region of Morelos. There are ever fewer islands of corn in an ocean of sugar. Of the village of Tequesquitengo, condemned to die because its free Indians refused to become a gang of peons, nothing remains but the church-tower cross. The immense plantations advance, swallowing up land, water, and woods. They leave no room even to bury the dead.

"If they want to plant, let them plant in pots."

Gunmen and conmen see to the actual plundering while the consumers of communities hold concerts in their gardens and breed polo ponies and pedigreed dogs.

Zapata, leader of the enslaved villagers, buries the viceregal land titles under the Anenecuilco church floor and throws himself into the struggle. His troops of Indians, well turned out and well mounted, if badly armed, grows as it goes.

(468)

1911: Mexico City
Madero

Meanwhile, the whole of the north is rising behind Francisco Madero; and after thirty continuous years on the throne, Porfirio Díaz collapses in a few months.

Madero, the new president, is a virtuous son of the liberal Constitution. He wants to save Mexico by judicial reform, while Zapata demands agrarian reform. Confronting the clamor of the campesinos, the new deputies promise to study their misery.

(44 and 194)

1911: The Fields of Chihuahua
Pancho Villa

Of all the northern leaders who have raised Madero to the presidency, Pancho Villa is the most loved and loving.

He likes to get married and keeps on doing it. Pistol to head, there is no priest who balks nor girl who resists. He also likes to dance the *tapatío* to the strains of the marimba, and to get into shoot-outs. Bullets bounce off his sombrero like raindrops.

He took to the desert early on: *"For me the war began when I was born."* He was little more than a child when he avenged his sister. Of the many deaths notched up since, the first was that of his boss, leaving him little choice but to become a horse thief.

He was born as Doroteo Arango. Pancho Villa was someone else entirely—a gang compañero, a friend, the best of friends. When the Rural Guards killed the real Pancho Villa, Doroteo Arango took his name and kept it. Against death and forgetting, he began calling himself Pancho Villa, so that his friend should continue to be.

(206)

1911: Machu Picchu
The Last Sanctuary of the Incas

isn't dead; it only sleeps. For centuries the Urubamba River, foaming and roaring, has exhaled its potent breath against these sacred stones, covering them with a blanket of dense jungle to guard their sleep. Thus has the last bastion of the Incas, the last foothold of the Indian kings of Peru, been kept secret.

Among snow mountains which appear on no maps, a North American archeologist, Hiram Bingham, stumbles upon Machu Picchu. A child of the region leads him by the hand over precipices to the lofty throne veiled by clouds and greenery. There, Bingham finds the white stones still alive beneath the verdure, and reveals them, awakened, to the world.

(53 and 453)

1912: Quito
Alfaro

A tall woman, dressed all in black, curses President Alfaro as she plunges a dagger into his corpse. Then she raises, on the point of a stick, a flaming banner, the bloody rag of his shirt.

Behind the woman in black march the avengers of Holy Mother Church. With ropes tied to his feet they drag away the nude body. Flowers rain from windows. Saint-eating, host-swallowing, gossipy old women cry *"Long live religion!"* The cobbled streets run with blood which the dogs can never lick away nor the rain wash off. The butchery ends in flames. A great bonfire is lit, and on it they throw what remains of old Alfaro. Then gunmen and thugs, hired by the landed gentry, stamp on his ashes.

Eloy Alfaro had dared to expropriate the lands of the Church, owner of much of Ecuador, and used the rents to create schools and hospitals. A friend of God but not of the Pope, he had legalized divorce and freed Indians jailed for debt. No one was so hated by the surpliced, nor so feared by the frock-coated.

Night falls. The air of Quito reeks of burned flesh. As on every Sunday, the military band plays waltzes and *pasillos* in the Grand Plaza bandstand.

(12, 24, 265, and 332)

Sad Verses from the Ecuadoran Songbook

Don't come near, anyone,
Stand aside or go.
My disease is contagious,
I'm full of woe.

I'm alone, born alone,
Of a mother forlorn,
All alone I stay,
A feather in a storm.

Why should a painted house
Make a blind man sing?
What are balconies to the street,
If he can't see a thing?

(294)

1912: Cantón Santa Ana
Chronicle of the Customs of Manabí

Eloy Alfaro was born on the coast of Ecuador, in the province of Manabí. In that hot land, region of insolence and violence, no one paid the least attention to his recent divorce law, pushed through against wind and tide. Here, it's simpler to become a widower than to get caught up in red tape. On the bed where two go to sleep, sometimes only one wakes up. Manabís are famous for short tempers, no money, and big hearts.

Martín Vera was a rare Manabí. His knife had rusted from remaining so long in its sheath. When the neighbors' hog invaded his little garden and ate his manioc plants, Martín went to talk to them, the Rosados, and asked them nicely to shut the creature in. On the second occasion, Martín offered to repair the rickety walls of the Rosados' pigsty for nothing. But the third time, as the hog romped about in his garden, Martín took a shot at it with his gun. Round as it was, the baneful animal fell flat. The Rosados hauled it back to their property to give it a porcine burial.

The Veras and the Rosados stopped greeting each other. Some days later, the executioner of the hog was crossing the Calvo cliffs, holding on to the mane of his mule, when a bullet left him hanging from one stirrup. The mule dragged Martín Vera home, too late for any kneeling woman to help him to a decent death.

The Rosados fled. When Martín's children hunted them down in an empty convent near Colimas, they lit a fire around the place. The Rosados, thirty in all, had to choose death. Some expired by fire, burnt to a crisp; others by bullet, riddled like colanders.

This happened a year ago. Now, the jungle has devoured the gardens of both families, leaving only a no-man's-land.

(226)

1912: Pajeú de Flores

Family Wars

In the deserts of northeast Brazil the elite inherit land and hatred: sad land, land dying of thirst; and hatred, which relatives perpetuate from generation to generation, vengeance to vengeance, forever and a day. In Ceará there is eternal war between the Cunha family and the Pataca family, and the Monteses and the Faitosas practice mutual extermination. In Paraíba it is the Dantases and the Nóbregases who kill each other. In Pernambuco, in the Pajeú River region, every newly born Pereira receives from his parents and godparents the order to hunt down his Carvalho; and every Carvalho comes into the world prepared to liquidate his Pereira.

Today, Virgulino da Silva Pereira, known as Lampião, fires his first shots at a Carvalho. Though still a child, he automatically becomes an outlaw, a *cangaceiro*. Life is not worth much around here, where the only hospital is the cemetery. If Lampião were the child of the rich, he would not have to kill on others' account; he would have it done for him.

(343)

1912: Daiquirí
Daily Life in the Caribbean: An Invasion

The Platt Amendment, handiwork of Senator Platt of Connecticut, is the passkey that the United States uses to enter Cuba at any hour. The amendment, part of the Cuban Constitution, authorizes the United States to invade and stand fast, and gives it the power to decide who is or is not a proper president for Cuba.

The current proper president, Mario García Menocal, who also presides over the Cuban American Sugar Company, applies the Platt Amendment, calling in the Marines to put unrest to rest. Too many blacks are in revolt, and none of them has a high enough opinion of private property. Two warships steam in and the Marines land on the beach at Daiquirí to protect the iron and copper mines of the Spanish American and Cuban Copper companies, threatened by black wrath, and the sugar mills all along the Guantánamo and Western Railroad tracks.

(208 and 241)

1912: Niquinohomo
Daily Life in Central America:
Another Invasion

Nicaragua pays the United States a colossal indemnity for *moral damages*, inflicted by fallen president Zelaya when he committed the grave offense of trying to impose taxes on North American companies.

As Nicaragua lacks funds, U.S. bankers lend the necessary monies to pay the indemnity, and since Nicaragua lacks guarantees, U.S. Secretary of State Philander Knox sends back the Marines to take charge of customs houses, national banks, and railroads.

Benjamin Zeledón heads the resistance. The chief of the patriots has a fresh-looking face and startled eyes. The invaders cannot bribe him because Zeledón spits on money, so they defeat him by treachery.

Augusto César Sandino, a no-account peon from a no-account village, sees Zeledón's corpse pass by, dragged through the dust, hands and feet bound to the saddle of a drunken invader.

(10 and 56)

1912: Mexico City

Huerta

looks like a malignant corpse. His shiny dark glasses are all that seem alive in his face.

Veteran bodyguard of Porfirio Díaz, Victoriano Huerta converted to democracy on the day the dictatorship fell. Now he is President Madero's right-hand man, and has dedicated himself to hunting down revolutionaries. In the north he catches Pancho Villa, in the south Zapata's lieutenant, Gildardo Magaña, and orders them shot. The firing squad are stroking their triggers when the presidential pardon interrupts the ceremony. *"Death came for me,"* sighs Villa, *"but missed the appointment."*

The resuscitated pair end up in the same cell in Tlatelolco prison. They pass days, months, chatting. Magaña talks of Zapata, of his plan for agrarian reform, and of Madero, who turns a deaf ear, so eager is he to offend neither campesinos nor landlords, *riding two horses at once.*

A small blackboard and a few books arrive. Pancho Villa knows how to read people, but not letters. Magaña teaches him, and together they enter, word by word, sword-thrust by sword-thrust, the castles of *The Three Musketeers*. Then they start the journey through *Don Quixote de la Mancha*, crazy roads of old Spain; and Pancho Villa, fierce warrior of the desert, strokes the pages with the hand of a lover.

Magaña tells him: *"This book . . . You know? A jailbird wrote it. One of us."*

(194 and 206)

1913: Mexico City
An Eighteen-Cent Rope

President Madero imposes a tax, a tiny tax, on the heretofore un-
touched oil companies, and North American ambassador Henry Lane
Wilson threatens invasion. Several warships are heading for the ports
of Mexico, announces the ambassador, while General Huerta rebels
and his troops bombard the National Palace.

The fate of Mexico is discussed in the smoking lounge of the
U.S. embassy. It is decided to invoke the shot-while-trying-to-escape
law, so they put Madero in a car, order him to get out of town, and
riddle him with bullets when he tries to.

General Huerta, the new president, attends a banquet at the
Jockey Club. There he announces that he has a good remedy, an
eighteen-cent rope, for Emiliano Zapata and Pancho Villa and the
other enemies of order.

(194 and 246)

1913: Jonacatepec
The Hordes Are Not Destroyed

Huerta's officers, old hands at massacring rebellious Indians, propose
to clean up the southern areas—burning villages and hunting down
campesinos. Anyone they meet falls dead or prisoner, for in the south,
who is not with Zapata?

Zapata's forces are hungry and sick, frayed, but the leader of the
landless knows what he wants, and his people believe in what he
does; neither fire nor deceit can prevail against that. While the capital's newspapers report that *the Zapata hordes have been totally
destroyed*, Zapata blows up trains, surprises garrisons and annihilates
them, occupies villages, attacks cities, and moves wherever he wants
across impenetrable mountains, through impassable ravines, fighting
and loving as though it's all in a day's work.

Zapata sleeps where he likes with anyone he likes, but of them
all he prefers two who are one.

(468)

Zapata and Those Two

We were twins. We were both named Luz for the day of our baptism and Gregoria for the day we were born. They called her Luz and me Gregoria and there we were, two young girls in the house, when Zapata's boys came along, and then their chief, trying to persuade my sister to go with him.

"Look, come with me."

And precisely one September 15 he came by and took her.

Afterward, in this continuous moving around, my sister died in Huautla of a disease that they call—what do they call it?—Saint Vitus, the Saint Vitus disease.

Three days and three nights chief Zapata was there with us, not eating or drinking a thing. We had only just lit the candles for my sister when ay, ay, ay, he took me by force. He said I belonged to him, because my sister and I were one . . .

(244)

1913: The Plains of Chihuahua
The North of Mexico Celebrates War and Fiesta

The cocks crow whenever they feel like it. This land has caught fire, gone crazy. Everyone is in rebellion.

"We're off to the war, woman."

"But why me?"

"Do you want me to die of starvation in the war? Who'll make my tortillas?"

Flocks of vultures follow the armed peons over plains and mountains. If life is worth nothing, what can death be worth? Men roll themselves like dice into the tumult, and find vengeance or oblivion, land to feed them or to cover them.

"Here comes Pancho Villa!" the peons exult.

"Here comes Pancho Villa!" cry the overseers, crossing themselves.

"Where, where is he?" asks General Huerta.

"In the north, south, east, and west, and also nowhere," replies the Chihuahua garrison commander.

Confronting the enemy, Pancho Villa is always the first to charge, right into the smoking jaws of the guns. When the battle gets hot, he just horse-laughs. His heart thumps like a fish out of water.

"There's nothing wrong with the general. He's just a bit emotional," his officers explain.

And so he is. With a single shot, for pure fun, he has been known to disembowel the messenger who gallops up with good news from the front.

(206 and 260)

1913: Culiacán
Bullets

There are bullets with imagination, Martín Luis Guzmán discovers. Bullets which amuse themselves in afflicting the flesh. He has known serious bullets, which serve human fury, but not these bullets that play with human pain.

For being a bad marksman with a good heart, the young novelist is assigned to direct one of Pancho Villa's hospitals. The wounded pile up in the dirt with no recourse but to clench their teeth, if they have any.

Checking the jammed wards, Guzmán confirms the improbable trajectories of these fanciful bullets, capable of emptying an eye-socket while leaving a body alive, or of sticking a piece of ear into the neck and a piece of neck into the foot. And he witnesses the sinister joy of bullets, which, having been ordered to kill a soldier, condemn him never again to sit down or never again to eat with his mouth.

(216)

1913: The Fields of Chihuahua
One of These Mornings I Murdered Myself,

on some dusty Mexican road, and the event left a deep impression on me.

This wasn't the first crime I committed. From the time I was born in Ohio seventy-one years ago and received the name Ambrose Bierce, until my recent death, I have played havoc with the lives of my parents and various relatives, friends, and colleagues. These touching episodes have splashed blood over my days—or my stories, which is all the same to me: the difference between the life I lived and the life I wrote is a matter for the jokers who execute human law, literary criticism, and the will of God in this world.

To put an end to my days, I joined the troops of Pancho Villa and chose one of those many stray bullets zooming through the Mexican sky these days. This method proved more practical than hanging, cheaper than poison, more convenient than firing with my own finger, and more dignified than waiting for disease or old age.

1914: Montevideo

Batlle

He writes articles slandering the saints and makes speeches attacking the company that sells real estate in the Great Beyond. When he assumed the presidency of Uruguay, he had no alternative but to swear before God and the Holy Evangels, but explained immediately that he didn't believe in any of that.

José Batlle y Ordoñez governs in defiance of the powers of heaven and earth. The Church has promised him a nice place in hell; companies he nationalized, or forced to respect their workers' unions and the eight-hour work day, will feed the fire; and the Devil will avenge his offenses against male-supremacists.

"He is legalizing licentiousness," say his enemies when he approves a law permitting women to sue for divorce.

"He is dissolving the family," they say, when he extends inheritance rights to illegitimate children.

"The female brain is inferior," they say, when he creates a women's university and announces that women will soon have the vote so that Uruguayan democracy need not walk on just one leg, and so that women will not forever be children passing from the hands of the father to those of the husband.

(35 and 271)

1914: San Ignacio

Quiroga

From the Paraná River jungle where he lives in voluntary exile, Horacio Quiroga applauds Batlle's reforms and *that ardent faith in noble things.*

But Quiroga is indeed far from Uruguay. He left the country some years ago, fleeing the shadow of death. A curse has darkened his life since he killed his best friend while trying to defend him; or perhaps he was cursed from the beginning.

In the jungle, a step away from the ruins of the Jesuit missions, Quiroga lives surrounded by bugs and palm trees. He writes stories without detours, just as he opens paths through the thicket with his machete. He works the word with the same rugged love as he does the soil, and wood, and iron.

What Quiroga seeks he could never find away from here. Here, yes, though only very occasionally. In this house which his hands built by the river, Quiroga has at times the joy of hearing voices more powerful than the call of death: rare and fleeting certainties of life, which while they last are as absolute as the sun.

(20, 357, 358, and 390)

1914: Montevideo

Delmira

In this rented room she had an appointment with the man who had been her husband. Wanting to possess her, wanting to stay with her, he made love to her, killed her, then killed himself.

The Uruguayan papers publish a photo of the body lying beside the bed: Delmira struck down by two bullets, naked like her poems, all unclothed in red.

Let's go further in the night, let's . . .

Delmira Agustini wrote in a trance. She sang to the fevers of love without shame, and was condemned by those who punish women for what they applaud in men, because chastity is a feminine duty, and desire, like reason, a male privilege. In Uruguay the laws march ahead of the people, who still separate soul from body as if they were Beauty and the Beast. Before the corpse of Delmira flow tears and phrases about this irreplaceable loss to national letters, but deep down the mourners feel some relief: the woman is dead, and better so.

But is she dead? Will not all the lovers burning in the nights of the world be the shadows of her voice and the echoes of her body? In the nights of the world won't they make a small place where her unfettered voice can sing and her radiant feet can dance?

(49 and 426)

1914: Ciudad Jiménez
Chronicler of Angry Peoples

From shock to shock, from marvel to marvel, John Reed travels the roads of northern Mexico. He is looking for Pancho Villa and finds him at every step.

Reed, chronicler of revolution, sleeps wherever night catches up with him. No one ever steals from him, or ever lets him pay for anything except dance music; and there's always someone to offer him a piece of tortilla or a place on his horse.

"Where do you come from?"

"From New York."

"Well, I don't know anything about New York, but I'll bet you don't see such fine cattle going through the streets as you see in the streets of Jiménez."

A woman carries a pitcher on her head. Another, squatting, suckles her baby. Another, on her knees, grinds corn. Enveloped in faded serapes, the men sit in a circle, drinking and smoking.

"Listen, Juanito, why is it your people don't like Mexicans? Why do they call us 'greasers'?"

Everyone has something to ask this thin, bespectacled, blond man who looks as if he were here by mistake.

"Listen, Juanito, how do you say 'mula' in English?"

"Goddamn stubborn—fathead mule . . ."

(368)

1914: Salt Lake City
Songster of Angry Peoples

They condemn him for singing red ballads that make fun of God, that wake up the worker, that curse money. The sentence doesn't say that Joe Hill is a proletarian troubadour, or worse, a foreigner seeking to subvert the good order of business. The sentence speaks of assault and crime. There is no proof, the witnesses change their stories each time they testify, and the defense lawyers act as if they were the prosecutors. But these details lack importance for the judges and for all who make decisions in Salt Lake City. Joe Hill will be bound to a chair with a cardboard circle pinned over his heart as a target for the firing squad.

Joe Hill came from Sweden. In the United States he wandered the roads. In the cities he cleaned spittoons and built walls; in the countryside he stacked wheat and picked fruit, dug copper in the mines, toted sacks on the piers, slept under bridges and in barns, sang anywhere at any hour, and never stopped singing. He bids his comrades farewell singing, now that he's off to Mars to disturb its social peace.

(167)

1914: Torreón
By Rail They March to Battle

In the red car, which displays his name in big gilt letters, General Pancho Villa receives John Reed. He receives him in his underpants, pours him coffee, and studies him for a long moment. Deciding that this gringo deserves the truth, he begins to talk.

"The chocolate politicians want to win without dirtying their hands. Those perfumed . . ."

Then he takes him to visit the field hospital, a train with a surgery and doctors to heal their own men and others: and he shows him the cars that take corn, sugar, coffee, and tobacco to the front. He also shows him the platform on which traitors are shot.

The railroads were the work of Porfirio Díaz, the key to peace and order, masterkey to the progress of a country without rivers or roads. They had been created not to transport an armed people but cheap raw materials, docile workers, and the executioners of rebellions. But General Villa makes war by train. From Camargo he turns loose a locomotive at full speed and smashes a trainful of soldiers. Villa's men enter Ciudad Juárez crouching in innocent coal cars, and after firing a few shots occupy it, more out of fun than necessity. By train the Villista troops roll to the front lines of the war. The locomotive gasps, painfully climbing the bare northern slopes. From behind a plume of black smoke come creaking shaking cars filled with soldiers and horses. On their roofs sprout rifles, sombreros, and stoves. Up there, among soldiers singing *mañanitas* and shooting into the air, children bawl and women cook—the women, the *soldaderas*, dressed in bridal gowns and silk shoes from the last looting.

(246 and 368)

1914: The Fields of Morelos
It's Time to Get Moving and Fight,

and the roars and rifle shots echo like mountain landslides. The army of Zapata—*down with the haciendas, up with the villages*—opens the way to Mexico City.

Around chief Zapata, General Genovevo de la O meditates and cleans his rifle, his face like a mustachioed sun, while Otilio Montaño, anarchist, discusses a manifesto with Antonio Díaz Soto y Gama, socialist.

Among Zapata's officers and advisers there is but one woman. Colonel Rosa Bobadilla, who won her rank in battle, commands a troop of cavalrymen and maintains a ban on drinking so much as a drop of tequila. They obey her, mysteriously, although they remain convinced that women are only good for adorning the world, making children, and cooking corn, chili, beans, or whatever God provides and permits.

(296 and 468)

1914: Mexico City
Huerta Flees

on the same ship that took Porfirio Díaz from Mexico.

Rags are winning the war against lace. A campesino tide beats against the capital. Zapata, *the Attila of Morelos*, and Pancho Villa, *the orangutan who eats raw meat and gnaws bones*, attack from north and south, avenging wrongs. Just before Christmas, the front pages of Mexico City's newspapers appear with black borders, mourning the arrival of the outlaws, barbarian violators of young ladies and locks.

Turbulent years. Now nobody knows who is who. The city trembles in panic and sighs with nostalgia. Only yesterday at the hub of the world were the masters in their big houses with their lackeys and pianos, candelabra and Carrara marble baths; and all around, serfs, the poor of the barrios, dizzy with *pulque*, drowning in garbage, condemned to the wages or tips which barely bought some occasional watered milk or *frijol* coffee or burro meat.

(194 and 246)

1915: Mexico City

Power Ungrasped

A timid knock, somewhere between wanting and not wanting. A door that half opens. An uncovered head, enormous sombrero clutched in hands pleading, for the love of God, for water or tortillas. Zapata's men, Indians in white pants, cartridge belts crossed on chests, wander the streets of the city that scorns and fears them. Nowhere are they invited in. In no time they run into Villa's men, also foreigners lost, blind.

Soft click of sandals, chas-ches, chas-ches, on the marble stairways, feet that are frightened by the pleasure of carpets, faces staring bewildered at themselves in the mirrors of waxed floors: Zapata's and Villa's men enter the National Palace as if begging pardon. Pancho Villa sits on the gilt armchair that was Porfirio Díaz's throne *to see how it feels*, while at his side Zapata, in a very embroidered suit, with an expression of being there without being there, murmurs answers to the reporters' questions.

The campesino generals have triumphed, but they don't know what to do with their victory: *"This shack is pretty big for us."*

Power is something for doctors, a threatening mystery that can only be deciphered by the cultured, those who understand the high art of politics, *those who sleep on downy pillows.*

When night falls, Zapata goes to a seedy hotel just a step away from the railway that leads to his country, and Villa to a military train. After a few days, they bid farewell to Mexico City.

The hacienda peons, the Indians of the communities, the pariahs of the countryside, have discovered the center of power and occupied it for a moment, as if on a visit, on tiptoe, anxious to end as soon as possible this trip to the moon. Strangers to the glory of victory, they end up going home to the lands where they know how to move around without getting lost.

No better news could be imagined by Huerta's successor, General Venustiano Carranza, whose battered troops are recovering with the aid of the United States.

(47, 194, 246, and 260)

1915: Tlaltizapán

Agrarian Reform

In an old mill in the village of Tlaltizapán, Zapata installs his head-quarters. Here, in his native district, far from the sideburned lords and their feathered ladies, far from the flashy, deceitful city, the Morelos rebel chief liquidates the great estates, nationalizes sugar-mills and distilleries without paying a centavo, and restores to the communities lands stolen through the centuries. Free villages are reborn, the conscience and memory of Indian traditions, and with them local democracy. Here neither bureaucrats nor generals make the decisions, but the assembled community in open forum. Selling or renting land is forbidden. Covetousness is forbidden.

In the shade of the laurels, in the village plaza, the talk is of more than fighting cocks, horses, and rain. Zapata's army, a league of armed communities, watches over the recovered land; they oil their guns and reload them with old Mauser and .30-.30 cartridges.

Young technicians are arriving in Morelos with tripods and other strange instruments to help the agrarian reform. The campesinos receive these budding engineers from Cuernavaca with a rain of flow-ers; but the dogs bark at the mounted messengers who gallop in from the north with the grim news that Pancho Villa's army is being wiped out.

(468)

1915: El Paso

Azuela

Exiled in Texas, a medic from Pancho Villa's army treats the Mexican revolution as a pointless outburst. According to Mariano Azuela's novel *The Underdogs*, this is a tale of drunken blind men who shoot without knowing why or against whom, who lash out like animals

seeking things to steal or women to tumble on the ground in a land
that stinks of gunpowder and frying grease.

(33)

1916: Tlaltizapán
Carranza

The clink of Villa's horsemen's spurs can still be heard in the mountains, but it is no longer an army. From trenches defended by barbed
wire, machineguns have made a clean sweep in four long battles of
Villa's fiery cavalry, ground to dust in stubbornly repeated suicide
charges.

Venustiano Carranza, president in spite of Villa and Zapata,
launches the war in the south: *"This business of dividing up the land
is crazy,"* he says. One decree announces that lands distributed by
Zapata will be returned to their old owners; another promises to shoot
anyone who is, or looks like, a Zapatista.

Shooting and burning with rifles and torches, government forces
swoop down on the flourishing fields of Morelos. They kill five hundred
people in Tlaltizapán, and many more elsewhere. The prisoners are
sold in Yucatán as slave labor for the henequén plantations, as in the
days of Porfirio Díaz; and crops, herds, all war booty is taken to the
markets of the capital.

In the mountains, Zapata resists. When the rainy season approaches, the revolution is suspended for planting; but later, stubbornly, incredibly, it goes on.

(246, 260, and 468)

1916: Buenos Aires
Isadora

Barefoot, naked, scantily draped in the Argentine flag, Isadora Duncan dances to the national anthem in a students' café in Buenos Aires,
and the next morning the whole world knows of it. The impresario
breaks his contract, good families cancel their reservations at the
Colón Theater, and the press demands the immediate expulsion of

this disgraceful North American who has come to Argentina to sully patriotic symbols.

Isadora cannot understand it. No Frenchman protested when she danced the Marseillaise in nothing but a red shawl. If one can dance an emotion, if one can dance an idea, why not an anthem?

Liberty offends. This woman with shining eyes is the declared enemy of schools, matrimony, classical dance, and everything that cages the wind. She dances for the joy of dancing; dances what she wants, when she wants, how she wants; and orchestras hush before the music that is born of her body.

(145)

1916: New Orleans

Jazz

From the slaves comes the freest of all music, jazz, which flies without asking permission. Its grandparents are the blacks who sang at their work on their owners' plantations in the southern United States, and its parents are the musicians of black New Orleans brothels. The whorehouse bands play all night without stopping, on balconies that keep them safe above the brawling in the street. From their improvisations is born the new music.

With his savings from delivering newspapers, milk, and coal, a short, timid lad has just bought his own trumpet for ten dollars. He blows and the music stretches out, out, greeting the day. Louis Armstrong, like jazz, is the grandson of slaves, and has been raised, like jazz, in the whorehouse.

(105)

1916: Columbus

Latin America Invades the United States

Rain falls upward. Hen bites fox and hare shoots hunter. For the first and only time in history, Mexican soldiers invade the United States.

With the tattered force remaining, five hundred men out of the many thousands he once had, Pancho Villa crosses the border and, crying *Viva Mexico!* showers bullets on the city of Columbus, Texas.

(206 and 260)

1916: León
Darío

In Nicaragua, occupied land, humiliated land, Rubén Darío dies.

The doctor kills him, fatally puncturing his liver. The embalmer, the hairdresser, the makeup man, and the tailor torment his remains.

A sumptuous funeral is inflicted upon him. The warm February air in the city of León smells of incense and myrrh. The most distinguished señoritas, festooned in lilies and heron feathers, serve as Canephoras and Virgins of Minerva strewing flowers along the route of the funeral procession.

Surrounded by candles and admirers, the corpse of Darío wears a Greek tunic and laurel crown by day, by night a formal black frock coat and gloves to match. For a whole week, day and night, night and day, he is scourged with never-ending recitals of shoddy verses, and regaled with speeches proclaiming him Immortal Swan, Messiah of the Spanish Lyre, and Samson of the Metaphor.

Guns roar. The government contributes to the martyrdom by piling War Ministry honors on the poet who preached peace. Bishops brandish crosses; steeple bells ring out. In the culminating moment of this flagellation, the poet who believed in divorce and lay education is dropped into the hole converted, a prince of the Church.

(129, 229, and 454)

1917: The Fields of Chihuahua and Durango
Eagles into Hens

A punitive expedition, ten thousand soldiers with plentiful artillery enter Mexico to make Pancho Villa pay for his impudent attack on the North American city of Columbus.

"We'll bring back that assassin in an iron cage," proclaims General John Pershing, and the thunder of his guns echoes the words.

Across the drought-stricken immensities of northern Mexico, General Pershing finds various graves—*Here lies Pancho Villa*—

without a Villa in any of them. He finds snakes and lizards and silent stones, and campesinos who murmur false leads when beaten, threatened, or offered all the gold in the world.

After some months, almost a year, Pershing returns to the United States. He brings back a long caravan of soldiers fed up with breathing dust, with the people throwing stones, with the lies in each little village in that gravelly desert. Two young lieutenants march at the head of the humbled procession. Both have had in Mexico their baptism of fire. For Dwight Eisenhower, newly graduated from West Point, it is an unlucky start on the road to military glory. George Patton spits as he leaves *this ignorant and half-savage country.*

From the crest of a hill, Pancho Villa looks down and comments: *"They came like eagles and they leave like wet hens."*

(206 and 260)

1918: Córdoba

Moldy Scholars

At the Argentine university of Córdoba degrees are no longer denied to those unable to prove their white lineage as was the case a few years ago, but *Duties toward Servants* is still a subject studied in the Philosophy of Law course, and students of medicine still graduate without having set eyes on a sick person.

The professors, venerable specters, copy a Europe several centuries gone, a lost world of gentlemen and pious ladies, the sinister beauty of a colonial past. The merits of the parrot and the virtues of the monkey are rewarded with trimmings and tassels.

The Córdoba students, fed up, explode with disgust. They go on strike against these jailers of the spirit, calling on students and workers throughout Latin America to fight for a culture of their own. From Mexico to Chile come mighty echoes.

(164)

1918: Córdoba

"The Pains That Linger Are the Liberties We Lack," Proclaims the Student Manifesto

. . . We have resolved to call all things by their right names. Córdoba is redeeming itself. From today we count for our country one shame less and one freedom more. The pains that linger are the liberties we lack. We believe we are not wrong, the resonances of the heart tell us so: we are treading on the skirts of the revolution, we are living an American hour . . .

The unversities have till now been a secular refuge for the mediocre, income of the ignorant, secure hospital for the invalid, and —which is even worse—the place where all forms of tyranny and insensitivity have found a professor to teach them. The universities thus faithfully reflect those decadent societies which offer the sad spectacle of senile immobility. For that reason, science, confronting these mute and shut-in establishments, passes by in silence or enters into bureaucratic service, mutilated and grotesque . . .

(164)

1918: Ilopango

Miguel at Thirteen

He arrives at the Ilopango barracks driven by a hunger that has sunk his eyes into the depths of his head.

In the barracks, in exchange for food, Miguel begins running errands and shining lieutenants' boots. He learns fast to split coconuts with one blow of the machete as if they were necks, and to fire a carbine without wasting cartridges. Thus he becomes a soldier.

At the end of a year of barracks life, the wretched boy gives out. After putting up for so long with drunken officers who beat him for no reason, Miguel escapes. And that night, the night of his flight, is the night of the Ilopango earthquake. Miguel hears it from far away.

For a whole day and the next day too, the earth shakes El Salvador, this little country of warm people, until between tremor and tremor the real quake comes, the super-earthquake that bursts and shatters everything. It brings down the barracks to the last stone, crushing officers and soldiers alike—but not Miguel.

And so occurs the third birth of Miguel Mármol, at thirteen years of age.

(126)

1918: The Mountains of Morelos
Ravaged Land, Living Land

The hogs, the cows, the chickens, are they Zapatistas? And the jugs, the pans, the stewpots, what of them? Government troops have exterminated half the population of Morelos in these years of stubborn peasant war, and taken away everything. Only stones and charred stalks remain in the fields; the wreckage of a house, a woman heaving a plow. Of the men, any not dead or exiled have become outlaws.

But the war continues. The war will continue as long as corn sprouts in secret mountain crannies, as long as Zapata's eyes flash.

(468)

1918: Mexico City
The New Bourgeoisie Is Born Lying

"We fight for the land," says Zapata, *"and not for illusions that give us nothing to eat . . . With or without elections, the people are chewing the cud of bitterness."*

While taking the land from the campesinos of Morelos and wrecking their villages, President Carranza talks about agrarian reform. While applying state terror against the poor, he grants them the right to vote for the rich and offers illiterates freedom of the press.

The new Mexican bourgeoisie, voracious child of war and plunder, sings hymns of praise to the Revolution while gobbling it down with knife and fork from an embroidered tablecloth.

(468)

1919: Cuautla

This Man Taught Them That Life Is Not Only Fear of Suffering and Hope for Death

It had to be done by treachery. Shamming friendship, a government officer leads him into the trap. A thousand soldiers are waiting, a thousand rifles tumble him from his horse.

Afterward they haul him to Cuautla and exhibit him face up.

Campesinos from everywhere flock there for the silent march-past, which lasts several days. Approaching the body, they remove their sombreros, look attentively, and shake their heads. No one believes it. There's a wart missing, a scar too many; that suit isn't his; this face swollen by so many bullets could be anybody's.

The campesinos talk in slow whispers, peeling off words like grains of corn:

"They say he went with a compadre to Arabia."

"Hell, Zapata doesn't chicken out."

"He's been seen on the Quilamula heights."

"I know he's sleeping in a cave in Cerro Prieto."

"Last night his horse was drinking in the river."

The Morelos campesinos don't now believe, nor will they ever believe, that Emiliano Zapata could have committed the infamy of dying and leaving them all alone.

(468)

Ballad of the Death of Zapata

Little star in the night
that rides the sky like a witch,
where is our chief Zapata
who was the scourge of the rich?

Little flower of the fields
and valleys of Morelos,
if they ask for Zapata,
say he's gone to try on halos.

Little bubbling brook,
what did that carnation say to you?
It says our chief didn't die.
that Zapata's on his way to you.

(293)

1919: Hollywood
Chaplin

In the beginning were rags.

From the rag bag of the Keystone studios, Charles Chaplin chose the most useless garments, the too big, too small, too ugly, and put them together, as if picking through a garbage can. Some outsized pants, a dwarf's jacket, a bowler hat, and some huge dilapidated shoes. To that he added a prop mustache and cane. Then this little heap of rejected rags stood up, saluted its author with a ridiculous bow, and set off walking like a duck. After a few steps he collided with a tree and asked its pardon, doffing his hat.

And so came to life Charlie the Tramp, outcast and poet.

(121 and 383)

1919: Hollywood
Keaton

The man who never laughs creates laughter.

Like Chaplin, Buster Keaton is a Hollywood magician. His outcast hero—straw hat, stone face, cat's body—in no way resembles Charlie the Tramp, but is caught in the same absurd war with cops, bullies, and machines. Always impassive, icy outside, burning inside, he walks with great dignity on walls, on air, on the bottom of the sea.

Keaton is not as popular as Chaplin. His films entertain, but with too much mystery, too much melancholy.

(128 and 382)

1919: Memphis

Thousands of People Flock to the Show,

and many are women with babies in their arms. The family performance reaches its high point when Ell Persons, tied to a stake, is baptized with gasoline and the flames draw his first howls.

Not long afterward, the audience departs in an orderly fashion, complaining of the brevity of these things. Some stir the cinders seeking a bone as a souvenir.

Ell Persons is one of the seventy-seven blacks who have been roasted alive or hanged by white crowds this year in the southern United States for committing a murder or a rape—that is to say, for looking at a white woman, possibly with a lascivious gleam; or for saying "Yes" instead of "Yes, ma'am"; or for not removing his hat before speaking.

Among these lynched "niggers," some have worn the military uniform of the United States of America and hunted Pancho Villa through Mexico's northern deserts, or are newly returned from the world war.

(51, 113, and 242)

1921: Rio de Janeiro

Rice Powder

President Epitácio Pessoa makes a recommendation to the managers of Brazilian football. For reasons of patriotic prestige, he suggests that no player with black skin be sent to the coming South American soccer championships.

It happens, however, that Brazil won last year thanks to the mulatto Artur Friedenreich, who scored the winning goal and whose boots, grimed with mud, are still on display in a jeweler's window. Friedenreich, born of a German and a black, is Brazil's best player. He always arrives on the field last. It takes him at least half an hour in the dressingroom to iron out his frizz, so that during the game not a hair will move, even when he heads the ball.

Football, that elegant after-Mass diversion, is something for whites. *"Rice powder! Rice powder!"* yell the fans at Carlos Alberto, another mulatto player on the Fluminense club who whitens his face with it.

(279)

1921: Rio de Janeiro
Pixinguinha

It is announced that the Batons will soon be appearing on the Paris stage, and indignation mounts in the Brazilian press. What will Europeans think? Will they imagine Brazil is an African colony? The Batons' repertory contains no operatic arias or waltzes, only *maxixes*, *lundús*, *cortajacas*, *batuques*, *cateretês*, *modinhas*, and the newborn *samba*. It is an orchestra of blacks who play black music. Articles exhort the government to head off the disgrace. The foreign ministry promptly explains that the Batons are not on an official mission.

Pixinguinha, one of the blacks in the ensemble, is the best musician in Brazil. He doesn't know it, nor does it interest him. He is too busy seeking on his flute, with devilish joy, sounds stolen from the birds.

(75)

1921: Rio de Janeiro
Brazil's Fashionable Author

inaugurates a swimming pool in a sports club. Coelho Neto's speech exalting the virtues of the pool draws tears and applause. Coelho Neto invokes the powers of sea, sky, and earth *on this solemn occasion of such magnitude that we cannot evaluate it without tracing, through the Shadows of Time, its projection into the Future.*

Sweets for the rich, denounces Lima Barreto, an author not in vogue and accursed both as a mulatto and a rebel, who, cursing back, dies in some godforsaken hospital.

Lima Barreto mocks the pomposities of writers who parrot the literature of ornamental culture. They sing the glories of a happy Brazil, without blacks, workers, or the poor; a Brazil populated with sage economists whose most original idea is to impose more taxes on the people, a Brazil with two hundred and sixty-two generals whose job is to design new uniforms for next year's parade.

(36)

1922: Toronto
This Reprieve

saves thousands condemned to early death. Neither royal nor presidential, it has been extended by a Canadian doctor who a week ago, with seven cents in his pocket, was looking for a job.

On a hunch that deprived him of sleep, and after much error and discouragement, Fred Banting discovers that insulin, secreted by the pancreas, reduces sugar in the blood; and thus he commutes the many death sentences imposed by diabetes.

(54)

1922: Leavenworth
For Continuing to Believe That
All Belongs to All

Ricardo, most talented and dangerous of the Flores Magón brothers, has been absent from the revolution he did so much to start. While Mexico's fate was played out on its battlefields, he was breaking stones, shackled in a North American prison.

A United States court had sentenced him to twenty years' hard labor for signing an anarchist manifesto against private property. He was many times offered a pardon, if only he would ask for it. He never asked.

"When I die, perhaps my friends will write on my grave: 'Here Lies a Dreamer,' and my enemies: 'Here Lies a Madman.' But no one will dare write: 'Here Lies a Coward and Traitor to his Ideas.'"

In his cell, far from his land, they strangle him. *Heart failure*, says the medical report.

(44 and 391)

1922: The Fields of Patagonia
The Worker-Shoot

Three years ago young aristocrats of the Argentine Patriotic League went hunting in the barrios of Buenos Aires. The safari was a success. The rich kids killed workers and Jews for a whole week without a license, and no one went to jail.

Now it's the army that is using workers for target practice in the frozen lands of the south. The boys of the Tenth Cavalry under Lieutenant Colonel Héctor Benigno Varela roam the great estates of Patagonia shooting peons on strike. Fervent Patriotic League volunteers accompany them. No one is executed without a trial. Each trial lasts less time than it takes to smoke a cigarette.

Estancia owners and officers act as judges. The condemned are buried by the heap in common graves they dig themselves.

President Hipólito Yrigoyen in general doesn't approve of this method of finishing off anarchists and reds, but lifts not a finger against the murderers.

(38 and 365)

1923: Guayas River
Crosses Float in the River,

hundreds of crosses crowned with mountain blossoms, flowery squadrons of tiny ships cruising on the swell of waves and memory. Each cross recalls a murdered worker. People have thrown these floating crosses into the water so that the workers lying in the riverbed may rest in peace.

It happened a year ago, in the port of Guayaquil, which for several hours was in the hands of the workers. Fed up with eating hunger, they had called the first general strike in Ecuador's history—not even government officials were able to circulate without a pass from the unions. The women—washerwomen, tobacco workers, cooks, peddlers—had formed the Rosa Luxemburg Committee; they were the most defiant.

"Today the rabble got up laughing. Tomorrow they'll go to bed crying," announced Carlos Arroyo, president of the Chamber of Deputies. And the president of the republic, José Luis Tamayo, ordered

General Enrique Barriga to take care of the matter: *"At any cost."*

At the first shots, many workers tried to escape, scattering like ants from an anthill squashed by a foot. These were the first to fall.

No one knows how many were thrown into the Guayas river to sink, their bellies slashed with bayonets.

(192, 332, and 472)

1923: Acapulco

The Function of the Forces of Order in the Democratic Process

As soon as the Tom Mix film ends, Juan Escudero surprises the audience by stepping in front of the screen of Acapulco's only cinema and delivering a harangue against bloodsucking merchants. By the time the boys in uniform pile on him, the Workers' Party of Acapulco has already been born, baptized by acclamation.

In no time at all, the Workers' Party has grown and won the elections and stuck its black-and-red flag over city hall. Juan Escudero—tall, thick sideburns, pointed mustache—is the new mayor, the socialist mayor. In the blink of an eye he turns the palace into a headquarters for cooperatives and unions, launches a literacy campaign, and defies the power of the three companies that own the water, air, ground, and grime of this filthy Mexican port abandoned by God and the federal government. Then the owners of everything organize new elections, so that the people may correct their error, but the Workers' Party of Acapulco wins again. So there's no way out but to call in the army, which promptly normalizes the situation. The victorious Juan Escudero receives two bullets, one in the arm and the other in the forehead, a mercy-shot from close range, while the soldiers set fire to city hall.

But Escudero survives, and continues winning elections. In a wheelchair, mutilated, hardly able to talk, Escudero conducts a victorious new campaign for deputy by dictating speeches to a youngster who deciphers his mumblings and repeats them aloud on campaign platforms.

The owners of Acapulco decide to pay thirty thousand pesos so that this time the military patrol will shoot properly. In the company ledgers these outlays are duly entered, but not their purpose. And finally Juan Escudero falls, very much shot, dead of total death you might say, thank you, gentlemen.

(441)

1923: Azángaro
Urviola

His family wanted him to be a doctor. Instead he became an Indian, as if his double-humped back and dwarf stature were not curse enough. Ezequiel Urviola quit his law career in Puno vowing to follow in the footsteps of Túpac Amaru. Since then he speaks Quechua, wears sandals, chews coca, and plays the *quena* flute. Day and night he comes and goes, inciting revolt in the Peruvian sierra, where the Indians have proprietors like the mules and the trees.

The police dream of catching the hunchback Urviola; the landlords pledge it; but the little shrimp turns into an eagle flying over the mountains.

(370)

1923: Callao
Mariátegui

A ship brings José Carlos Mariátegui back to Peru after some years in Europe. When he left he was a bohemian nighthawk from Lima who wrote about horses, a mystical poet who felt deeply and understood little. Over in Europe he discovered America. Mariátegui found Marxism and found Mariátegui, and this was how he learned to see from afar the Peru he couldn't see close up.

Mariátegui believes that Marxism means human progress as indisputably as smallpox vaccine or the theory of relativity, but to Peruvianize Peru one has to start by Peruvianizing Marxism, which is not a catechism or the tracing of some master plan, but a key to enter deep into this country. And the clues to the depths of his country are in the Indian communities, dispossessed by the sterile landowner system but unconquered in their socialist traditions of work and life.

(321, 277, and 355)

1923: Buenos Aires

Snapshot of a Worker-Hunter

He peruses the firearms catalogs lasciviously, as if they were pornography. For him the uniform of the Argentine army is as beautiful as the smoothest of human skin. He likes skinning alive the foxes that fall into his traps, but prefers making target practice of fleeing workers, the more so if they are reds, and more yet if they are foreign reds.

Jorge Ernesto Pérez Millán Temperley enlisted as a volunteer in the troop of Lieutenant Colonel Varela, and last year marched to Patagonia for the sport of liquidating any strikers who came within range. Later, when the German anarchist Kurt Wilckens threw the bomb that blew up Lieutenant Colonel Varela, this hunter of workers swore loudly to avenge his superior.

And avenge him he does. In the name of the Argentine Patriotic League, Jorge Ernesto Pérez Millán Temperley fires a Mauser bullet into the chest of Wilckens as he sleeps in his cell, then has himself immediately photographed for posterity, gun in hand, striking a martial pose of duty done.

(38)

1923: Tampico

Traven

A phantom ship, an old hulk destined to be wrecked, arrives off the coast of Mexico. Among its crew, vagabonds without name or nation, is a survivor of the suppressed revolution in Germany.

This comrade of Rosa Luxemburg, fugitive from hunger and the police, writes his first novel in Tampico and signs it B. Traven. With that name he will become famous without anyone ever knowing which face or voice or footstep is his. Traven decides to be a mystery, so that no bureaucracy can label him. All the better to mock a world where the marriage contract and inheritance matter more than love and death.

(398)

1923: The Fields of Durango

Pancho Villa Reads the
Thousand and One Nights,

deciphering the words out loud by candlelight, because this is the book that gives him the best dreams; and afterward, he awakens early to pasture the cows with his old battle comrades.

Villa is still the most popular man in the fields of northern Mexico, and officialdom doesn't like it a bit. Today it is three years since his men turned the Canutillo hacienda into a cooperative, which now has a hospital and a school, and a world of people have come to celebrate.

Villa is listening to his favorite *corridos* when Don Fernando, a pilgrim from Granada, mentions that John Reed has just died in Moscow.

Pancho Villa orders the party stopped. Even the flies pause in flight.

"So old Juan died? My old pal, Juan?"

"Himself."

Villa half believes and half not.

"I saw it in the papers," Don Fernando says, excusing himself. "He's buried over there with the heroes of the revolution."

Nobody breathes. Nobody disturbs the silence. Don Fernando murmurs: "It was typhus, not a bullet."

And Villa nods his head: "So old Juan died."

Then repeats: "So old Juan's dead."

He falls silent. Looking into the distance, he finally says: "I never even heard the word 'socialism' until he explained it to me."

All at once he rises, and extending his arms, rebukes the silent guitar-players: "And the music? What happened to the music? Play!"

(206)

1923: Mexico City/Parral

The People Donated a Million Dead to the
Mexican Revolution

in ten years of war so that military chieftains could finally take possession of the best lands and the most profitable businesses. These officers of the revolution share power and glory with Indian-fleecing doctors and the politicos-for-hire, brilliant banquet orators who call Obregón *the Mexican Lenin.*

On this road to national reconciliation there is no problem that can't be overcome by a public-works contract, a land concession, or the sort of favor that flows out of an open purse. Álvaro Obregón, the president, defines his style of government with a phrase soon to become a classic in Mexico: *"There's no general who can resist a salvo of fifty thousand pesos."*

But Obregón gets it wrong with General Villa.

Nothing can be done with him except to shoot him down.

Villa arrives in Parral by car in the early morning. At the sight of him someone signals with a red scarf. Twelve men respond by squeezing triggers.

Parral was his favorite city. *"I like Parral so much, so much . . ."* And the day when the women and children of Parral chased out the gringo invaders with stones, the horses inside Pancho broke free, and he let out a tremendous yell of joy: *"I just love Parral to death!"*

(206, 246, and 260)

1924: Mérida, Yucatán

More on the Function of the Forces of Order in the Democratic Process

Felipe Carrillo Puerto, also invulnerable to the gun from which Obregón fires pesos, faces a firing squad one damp January morning.

"Do you want a confessor?"

"I'm not a Catholic."

"How about a notary?"

"I've nothing to leave."

He had been a colonel in Zapata's army in Morelos before founding the Socialist Workers' Party in Yucatán. There Carrillo Puerto delivered his speeches in Mayan, explaining that Marx was a brother of Jacinto Canek and Cecilio Chi and that socialism, the inheritor of the communitarian tradition, gave a future dimension to the glorious Indian past.

Until yesterday he headed the socialist government of Yucatán. Innumerable frauds and private interests had not been able to keep the socialists from an easy electoral victory, nor afterward keep them from fulfilling their promises. Their sacrileges against the hallowed big estates, the slave labor system and various imperial monopolies aroused the rage of those who ran the henequén plantations, not to speak of the International Harvester Company. The archbishop went into convulsions over lay education, free love, and red baptisms—so called because children received their names on a mattress of red flowers, and along with those names, wishes for a long life of socialist militancy. So what could be done, but call in the army to bring the scandal to an end?

The shooting of Felipe Carrillo Puerto repeats the history of Juan Escudero in Acapulco. The government of the humiliated has lasted a couple of years in Yucatán. The humiliated govern with the weapons of reason. The humiliators don't have the government, but they do have the reason of weapons. And as in all of Mexico, death rides the dice of destiny.

(330)

1924: Mexico City
Nationalizing the Walls

Easel art invites confinement. The mural, on the other hand, offers itself to the passing multitude. The people may be illiterate but they are not blind; so Rivera, Orozco, and Siqueiros assault the walls of Mexico. They paint something new and different. On moist lime is born a truly national art, child of the Mexican revolution and of these days of births and funerals.

Mexican muralism crashes head on into the dwarfed, castrated art of a country trained to deny itself. All of a sudden, still lifes and defunct landscapes spring dizzily to life, and the wretched of the earth become subjects of art and history rather than objects of use, scorn, or pity.

Complaints pelt down on the muralists, but praise, not a drop. Still, mounted on their scaffoldings, they stick to their jobs. Sixteen hours without a break is the working day for Rivera, eyes and belly of a toad, teeth like a fish. He keeps a pistol at his waist.

"To set a line for the critics," he says.

(80 and 387)

1924: Mexico City
Diego Rivera

resurrects Felipe Carrillo Puerto, redeemer of Yucatán, with a bullet wound in his chest but uninformed of his own death, and paints Emiliano Zapata arousing his people, and paints the people, all the peoples of Mexico, united in an epic of work and war and fiesta, on sixteen hundred square meters of wall in the Ministry of Education. While he washes the world with colors, Diego amuses himself by lying. To anyone who wants to listen he tells lies as colossal as his belly, as his passion for creating, and as his woman-devouring insatiability.

Barely three years ago he returned from Europe. Over there in Paris, Diego was a vanguard painter who got tired of the "isms"; and just as his star was fading, and he was painting just from boredom, he returned to Mexico and the lights of his country hit him in the face, setting his eyes aflame.

(82)

1924: Mexico City
Orozco

Diego Rivera rounds out, José Clemente Orozco sharpens. Rivera paints sensualities: bodies of corn flesh, voluptuous fruits. Orozco paints desperations: skin-and-bone bodies, a maguey mutilated and bleeding. What is happiness in Rivera is tragedy in Orozco. In Rivera there is tenderness and radiant serenity; in Orozco, severity and contortion. Orozco's Mexican revolution has grandeur, like Rivera's; but where Rivera speaks to us of hope, Orozco seems to say that whoever steals the sacred fire from the gods will deny it to his fellow men.

(83 and 323)

1924: Mexico City

Siqueiros

Surly, withdrawn, turbulent inside—that's Orozco. Spectacular, bombastic, turbulent on the outside—that's David Alfaro Siqueiros. Orozco practices painting as a ceremony of solitude. For Siqueiros it is an act of militant solidarity. *"There is no other way except ours,"* says Siqueiros. To European culture, which he considers sick, he opposes his own muscular energy. Orozco doubts, lacks faith in what he does. Siqueiros bulls ahead, sure that his patriotic brashness is no bad medicine for a country with a severe inferiority complex.

(27)

The People Are the Hero of Mexican Mural Painting, Says Diego Rivera

The true novelty of Mexican painting, in the sense that we initiated it with Orozco and Siqueiros, was to make the people the hero of mural painting. Until then the heroes of mural painting had been gods, angels, archangels, saints, war heroes, kings and emperors, prelates, and great military and political chiefs, the people appearing as the chorus around the star personalities of the tragedy . . .

(79)

1924: Regla

Lenin

The mayor of the Cuban community of Regla calls everybody together. From the neighboring city of Havana has come news of the death of Lenin in the Soviet Union. The mayor issues a proclamation of mourning. The proclamation says that *the aforementioned Lenin won well-deserved sympathy among the proletarian and intellectual elements of this municipal district. Accordingly, at 5:00 P.M. Sunday next its residents will observe two minutes of silence and meditation, during which persons and vehicles will maintain absolute stillness.*

At precisely five o'clock on Sunday afternoon, the mayor of Regla climbs up Fortín hill. Despite a heavy downpour, over a thousand people accompany him to observe the two minutes of silence and meditation. Afterward, the mayor plants an olive tree on top of the hill in homage to the man who was always planting the red flag over there, in the middle of the snow.

(215)

1926: San Albino
Sandino

is short and thin as a rake. A stray wind would blow him away were he not so firmly planted in the soil of Nicaragua.

In this land, his land, Augusto César Sandino stands tall and speaks of what the land has said to him, for when Sandino stretches out to sleep, his land whispers sorrow and sweetness to him.

Sandino speaks of the secrets of his invaded and humiliated land, and asks, *How many of you love it as much as I do?*

Twenty-nine San Albino miners step forward.

These are the first soldiers in Nicaragua's army of liberation. Illiterate, they toil fifteen hours a day hacking gold out of the ground for a North American firm and sleep piled up in a shed. They blow up the mine with dynamite and follow Sandino into the mountains.

Sandino goes on a small white burro.

(118 and 361)

1926: Puerto Cabezas
The Most Admirable Women on Earth

are the whores of Puerto Cabezas. From pillow talk they know the exact spot under water where U.S. Marines have buried forty rifles and seven thousand cartridges. Thanks to these women, who risk their lives in defiance of the foreign occupation troops, Sandino and his men rescue from the waters, by torchlight, their first weapons and first ammunition.

(361)

1926: Juazeiro do Norte

Father Cicero

Once Juazeiro was a nothing of a hamlet—four shacks God seemed to have spat into the void when, one fine day, He pointed a finger at this garbage heap and decided it was to be a Holy City. Since then, the afflicted flock here by the thousands. Every road of martyrdom and miracle leads here. Squalid pilgrims from all Brazil, long lines of rags and stumps of limbs, have turned Juazeiro into the richest city of the northeastern hinterland. In this faith-restoring new Jerusalem, memorials to the forgotten, polestar of the lost, the modest Salgadinho stream is now known as the River Jordan. Surrounded by pious women brandishing their bleeding bronze crucifixes, Father Cicero announces that Jesus Christ is on his way.

Father Cicero Romão Baptista is the master of the lands and souls. This savior of the shipwrecked in the desert, tamer of madmen and criminals, gives children to sterile women, rain to dry ground, light to the blind, and, to the poor, some crumbs from the bread he eats.

(133)

1926: Juazeiro do Norte

By Divine Miracle a Bandit
Becomes a Captain

Lampião's warriors fire off bullets and sing songs. Tolling bells and fireworks welcome them to the city of Juazeiro. The *cangaceiros* display a complete arsenal and a luxuriance of medals on their leather armor.

At the foot of the statue of Father Cicero, Father Cicero blesses the chief of the gang. It is well known that the bandit Lampião never touches a house containing an image of Father Cicero, or kills any devotee of the miracle-working saint.

In the name of the government of Brazil, Father Cicero confers on Lampião the rank of captain, three blue stripes on either shoulder, and hands out to his men impeccable Mausers in exchange for their old Winchester rifles. In return, Captain Lampião promises to defeat the rebels under Lieutenant Luis Carlos Prestes, who roam Brazil preaching democracy and other devilish ideas; but he has hardly left this city before he forgets about the Prestes Column and returns to his old routine.

(120, 133, and 263)

1926: New York

Valentino

Last night, in an Italian bar, Rudolph Valentino collapsed, struck down by a pasta banquet.

Millions of women on five continents have been widowed. They adored the elegant, feline Latin on the screen-altar of the movie theater, itself a temple for all peoples in all cities. With him they galloped to the oasis, spurred by the wind of the desert, and with him participated in tragic bullfights, entered mysterious palaces, danced on mirrored floors, and undressed in the bedrooms of Indian Prince and Son of the Sheik. Pierced by the languid gimlet of his eyes and crushed by his arms, they swooned into deep silken beds.

He didn't even realize. Valentino, the Hollywood god who casually smoked while kissing and annihilated with a glance, he who daily received a thousand love letters, in reality slept alone and dreamed of Mother.

(443)

1927: Chicago

Louie

She lived on New Orleans' Perdido Street—the street of the lost— where the dead were laid out with a saucer on the chest for the neighbors' coins to pay for the funeral. When she dies, her son Louis takes pleasure in giving her a fine funeral—the deluxe funeral she would have dreamed of at the end of the dream in which God made her white and a millionaire.

Louis Armstrong, who grew up with no more to eat than leftovers and music, fled New Orleans for Chicago with only a trumpet for baggage and a fish sandwich for company. A few years have passed and he is getting fat. He eats to avenge himself. And if he returned to the South now, maybe he'd be welcomed in some of the places barred to blacks and out of bounds for the poor. He could probably walk down most any street in town. He's the king of jazz and no one argues it. His trumpet whispers, moans, wails, howls like a wounded beast, and laughs uproariously, celebrating with euphoria and immense power the absurdity of life.

(105)

1927: New York

Bessie

This woman sings her sufferings with the voice of glory and no one can listen and pretend he doesn't hear or he's not moved. Lungs of deep night: Bessie Smith, immensely fat, immensely black, curses the thieves of Creation. Her blues are the hymns of poor drunk black women of the slums. They announce that the whites and the supermen and the rich who humiliate the world will be dethroned.

(165)

1927: Rapallo

Pound

It is twenty years since Ezra Pound pulled out of America. Son of poets, father of poets, Pound seeks beneath the Italian sun new images, worthy accompaniments to the bison of Altamira, unknown words for talking to gods more ancient than the fish.

Along the road, he makes the wrong friends.

(261, 349, and 437)

1927: Charlestown

"Lovely day,"

says the governor of the state of Massachusetts.

At midnight on this August Monday, two Italian workers will occupy the electric chair of Charlestown prison's death house. Nicola Sacco, shoemaker, and Bartolomeo Vanzetti, fish peddler, will be executed for crimes they did not commit.

The lives of Sacco and Vanzetti are in the hands of a businessman who has made forty million dollars selling Packard cars. Alvan Tufts Fuller, governor of Massachusetts, a small man behind a big desk of carved wood, declines to yield to the protests rumbling from every direction. He honestly believes in the correctness of the trial and the validity of the evidence. He also believes that all the damned anarchists and filthy foreigners who come to ruin this country deserve to die.

(162 and 445)

1927: Araraquara
Mário de Andrade

challenges everything servile, saccharine, grandiloquent in official culture. He is a creator of words, words dying of envy for music, which nonetheless are capable of seeing and speaking everything to Brazil, and also of savoring it, Brazil the tasty hot peanut.

On holidays, for the fun of it, Mário de Andrade transcribes the sayings and deeds of one Macunaíma, a hero with no character, just as he hears them from the golden beak of a parrot. According to the parrot, Macunaíma was an ugly black man, born in the heart of the jungle, who didn't bother saying a word until he was six—for sheer laziness, and preoccupied as he was with decapitating ants, spitting in his brothers' faces, and fondling his female relatives. Macunaíma's wild adventures cover all times and all spaces in Brazil, while stripping saints of their robes, and puppets of their heads.

Macunaíma is more real than his author. Like every flesh-and-blood Brazilian, Mário de Andrade is a figment of the imagination.

(23)

1927: Paris
Villa-Lobos

From behind the enormous cigar floats a cloud of smoke. Enveloped within it, happy and in love, Heitor Villa-Lobos whistles a vagabond tune.

In Brazil, hostile critics claim he composes music to be played by epileptics for an audience of paranoiacs, but in France he is received with ovations. The Paris press enthusiastically applauds his audacious harmonies and his vigorous sense of nationality. They publish articles on the maestro's life. One newspaper recounts how Villa-Lobos was once bound to a grill and almost roasted alive by cannibal Indians while out strolling in the Amazon jungle with a Victrola in his arms playing Bach.

At one of the many parties they throw for him between concerts in Paris, a lady asks him if he has eaten people raw, and how he liked it.

(280)

1927: The Plains of Jalisco
Behind a Huge Cross of Sticks

charge the *Cristeros,* rebelling in Jalisco and other states of Mexico in search of martyrdom and glory. They shout *Vivas!* for a Christ the King crowned with jewels instead of thorns, and *Vivas!* for the Pope, who has not resigned himself to the loss of the few clerical privileges still remaining in Mexico.

These poor campesinos have just been dying for a revolution that promised them land. Now, condemned to a living death, they start dying for a Church that promises them heaven.

(297)

1927: San Gabriel de Jalisco
A Child Looks On

The mother covers his eyes so he cannot see his grandfather hanging by the feet. And then the mother's hands prevent his seeing his father's body riddled by the bandits' bullets, or his uncle's twisting in the wind over there on the telegraph posts.

Now the mother too has died, or perhaps has just tired of defending her child's eyes. Sitting on the stone fence that snakes over the slopes, Juan Rulfo contemplates his harsh land with a naked eye. He sees horsemen—federal police or *Cristeros,* it makes no difference—emerging from smoke, and behind them, in the distance, a fire. He sees bodies hanging in a row, nothing now but ragged clothing emptied by the vultures. He sees a procession of women dressed in black.

Juan Rulfo, a child of nine, is surrounded by ghosts who look like him.

Here there is nothing alive—the only voices those of howling coyotes, the only air the black wind that rises in gusts from the plains of Jalisco, where the survivors are only dead people pretending.

(48 and 400)

1927: El Chipote

The War of Jaguars and Birds

Fifteen years ago the Marines landed in Nicaragua for a while, *to protect the lives and properties of United States citizens*, and forgot to leave. Against them now loom these northern mountains. Villages are scarce here; but anyone who hasn't actually become one of Sandino's soldiers is his spy or messenger. Since the dynamiting of the San Albino mine and the first battle, at Muy Muy, the liberating force keeps growing.

The whole Honduran army is mobilized on the border to prevent arms from reaching Sandino from across the river, but the guerrillas, unconcerned, acquire rifles from fallen enemies and carve bullets out of the trees in which they imbed themselves; nor is there any shortage of machetes for chopping off heads, or sardine-can grenades filled with glass, nails, screws, and dynamite for scattering the enemy.

U.S. airplanes bomb haphazardly, destroying villages. And Marines roam the forests, between abysses and high peaks, roasted by the sun, drowned by the rain, asphyxiated by dust, burning and killing all they find. Even the little monkeys throw things at them.

They offer Sandino a pardon and ten dollars for every day he has been in rebellion. Captain Hatfield hints at a surrender.

From his stronghold in El Chipote, a mysterious peak wreathed in mist, comes the reply: *I don't sell out or surrender.* It closes: *Your obedient servant, who desires to put you in a handsome coffin with beautiful bouquets of flowers.* And then Sandino's signature.

His soldiers bite like jaguars and flit like birds. When least expected, they lash out in a single jaguar leap, and before the enemy can even react are already striking from the rear or the flanks, only to disappear with a flap of wings.

(118 and 361)

1928: San Rafael del Norte
Crazy Little Army

Four Corsairs bombard El Chipote, already encircled and harassed by salvos from Marine artillery. For days and nights now the whole region thunders and trembles, until the invaders fix bayonets and charge the stone trenches bristling with rifles. This heroic action ends with neither dead nor wounded, because the attackers find only soldiers of straw and guns of sticks.

U.S. papers promptly report the victory without mentioning that the Marines have demolished a legion of dolls with wide-brimmed hats and black-and-red kerchiefs. They do verify, however, that Sandino himself is among the victims.

In the remote village of San Rafael del Norte, Sandino listens to his men singing by the light of campfires. There he receives word of his death.

"God and our mountains are with us. And after all is said and done, death is no more than a little moment of pain."

Over the past months thirty-six warships and six thousand more Marines have arrived as reinforcements in Nicaragua. Yet, of seventy-five big and small battles, almost all have been lost, and the quarry has slipped through their fingers, no one knows how.

Crazy little army, the Chilean poet Gabriela Mistral calls Sandino's battered warriors, these masters of daring and devilment.

(118, 361, and 419)

"It Was All Very Brotherly"

JUAN PABLO RAMÍREZ: *We made dolls of straw and stuck them there. As decoys we fixed up sticks topped by sombreros. And it was fun . . . They spent a week firing at them, bombing them, and I pissed in my pants laughing!*

ALFONSO ALEXANDER: *The invaders were like the elephant and we the snake. They were immobility, we were mobility.*

PEDRO ANTONIO ARAÚZ: *The Yanquis died sad deaths, the ingrates. They just didn't know how things work in our country's mountains.*

SINFOROSO GONZÁLEZ ZELEDÓN: *The campesinos helped us, they worked with us, they felt for us.*

COSME CASTRO ANDINO: *We weren't drawing any pay. When we got to a village and the campesinos gave us food, we shared it. It was all very brotherly.*

(236)

1928: Washington

Newsreel

In an emotional ceremony in Washington, ten Marine officers receive the Cross of Merit *for distinguished service and extraordinary heroism* in the war against Sandino.

The *Washington Herald* and other papers devote pages to the crimes of the *outlaw band* who slit Marines' throats. They also publish documents newly arrived from Mexico, with impressive numbers of spelling mistakes, proving that Mexican president Calles is sending bolshevik weapons and propaganda to Sandino through Soviet diplomats. Official State Department sources explain that Calles began revealing his communist sympathies when he raised taxes on U.S. oil companies operating in Mexico, and fully confirmed them when his government established diplomatic relations with the Soviet Union.

The U.S. government warns that it *will not permit Russian and Mexican soldiers to implant the Soviet in Nicaragua.* According to official State Department spokesmen, Mexico is *exporting bolshevism.* After Nicaragua the next target of Soviet expansion in Central America will be the Panama Canal.

Senator Shortridge declares that the citizens of the United States *deserve as much protection as those of ancient Rome,* and Senator Bingham says: *We are obliged to accept our function as international policemen.* Senator Bingham, the famous archaeologist who sixteen years ago discovered the ruins of Machu Picchu in Peru, has never concealed his admiration for the works of dead Indians.

For the opposition, Senator Borah denies his country's right to act as the censor of Central America, and Senator Wheeler suggests that the government send Marines to Chicago, not Nicaragua, if it really wants to take on bandits. The *Nation* magazine, for its part, takes the view that for the U.S. president to call Sandino a bandit is like George III of England labeling George Washington a thief.

(39 and 419)

1928: Managua
Profile of Colonial Power

North American children study geography from maps showing Nicaragua as a colored blob labeled *Protectorate of the United States of America.*

When the United States decided that Nicaragua could not govern itself, there were forty public schools in its Atlantic coast region. Now there are six. The tutelary power has not put in a railroad, opened a single highway, or founded a university. At the same time, the occupied country falls farther into debt, paying the costs of its own occupation, while the occupiers continue to occupy—to guarantee the payment of the expenses of the occupation.

The Nicaraguan customs offices are in the hands of North American creditor banks, which appoint Clifford D. Ham comptroller of customs and general tax collector. Ham is also the Nicaraguan correspondent for the United Press news agency, The vice-comptroller of customs and vice-collector of taxes, Irving Lindbergh, is the correspondent for the Associated Press. So Ham and Lindbergh not only usurp the tariffs of Nicaragua, they also usurp the information. It is they who inform international public opinion about the misdeeds of Sandino, *criminal bandit and bolshevik agent.* A North American colonel leads the Nicaraguan army—the National Guard—and a North American captain leads the Nicaraguan police.

North American General Frank McCoy administers the National Electoral Junta. Four hundred and thirty-two U.S. Marines and twelve U.S. airplanes preside over the voting tables. The Nicaraguans vote, the North Americans elect. The new president is barely chosen before he announces that the Marines will stay.

This unforgettable civic fiesta has been organized by General Logan Feland, commander of the occupation forces. General Feland, all muscle and eyebrows, crosses his feet under the desk. In the matter of Sandino, he yawns and says, *"This bird has to fall one day."*

(39 and 419)

1928: Mexico City

Obregón

At the Náinari hacienda in Mexico's Yaqui Valley, the dogs howled.

"*Shut them up!*" ordered General Álvaro Obregón.

But the dogs barked more than ever.

"*Have them fed!*" ordered the general.

But the dogs ignored the food and continued their uproar.

"*Throw them fresh meat!*"

But the fresh meat had no effect. Even when they were beaten, the din went on.

"*I know what they want,*" said Obregón with resignation.

This happened on May 17. On July 9, in Culiacán, Obregón was sipping a tamarind drink in the shade of a porch, when the cathedral bells tolled and the poet Chuy Andrade, slightly drunk, said, "*They're tolling for you, friend.*"

And the next day, in Escuinapa, after a banquet of shrimp tamales, Obregón was boarding a train when Elisa Beaven, a good friend, pressed his arm and pleaded with him in her hoarse voice, "*Don't go. They're going to kill you.*"

But Obregón entered the train anyway and rode to the capital. After all, he had known how to muscle and hustle his way ahead in the days when bullets buzzed like hornets. He was the killer of killers, the conqueror of conquerors, and had won power, and glory, and money, without losing anything but the hand that Pancho Villa blew off; so he wasn't about to back off now that he knew his days were numbered. He simply went ahead, blithely but sadly. He had, after all, lost his one innocence: the happiness of unconcern about his own death.

Today, July 17, 1928, two months after the dogs barked in Náinari, a Christ-the-King fanatic kills reelected President Álvaro Obregón in a Mexico City restaurant.

(4)

1928: Villahermosa

The Priest Eater

Obregón is hardly dead, felled by the bullets of an ultra-Catholic, when Governor Manuel Garrido of the Mexican state of Tabasco decrees vengeance. He orders the cathedral demolished to the last stone, and from the bronze of the bells erects a statue of the late lamented.

Garrido believes that Catholicism shuts workers into a cage of fear, terrorizing them with the threat of eternal fire. For freedom to come to Tabasco, says Garrido, religion must go; and he kicks it out, decapitating saints, wrecking churches, yanking crosses out of cemeteries, forcing priests to marry, and renaming all places named after saints. The state capital, San Juan Bautista, becomes Villahermosa. And in a solemn ceremony he has a stud bull called "Bishop" and an ass, "Pope."

(283)

1928: Southern Santa Marta

Bananization

They were no more than lost villages on the Colombian coast, a strip of dust between river and cemetery, a yawn between two siestas, when the yellow train of the United Fruit Company pulled in. Coughing smoke, the train had crossed the swamps and penetrated the jungle and emerged here in brilliant clarity, announcing with a whistle that the age of the banana had come.

The region awoke to find itself an immense plantation. Ciénaga, Aracataca, and Fundación got telegraph and post offices and new streets with poolrooms and brothels. Campesinos, who arrived by the thousands, left their mules at the hitching posts and went to work.

For years these workers proved obedient and cheap as they hacked at the undergrowth and roots with their machetes for less than a dollar a day, and consented to live in filthy sheds and die of malaria or tuberculosis.

Then they form a union.

(186 and 464)

1928: Aracataca

The Curse

Swelter and languor and rancor. Bananas rot on the trees. Oxen sleep before empty carts. Trains stand dead on their tracks, not a single bunch of fruit reaching them. Seven ships wait anchored at the Santa Marta piers: in their fruit-less holds, the ventilators have stopped whirring.

Four hundred strikers are behind bars, but the strike goes relentlessly on.

In Aracataca, United Fruit throws a supper in honor of the regional Civil and Military Chief. Over dessert, General Carlos Cortés Vargas curses the workers, *armed evildoers*, and their *bolshevik agitators*, and announces that tomorrow he'll march to Ciénaga at the head of the forces of order, to get on with the job.

(93 and 464)

1928: Ciénaga

Carnage

On the shores of Ciénaga, a high tide of banners. Men with machetes at their waists, women toting pots and children wait here amid the campfires. The company has promised that tonight it will sign an agreement ending the strike.

Instead of the manager of United Fruit comes General Cortés Vargas. Instead of an agreement he reads them an ultimatum.

No one moves. Three times the warning bugle blares. And then, in an instant, the world explodes, sudden thunder of thunders, as machineguns and rifles empty. The plaza is carpeted with dead.

The soldiers sweep and wash all night long, while corpses are thrown into the sea. In the morning there is nothing.

"In Macondo nothing has happened, nor is happening, nor ever will happen."

(93 and 464)

1928: Aracataca

García Márquez

The roundup is on for the wounded and hiding strikers. They are hunted like rabbits, with broadsides from a moving train, and in the stations netted like fish. One hundred and twenty are captured in Aracataca in a single night. The soldiers awaken the priest and grab the key to the cemetery. Trembling in his underwear, the priest listens as the shootings begin.

Not far away, a little boy bawls in his crib.

The years will pass and this child will reveal to the world the secrets of a region so attacked by a plague of forgetfulness that it lost the names of things. He will discover the documents that tell how the workers were shot in the plaza, and how Big Mamma is the owner of lives and haciendas and of the rain that has fallen and will fall, and how between rain and rain Remedios the Beautiful goes to heaven, and in the air passes a little old plucked angel who is falling into a henhouse.

(187 and 464)

1928: Bogotá

Newsreel

The press reports on recent events in the banana zone. According to official sources, the excesses of the strikers have left a total of forty plantations burned, thirty-five thousand meters of telegraph wires destroyed, and eight workers killed when they tried to attack the army.

The president of the republic charges the strikers with treason and felony. *With their poisoned dagger they have pierced the loving heart of the Fatherland,* he declares. By decree, the president appoints General Cortés Vargas head of the National Police, and announces promotions and rewards for the other officers who participated in the events.

In a spectacular speech, the young liberal legislator Jorge Eliécer Gaitán contradicts the official story. He accuses the Colombian army of committing butchery under the orders of a foreign company. The United Fruit Company, which directed the massacre, according to

Gaitán, has subsequently reduced the daily wage that it pays in coupons, not money. The legislator stresses that the company exploits lands donated by the Colombian state, which are not subject to taxes.

(174 and 464)

1929: Mexico City
Mella

The dictator of Cuba, Gerardo Machado, orders him killed. Julio Antonio Mella is just another expatriate student in Mexico, intensely busy chasing around and publishing articles—for very few readers—against racism and the hidden face of colonialism; but the dictator is not mistaken in thinking him his most dangerous enemy. He has been a marked man ever since his fiery speeches rocked Havana's students. Mella blazed as he denounced the dictatorship and mocked the decrepitude of the Cuban university, a factory of professionals with the mentality of a colonial convent.

One night Mella is strolling arm in arm with his friend Tina Modotti, when the murderers shoot him down.

Tina screams, but doesn't cry. Not until she returns home at dawn and sees Mella's empty shoes waiting for her under the bed.

Until a few hours ago, this woman was so happy she was jealous of herself.

(290)

1929: Mexico City
Tina Modotti

The Cuban government has nothing to do with it, insist the right-wing Mexican papers. Mella was the victim of a crime of passion, *whatever the Muscovite bolshevik yids may say*. The press reveals that Tina Modotti, *a woman of dubious decency*, reacted coldly to the tragic episode and subsequently, in her statements to the police, fell into suspicious contradictions.

Modotti, an Italian photographer, has dug her feet deeply into Mexico in the few years she has been here. Her photographs mirror a grandeur in everyday things, and in people who work with their hands.

But she is guilty of freedom. She was living alone when she found Mella mixed up in a crowd demonstrating for Sacco and Vanzetti and for Sandino, and she hitched up with him unceremoniously. Previously she had been a Hollywood actress, a model, and a lover of artists; and she makes every man who sees her nervous. In short, she is a harlot—and to top it off, a foreigner and a communist. The police circulate photos showing her unforgivable beauty in the nude, while proceedings begin to expel her from Mexico.

(112)

1929: Mexico City
Frida

Tina Modotti is not alone before her inquisitors. Accompanying her, one on each arm, are Diego Rivera and Frida Kahlo: the immense painter-Buddha and his little Frida, also a painter, Tina's best friend, who looks like a mysterious oriental princess but swears and drinks tequila like a Jalisco mariachi.

Kahlo has a wild laugh, and has painted splendid canvases in oils ever since the day she was condemned to pain without end. She had known other pain from infancy, when her parents dressed her up with straw wings. But constant and crippling agony has come only since her accident, when a shard from a shattered street car pierced her body, like a lance, tearing at her bones.

Now she is a pain that survives as a person. They have operated in vain several times; and it was in her hospital bed that she started painting self-portraits, desperate homage to the life that remains for her.

(224 and 444)

1929: Capela
Lampião

The most famous gang in northeast Brazil attacks the town of Capela. Its chief, Lampião, who never smiles, fixes a reasonable sum as ransom, then offers a reduction, because we are in the drought season. While the town notables drum up the money, he strolls the streets.

The whole town follows him. His horrifying crimes have won him general admiration.

Lampião, the one-eyed king, master of the open spaces, sparkles in the sun. His glittering gold-wire glasses give him the look of an absent-minded professor; his gleaming dagger is as long as a sword. On each finger shimmers a diamond ring, and to the hairband around his forehead are sewn English pound notes.

Lampião wanders into the cinema, where they are showing a Janet Gaynor film. That night he dines at the hotel. The town telegraph operator, seated beside him, tastes the first mouthful of each dish. Then Lampião has a few drinks while reading Ellen G. White's *Life of Jesus*. He ends the day in the whorehouse. He picks the plumpest one, a certain Enedina. With her he spends the whole night. By dawn, Enedina is famous. For years men will line up outside her door.

(120 and 348)

1929: Atlantic City
The Crime Trust

Organized crime in the United States holds its first national convention, in the salons of the President Hotel. Attending are the qualified representatives of mobs operating in each of the major cities.

Olive branch, white flag: The convention resolves that rival gangs will stop killing one another and decrees a general amnesty. To guarantee peace, the executives of the crime industry follow the example of the oil industry. As Standard Oil and Shell have just done, the powerful gangsters divide markets, fix prices, and agree to eliminate the competition of small and middle fry.

In recent years, crime's impresarios have diversified their activities and modernized their methods. Now they not only engage in extortion, murder, pimping, and smuggling, but also own distilleries, hotels, casinos, banks, and supermarkets. They use the latest-model machineguns and accounting machines. Engineers, economists, and publicity experts direct the teams of technicians that avoid waste of resources and ensure a constant rise in profits.

Al Capone chairs the board of the most lucrative company in the game. He earns a hundred million dollars a year.

(335)

1929: Chicago
Al Capone

Ten thousand students chant the name of Al Capone on the sports field of Northwestern University. The popular Capone greets the multitude with a two-handed wave. Twelve bodyguards escort him. At the gate an armored Cadillac awaits him. Capone sports a rose in his lapel and a diamond stickpin in his tie, but underneath he wears a steel vest, and his heart beats against a .45.

He is an idol. No one provides as much business for funeral parlors, flower shops, and tailors who do invisible mending on small holes; and he pays generous salaries to policemen, judges, legislators, and mayors. Exemplary family man, Capone abominates short skirts and cosmetics. He believes woman's place is in the kitchen. Fervent patriot, he exhibits portraits of George Washington and Abraham Lincoln on his desk. Influential professional, he offers the best available service for breaking strikes, beating up workers, and sending rebels to the other world. He is ever alert to the red menace.

(335)

Al Capone Calls for Defense Against the Communist Danger

Bolshevism is knocking at our door. We must not let it in. We have to remain united and defend ourselves against it with full decisiveness. America must remain safe and uncorrupted. We must protect the workers from the red press and from red perfidy, and ensure that their minds stay healthy . . .

(153)

1929: New York
Euphoria

Millions are reading *The Man Nobody Knows*, the book by Bruce Barton that places heaven on Wall Street. According to the author, Jesus of Nazareth founded the modern world of business. Jesus, it turns out, was a market-conquering entrepreneur gifted with a genius for publicity, professionally assisted by twelve salesmen in his image and likeness.

With a faith bordering on the religious, capitalism believes in its own eternity. What North American citizen does not feel himself one of the elect? The Stock Exchange is a casino where everybody plays and no one loses. God has made them prosperous. The entrepreneur Henry Ford wishes he never had to sleep, so he could make more money.

(2 and 304)

From the Capitalist Manifesto of Henry Ford, Automobile Manufacturer

Bolshevism failed because it was both unnatural and immoral. Our system stands . . .

There can be no greater absurdity and no greater disservice to humanity in general, than to insist that all men are equal . . .

Money comes naturally as the result of service. And it is absolutely necessary to have money. But we do not want to forget that the end of money is not ease but the opportunity to perform more service. In my mind nothing is more abhorrent than a life of ease. None of us has any right to ease. There is no place in civilization for the idler . . .

In our first advertisement we showed that a motor car was a utility. We said: "We often hear quoted the old proverb, 'Time is money'—and yet how few business and professional men act as if they really believed its truth . . ."

(168)

1929: New York
The Crisis

Speculation grows faster than production and production faster than consumption, and everything grows at a giddy rhythm until, all of a sudden, in a single day, the collapse of the New York Stock Exchange reduces to ashes the profits of years. The most prized stocks become mere scraps of paper, useless even for wrapping fish.

Prices and salaries plummet along with stock quotations, and more than one businessman from his tower. Factories and banks close; farmers are ruined. Workers without jobs chafe their hands at burning garbage heaps and chew gum to pacify their stomachs. The largest enterprises collapse; and even Al Capone takes a fall.

(2 and 304)

1930: La Paz

A Touching Adventure of the Prince of Wales Among the Savages

The New York Stock Exchange pulls many governments down into the abyss. International prices crumble, and with them, one after another, the civilian presidents of Latin America—feathers plucked from the wings of the eagle—and new dictatorships are born, to make hunger hungrier.

In Bolivia, the collapse of the price of tin brings down President Hernando Siles and puts in his place a general on the payroll of Patiño, the tin king. A mob accompanying the military rises, attacks the government palace, is granted permission to loot it. Out of control, they make off with furniture, carpets, paintings, everything. Everything. They take whole bathrooms, including toilets, tubs, and drainpipes.

Just then the Prince of Wales visits Bolivia. The people expect a prince to arrive in the style God intended, riding on a white steed, a sword at his waist and golden locks streaming in the wind. They are disappointed by a gentleman with top hat and cane who gets off the train looking exhausted.

That evening the new president offers the prince a banquet in the stripped-down palace. At dessert, just when speeches are due to begin, His Highness whispers dramatic words into the ear of his interpreter, who transmits them to the aide-de-camp, who transmits them to the president. The president turns pale. The prince's foot nervously taps the floor. His wishes are commands; but in the palace there's no place, no way. Without hesitation the president appoints a committee, headed by the Foreign Minister and the Chief of the Armed Forces.

Impressively top-hatted and plumed, the retinue accompanies the prince at a dignified but brisk pace, almost a hop, across the Plaza de Armas. Arriving at the corner, they all enter the Paris Hotel. The

Foreign Minister opens the door marked GENTLEMEN and points the way for the heir to the imperial British crown.

(34)

1930: Buenos Aires

Yrigoyen

The world crisis also leaves Argentine president Hipólito Yrigoyen teetering at the edge of a precipice, doomed by the collapse of meat and wheat prices.

Silent and alone, a stubborn old hangover from another time, another world, Yrigoyen still refuses to use the telephone, has never entered a movie theater, distrusts automobiles, and doesn't believe in airplanes. He has conquered the people just by chatting, convincing them one by one, little by little, without speeches. Now the same people who yesterday unyoked the horses from his carriage and pulled him with their hands, revile him. The crowd actually throws his furniture into the street.

The military coup that overthrows him has been cooked up at the Jockey Club and the Círculo de Armas on the flames of this sudden crisis. The ailing patriarch, creaking with rheumatism, sealed his own fate when he refused to hand over Argentine petroleum to Standard Oil and Shell. Worse, he wanted to alleviate the price catastrophe by doing business with the Soviet Union.

Once more, for the good of the world, the hour of the sword has struck, writes the poet Leopoldo Lugones, ushering in the military era in Argentina.

At the height of the coup, a young captain, Juan Domingo Perón, observes some enthusiast dashing at top speed from the government palace, yelling, *"Long live the Fatherland! Long live the Revolution!"*

The enthusiast carries an Argentine flag rolled up under his arm. Inside the flag is a stolen typewriter.

(178, 341, and 365)

1930: Paris

Ortiz Echagüe, Journalist, Comments on the Fallen Price of Meat

Every time I return from Buenos Aires, the Argentines in Paris ask me: "How are the cows?"

One must come to Paris to appreciate the importance of the Argentine cow. Last night at El Garrón—a Montmartre cabaret where young Argentines experience the tough apprenticeship of life—some guys at a neighboring table asked me, with that small-hours familiarity, "Say, chum, how are the cows back home making out?"

"Pretty down and out," I said.

"And they can't get up?"

"Doesn't look good."

"You don't have any cows?"

I felt my pockets and said no.

"You don't know, old pal, how lucky you are." At that point three concertinas broke into sobs of nostalgia and cut the dialogue short.

"How are the cows?" I have been asked by maître d's and musicians, flower girls and waiters, pallid ballerinas, gold-braided porters, diligent grooms, and above all, by painted women, those poor baggy-eyed anemic women . . .

(325)

1930: Avellaneda

The Cow, the Sword, and the Cross

form the holy trinity of power in Argentina. Conservative Party toughs guard the altar.

In the heart of Buenos Aires, white-gloved gunmen use laws and decrees like machineguns in their holdups. Experts in double accounting and double morality, they needn't trouble themselves picking locks. They don't have doctorates for nothing. They know precisely what secret combinations will open the country's cashboxes.

Across the river, in Avellaneda, the Conservative Party sticks to honest shooting for its politics and business. Don Alberto Barceló, senator, makes and breaks lives from his throne there. Outcasts line up to receive from Don Alberto some small gratuity, fatherly advice, a chummy embrace. His brother, One-Arm Enrique, takes care of the brothel department. Don Alberto's responsibilities are lotteries and social peace. He smokes with a holder, spies on the world from beneath swollen lids. His henchmen break strikes, burn libraries, wreck printshops, and make short work of trade unionists, Jews, and all who forget to pay up and obey in this hour of crisis so conducive to disorder. Afterward, the good Don Alberto will give a hundred pesos to the orphans.

(166 and 176)

1930: Castex
The Last Rebel Gaucho

on the Argentine pampa is called Bairoletto, the son of peasants from Italy. He became an outlaw quite young, after shooting in the forehead a policeman who had humiliated him, and now he has no choice but to sleep outdoors. In the desert, beaten by the wind, he appears and disappears, lightning or mirage, riding an inky-black stallion that jumps seven-strand wire fences without effort. The poor protect him, and he avenges them against the powerful who abuse them and then swallow up their land. At the end of each raid, he engraves a B with bullets into the wings of the estancia's windmill, and seeds the wind with anarchist pamphlets foretelling revolution.

(123)

1930: Santo Domingo
The Hurricane

beats down with a roar, smashing ships against piers, shredding bridges, uprooting trees and whirling them through the air. Tin roofs, flying like crazy hatchets, decapitate people. This island is being leveled by winds, raked by lightning, drowned by rain and sea. The hurricane strikes as if revenging itself, or executing some fantastic curse. One might think that the Dominican Republic had been condemned, alone, to pay a debt due from the entire planet.

Later, when the hurricane moves on, the burning begins. Corpses and ruins have to be incinerated or plagues will finish off whatever remains alive and standing. For a week a vast cloud of black smoke hangs over the city of Santo Domingo.

So go the first days of the government of General Rafael Leónidas Trujillo, who has come to power on the eve of the cyclone, borne by a no less catastrophic fall in the international price of sugar.

(60 and 101)

1930: Ilopango
Miguel at Twenty-Five

The crisis also knocks the price of coffee for a loop. Beans spoil on the trees; a sickly odor of rotten coffee hangs in the air. Throughout Central America, growers put their workers out on the road. The few who still have work get the same rations as hogs.

In the worst of the crisis the Communist Party is born in El Salvador. Miguel, now a master shoemaker who works wherever he finds himself, is one of the founders. He stirs people up, wins recruits, hides and flees, the police always on his heels.

One morning Miguel, in disguise, approaches his house. It seems not to be watched. He hears his little boy crying and he enters. The child is alone, screaming his lungs out. Miguel has begun changing his diapers when he looks up and through the window sees police surrounding the place.

"Pardon me," he says to his shitty little half-changed boy, and springs up like a cat, slipping through a hole between some broken roof tiles just as the first shots ring out.

And so occurs the fourth birth of Miguel Mármol, at twenty-five years of age.

(126 and 404)

1930: New York
Daily Life in the Crisis

Unpleasantly, like a series of rude slaps in the face, the crisis wakes up North Americans. The disaster at the New York Stock Exchange has pricked the Great Dream, which promised to fill every pocket with money, every sky with planes, every inch of land with automobiles and skyscrapers.

Nobody is selling optimism in the market. Fashions sadden. Long faces, long dresses, long hair. The roaring twenties come to an end, and with them, the exposed leg and bobbed hair.

All consumption drops vertically. Sales are up only for cigarettes, horoscopes, and twenty-five-watt bulbs, which don't give much light, but don't draw much current. Hollywood prepares films about giant monsters on the loose: King Kong, Frankenstein, as inexplicable as the economy, as unstoppable as the crisis that sows terror in the streets of the city.

(15 and 331)

1930: Achuapa
Shrinking the Rainbow

Nicaragua, a country condemned to produce cheap desserts— bananas, coffee, and sugar—keeps on ruining the digestion of its customers.

The Sandinista chief Miguel Ángel Ortez celebrates the new year by wiping out a Marine patrol in the muddy ravines of Achuapa, and on the same day another patrol falls over a precipice in the vicinity of Ocotal.

In vain, the invaders seek victory through hunger, by burning huts and crops. Many families are forced to take to the mountains, wandering and unprotected. Behind them they leave pillars of smoke and bayonetted animals.

The campesinos believe that Sandino knows how to lure the rainbow to him; and as it comes it shrinks until he can pick it up with just two fingers.

(118 and 361)

1931: Bocay
The Trumpets Will Sound

By the light of aromatic pitch-pine chips, Sandino writes letters, orders, and reports to be read aloud in the camp on the military and political situation in Nicaragua (*Like a firecracker, the enemy will soon burn himself out . . .*), manifestos condemning traitors (*They will find no place to live, unless under seven spans of earth . . .*), and prophesies announcing that soon war trumpets will sound against oppressors everywhere, and sooner than later the Last Judgment will destroy injustice so that the world may at last be what it wanted to be when there was was still nothing.

(237)

Sandino Writes to One of His Officers: "We won't be able to walk for all the flowers . . ."

If sleep, hunger, or petty fears overtake you, ask God to comfort you . . . God will give us this other triumph, which will be the definitive one, because I am sure that after this battle they won't come back to get their change, and you will be covered with glory! When we enter Managua, we won't be able to walk for all the flowers . . .

(361)

1931: Bocay
Santos López

Whoever joins the liberating army gets no pay, no pay ever, only the right to be called *brother*. He has to find a rifle on his own, in battle, and maybe a uniform stripped from some dead Marine, to wear once the pants have been properly shortened.

Santos López has been with Sandino from day one. He had worked for the farmers who owned him since he was eight. He was twelve at the time of the San Albino mine rebellion, and became a water boy and messenger in Sandino's army, a spy among drunken or distracted enemies, and along with his other buddies, specialized in setting ambushes and creating diversions with cans and whatever noisy odds and ends he could lay his hands on to make a few people seem like a crowd.

Santos López turns seventeen on the day Sandino promotes him to colonel.

(236, 267, and 361)

1931: Bocay

Tranquilino

In Sandino's rickety arsenal the finest weapon is a Browning machine-gun of the latest model, rescued from a North American plane downed by rifle fire.

In the hands of Tranquilino Jarquín, this Browning shoots and sings.

Tranquilino is the cook. He shows one tooth when he smiles, sticks an orchid in his hat, and as he stirs the big steaming pot, meat-poor but rich in aroma, he tosses down a good swig of rum.

In Sandino's army drinking is forbidden, Tranquilino excepted. It took a lot to win that privilege. But without his little swigs this artist of wooden spoon and trigger doesn't function. When they put him on a water diet, his dishes are flat, his shots twisted and off-key.

(236 and 393)

1931: Bocay

Little Cabrera

Tranquilino makes music with the machinegun, Pedro Cabrera with the trumpet. For Tranquilino's Browning it's bursts of tangos, marches, and ballads, while Little Cabrera's trumpet moans protests of love and proclaims brave deeds.

To kiss his celestial trumpet each morning, Little Cabrera must freeze his body and shut his eyes. Before dawn he wakens the soldiers, and at night lulls them to sleep, blowing low, low, lingering notes.

Musician and poet, warm heart and itchy feet, Little Cabrera has been Sandino's assistant since the war began. Nature has given him a yard and a half of stature and seven women.

(393)

1931: Hanwell

The Winner

Charlie the Tramp visits Hanwell School. He walks on one leg, as if skating. He twists his ear and out spurts a stream of water. Hundreds of children, orphaned, poor, or abandoned, scream with laughter. Thirty-five years ago, Charlie Chaplin was one of these children. Now he recognizes the chair he used to sit on and the corner of the dismal gym where he was birched.

Later he had escaped to London. In those days, shop windows displayed sizzling pork chops and golden potatoes steeped in gravy; Chaplin's nose still remembers the smell that filtered through the glass to mock him. And still engraved in his memory are the prices of other unattainable treats: a cup of tea, one halfpenny; a bit of herring, one penny; a tart, twopence.

Twenty years ago he left England in a cattle boat. Now he returns, the most famous man in the world. A cloud of journalists follows him like his shadow, and wherever he goes crowds jostle to see him, touch him. He can do whatever he wants. At the height of the talkie euphoria, his silent films have a devastating success. And he can spend whatever he wants—although he never wants. On the screen, Charlie the Tramp, poor leaf in the wind, knows nothing of money; in reality, Charles Chaplin, who perspires millions, watches the pennies and is incapable of looking at a painting without calculating its price. He will never share the fate of Buster Keaton, a man with open pockets, from whom everything flies away as soon as he earns it.

(121 and 383)

1932: Hollywood

The Loser

Buster Keaton arrives at the Metro studios hours late, dragging the hangover of last night's drinking spree: feverish eyes, coppery tongue, dishrag muscles. Who knows how he manages to execute the clownish pirouettes and recite the idiotic jokes ordered by the script.

Now his films are talkies and Keaton is not allowed to improvise; nor may he do retakes in search of that elusive instant when poetry discovers imprisoned laughter and unchains it. Keaton, genius of liberty and silence, must follow to the letter the charlatan scenarios written by others. In this way costs are halved and talent eliminated, according to the production norms of the movie factories of the sound-film era. Left behind forever are the days when Hollywood was a mad adventure.

Every day Keaton feels more at home with dogs and cows. Every night he opens a bottle of bourbon and implores his own memory to drink and be still.

(128 and 382)

1932: Mexico City

Eisenstein

While in Mexico they accuse him of being a *bolshevik, homosexual, and libertine*; in Hollywood they call him a *red dog and friend of murderers*.

Sergei Eisenstein has come to Mexico to film an indigenous epic. Before it is half-produced, the guts are ripped out. The Mexican censor bans some scenes because the truth is all very well, but not so much of it, thank you. The North American producer leaves the filmed footage in the hands of whoever may want to cut it to pieces.

Eisenstein's film *Que Viva México* ends up as nothing but a pile of grandiose scraps, images lacking articulation put together incoherently or with deceit, dazzling letters torn loose from a word that was never before spoken about this country, this delirium sprung from the place where the bottom of the sea meets the center of the earth: pyramids that are volcanoes about to erupt, creepers interwoven like hungry bodies, stones that breathe . . .

(151 and 305)

1932: The Roads of Santa Fe

The Puppeteer

didn't know he was one until the evening when, high on a balcony in Buenos Aires with a friend, he noticed a haycart passing down the street. On the hay lay a young boy smoking, face to the sky, hands behind his neck, legs crossed. Both he and his friend felt an irrepressible urge to get away. The friend took off with a woman toward the mysterious frozen lands to the South of the South; and the puppeteer discovered puppeteering, craft of the free, and hit the road on a cart pulled by two horses.

From town to town along the banks of the River Paraná, the cart's wooden wheels leave long scars. The name of the puppeteer, conjurer of happiness, is Javier Villafañe. Javier travels with his children whose flesh is paper and paste. The best beloved of them is Master Globetrotter: long sad nose, black cape, flying necktie. During the show he is an extension of Javier's hand, and afterward, he sleeps and dreams at his feet, in a shoebox.

1932: Izalco
The Right to Vote and Its Painful Consequences

General Maximiliano Hernández Martínez, president by coup d'état, convokes the people of El Salvador to elect deputies and mayors. Despite a thousand traps, the tiny Communist Party wins the elections. The general takes umbrage. Scrutiny of ballots is suspended *sine die*.

Swindled, the Communists rebel. Salvadorans erupt on the same day that the Izalco volcano erupts. As boiling lava runs down the slopes and clouds of ashes blot out the sky, red campesinos attack the barracks with machetes in Izalco, Nahuizalco, Tacuba, Juayúa, and other towns. For three days America's first soviets come to power.

Three days. Three months of slaughter follow. Farabundo Martí and other Communist leaders face firing squads. Soldiers beat to death the Indian chief José Feliciano Ama, leader of the revolution in Izalco. They hang Ama's corpse in the main plaza and force schoolchildren to watch the show. Thirty thousand campesinos, denounced by their employers, or condemned on mere suspicion or old wives' tales, dig their own graves with their hands. Children die too, for Communists, like snakes, need to be killed young. Wherever a dog or pig scratches up the earth, remains of people appear. One of the firing-squad victims is the shoemaker Miguel Mármol.

(9, 21, and 404)

1932: Soyapango
Miguel at Twenty-Six

As they take them away bound in a truck, Miguel recognizes his childhood haunts.

"What luck," he thinks, *"I'm going to die where my umbilical cord was buried."*

They beat them to the ground with rifle butts, then shoot them in pairs. The truck's headlights and the moon give more than enough light.

After a few volleys, it's the turn of Miguel and a man who sells engravings, condemned for being Russian. The Russian and Miguel, standing before the firing squad, grip each other's hands, which are bound behind their backs. Miguel itches all over and desperately needs to scratch; this fills his mind as he hears: *"Ready! Aim! Fire!"*

Miguel regains consciousness under a pile of bodies dripping blood. He feels his head throbbing and bleeding, and the pain of the bullets in his body, soul, and clothes. He hears the click of a rifle reloading. A coup de grâce.

Another. Another. His eyes misted with blood, Miguel awaits the final shot, but feels a machete chopping at him instead.

The soldiers kick the bodies into a ditch and throw dirt over them. Hearing the trucks drive off, Miguel, wounded and cut, tries to move. It takes him centuries to crawl out from under so much death and earth. Finally, managing to walk at a ferociously slow pace, more falling than standing, he very gradually gets out, wearing the sombrero of a comrade whose name was Serafín.

And so occurs the fifth birth of Miguel Mármol, at twenty-six.

(126)

1932: Managua

Sandino Is Advancing

in a great sweep that reaches the banks of Lake Managua. The occupation troops fall back in disarray. Meanwhile, two photographs appear in the world's newspapers. One shows Lieutenant Pensington of the United States Navy holding up a trophy, a head chopped from a Nicaraguan campesino. From the other smiles the entire general staff of the Nicaraguan National Guard, officers wearing high boots and safari headgear. At their center is seated the director of the Guard, Colonel Calvin B. Matthews. Behind them is the jungle. At the feet of the group, sprawled on the ground, is a dog. The jungle and the dog are the only Nicaraguans.

(118 and 361)

1932: San Salvador

Miguel at Twenty-Seven

Of those who saved Miguel, no one is left. Soldiers have riddled with bullets the comrades who found him in a ditch, those who carried him across the river on a chair of hands, those who hid him in a cave, and those who managed to bring him to his sister's home in San Salvador. When his sister saw the specter of Miguel stitched with bullets and crisscrossed with machete cuts, she had to be revived with a fan. Praying, she began a novena for his eternal rest.

The funeral service proceeds. Miguel begins to recover as best he can, hidden behind the altar set up in his memory, with nothing but the chichipince-juice ointment his sister applies with saintly patience to his purulent wounds. Lying behind the curtain, burning with fever, Miguel spends his birthday listening to disconsolate relatives and neighbors awash in oceans of tears, extolling his memory with nonstop prayers.

On one of these nights a military patrol stops at the door.

"Who are you praying for?"

"For the soul of my brother, the departed."

The soldiers enter, approach the altar, wrinkle their noses.

Miguel's sister clutches her rosary. The candles flicker before the image of our Lord Jesus Christ. Miguel has the sudden urge to cough. The soldiers cross themselves. "May he rest in peace," they say, and continue on their way.

And so occurs the sixth birth of Miguel Mármol, at twenty-seven.

(126)

1933: Managua

The First U.S. Military Defeat
in Latin America

On the first day of the year the Marines leave Nicaragua with all their ships and planes. The scraggy general, the little man who looks like a capital T with his wide-brimmed sombrero, has humbled an empire.

The U.S. press deplores the many dead in so many years of occupation, but stresses the value of the training of their aviators. Thanks to the war against Sandino, the United States has for the first time been able to experiment with aerial bombing from Fokker and Curtiss planes specially designed to fight in Nicaragua.

The departing Colonel Matthews is replaced by a sympathetic and faithful native officer, Anastasio Tacho Somoza, as head of the National Guard, now called the Guardia Nacional.

As soon as he reaches Managua, the triumphant Sandino says: *"Now we're free. I won't fire another shot."*

The president of Nicaragua, Juan Bautista Sacasa, greets him with an embrace. General Somoza embraces him too.

(118 and 361)

1933: Camp Jordán

The Chaco War

Bolivia and Paraguay are at war. The two poorest countries in South America, the two with no ocean, the two most thoroughly conquered and looted, annihilate each other for a bit of map. Concealed in the folds of both flags, Standard Oil and Royal Dutch Shell are disputing the oil of the Chaco.

In this war, Paraguayans and Bolivians are compelled to hate each other in the name of a land they do not love, that nobody loves. The Chaco is a gray desert inhabited by thorns and snakes; not a songbird or a person in sight. Everything is thirsty in this world of horror. Butterflies form desperate clots on the few drops of water. For Bolivians, it is going from freezer to oven: They are hauled down from the heights of the Andes and dumped into these roasting scrub-lands. Here some die of bullets, but more die of thirst.

Clouds of flies and mosquitos pursue the soldiers, who charge through thickets, heads lowered, on forced marches against enemy lines. On both sides barefoot people are the down payment on the errors of their officers. The slaves of feudal landlord and rural priest die in different uniforms, at the service of imperial avarice.

One of the Bolivian soldiers marching to death speaks. He says nothing about glory, nothing about the Fatherland. He says, breathing heavily, *"A curse on the hour that I was born a man."*

(354 and 402)

Céspedes

On the Bolivian side, this pitiful epic will be related by Augusto Céspedes:

A squadron of soldiers in search of water start digging a well with picks and shovels. The little rain that has fallen has already evaporated, and there is no water anywhere. At twelve meters the water hunters come upon liquid mud. But at thirty meters, at forty-five, the pulley brings up bucketfuls of sand, each one drier than the last. The soldiers keep on digging, day after day, into that well of sand, ever deeper, ever more silent. And when the Paraguayans, likewise hounded by thirst, launch an attack, the Bolivians die defending the well as if it contained water.

(96)

Roa Bastos

From the Paraguayan side, Augusto Roa Bastos will tell the story. He too will speak of wells that become graves, and of the multitude of dead, and of the living who are only distinguishable from them by the fact that they move, though like drunkards who have forgotten the way home. He will accompany the lost soldiers, who haven't a drop of water, not even to shed as tears.

(380)

1934: Managua
Horror Film: Scenario for Two Actors and a Few Extras

Somoza leaves the house of Arthur Bliss Lane, ambassador of the United States.

Sandino arrives at the house of Sacasa, president of Nicaragua.

While Somoza sits down to work with his officers, Sandino sits down to supper with the president.

Somoza tells his officers that the ambassador has just given his unconditional support to the killing of Sandino.

Sandino tells the president about the problems of the Wiwilí cooperative, where he and his soldiers have been working the land for over a year.

Somoza explains to his officers that Sandino is a communistic enemy of order, who has many more weapons concealed than those he has turned in.

Sandino explains to the president that Somoza won't let him work in peace.

Somoza discusses with his officers whether Sandino should die by poison, shooting, airplane accident, or ambush in the mountains.

Sandino discusses with the president the growing power of the Guardia Nacional, led by Somoza, and warns that Somoza will soon blow him away to sit in the presidential chair himself.

Somoza finishes settling some practical details and leaves his officers.

Sandino finishes his coffee and takes leave of the president.

Somoza goes off to a poetry reading and Sandino goes off to his death.

While Somoza listens to the sonnets of Zoila Rosa Cárdenas, young luminary of Peruvian letters who honors this country by her visit, Sandino is shot in a place called The Skull, on Lonesome Road.

(339 and 405)

1934: Managua

The Government Decides That Crime Does Not Exist

That night, Colonel Santos López escapes the trap in Managua. On a bleeding leg, his seventh bullet wound in these years of war, he climbs over roofs, drops to the ground, jumps walls, and finally begins a nightmare crawl northward along the railroad tracks.

The next day, while Santos López is still dragging his wounded leg along the lake shore, a wholesale massacre takes place in the mountains. Somoza orders the Wiwilí cooperative destroyed, and the new Guardia Nacional strikes with total surprise, wiping out Sandino's former soldiers, who were sowing tobacco and bananas and had a hospital half built. The mules are saved, but not the children.

Soon after, banquets in homage to Somoza are given by the United States embassy in Managua and by the most exclusive clubs of León and Granada.

The government issues orders to forget. An amnesty wipes out all crimes committed since the eve of Sandino's death.

(267 and 405)

1934: San Salvador

Miguel at Twenty-Nine

Hunted as ever by the Salvadoran police, Miguel finds refuge in the house of the Spanish consul's lover.

One night a storm sweeps in. From the window, Miguel sees that, far over there where the river bends, the rising waters are threatening the mud-and-cane hut of his wife and children. Leaving his hideout in defiance of both gale and night patrol, Miguel hurries to his family.

They spend the night huddled together inside the fragile walls, listening to the roar of wind and river. At dawn, when winds and waters subside, the little hut is slightly askew and very damp, but still standing. And so Miguel says goodbye to his family and returns to his refuge.

But it is nowhere to be found. Of that solidly built house not a brick remains. The fury of the river has undermined the ravine, torn away the foundations, and carried off to the devil the house, the consul's lover, and the servant girl.

And so occurs the seventh birth of Miguel Mármol, at twenty-nine years of age.

(126)

1935: The Villamontes-Boyuibe Road
After Ninety Thousand Deaths

the Chaco War ends. It is three years since the first Paraguayan and Bolivian bullets were exchanged in a hamlet called Masamaclay, which in the Indian language means *place where two brothers fought*.

At noon the news reaches the front. The guns fall silent. The soldiers stand up, very slowly, and even more slowly emerge from the trenches. Ragged ghosts, blinded by the sun, they lurch across the no-man's-land between Bolivia's Santa Cruz regiment and Paraguay's Toledo regiment—the scraps, the shreds. Newly received orders prohibit fraternization with those who just now were enemies. Only the military salute is allowed; and so they salute each other. But someone lets loose a great howl, and then there is no stopping it. The soldiers break ranks, throw caps, weapons, anything, everything into the air and run in mad confusion, Paraguayans to Bolivians, Bolivians to Paraguayans, shouting, singing, weeping, embracing one another as they roll in the hot sand.

(354 and 402)

1935: Maracay
Gómez

The dictator of Venezuela, Juan Vicente Gómez, dies and keeps on ruling. For twenty-seven years no one has been able to budge him, and now no one dares crack a joke about his corpse. When the coffin of the terrible old man is unquestionably buried beneath a heap of earth, the prisoners finally break down the jail doors, and only then does the cheering and looting begin.

Gómez died a bachelor. He has sired mountains of children, loving as if relieving himself, but has never spent a whole night in a woman's arms. The dawn light always found him alone in his iron bed beneath the image of the Virgin Mary and alongside his chests filled with money.

He never spent a penny, paying for everything with oil. He distributed oil in gushers, to Gulf, Standard, Texaco, Shell, and with oil wells paid for the doctor who probed his bladder, for the poets whose sonnets hymned his glory, and for the executioners whose secret tasks kept his order.

(114, 333, and 366)

1935: Buenos Aires
Borges

Everything that brings people together, like football or politics, and everything that multiples them, like a mirror or the act of love, gives him the horrors. He recognizes no other reality than what exists in the past, in the past of his forefathers, and in books written by those who knew how to expound that reality. The rest is smoke.

With great delicacy and sharp wit, Jorge Luis Borges tells the *Universal History of Infamy*. About the national infamy that surrounds him, he doesn't even inquire.

(25 and 59)

1935: Buenos Aires
These Infamous Years

In London, the Argentine government signs a commercial treaty selling the country for halfpence. In the opulent estates north of Buenos Aires, the cattlocracy dance the waltz in shady arbors; but if the entire country is worth only halfpence, how much are its poorest children worth? Working hands go at bargain prices and you can find any number of girls who will strip for a cup of coffee. New factories sprout, and around them tin-can barrios, harried by police and tuberculosis, where yesterday's maté, dried in the sun, stifles hunger. The Argentine police invent the electric prod to convince those in doubt and straighten out those who buckle.

In the Buenos Aires night, the pimp seeks a girl wanting a good time, and the girl seeks a man who'll give her one; the racetrack gambler seeks a hot tip; the con man, a sucker; the jobless, a job in the early editions. Coming and going in the streets are the bohemian, the roué, and the cardsharp, all solitary in their solitude, while Discepolín's last tango sings that the world was and will continue to be a dirty joke.

(176, 365, and 412)

1935: Buenos Aires

Discepolín

He is one long bone with a nose, so thin that injections are put through his overcoat, the somber poet of Buenos Aires in the infamous years.

Enrique Santos Discépolo creates his first tangos, *sad thoughts that can be danced,* as a touring-company comedian lost in the provinces. In ramshackle dressing rooms he makes the acquaintance of huge, almost human-size fleas, and for them he hums tangos that speak of those with neither money nor faith.

(379)

1935: Buenos Aires

Evita

To look at, she's just a run-of-the-mill stick of a girl, pale, washed-out, not ugly, not pretty, who wears secondhand clothes and solemnly repeats the daily routines of poverty. Like the others, she lives hanging on to each episode of the radio soaps, dreams every Sunday of being Norma Shearer, and every evening goes to the railway station to see the Buenos Aires train pass by. But Eva Duarte has turned fifteen and she's fed up; she climbs aboard the train and takes off.

This little creature has nothing at all. No father, no money, no memories to hold on to. Since she was born in the town of Los Toldos, of an unmarried mother, she has been condemned to humiliation, and now she is a nobody among the thousands of nobodies the trains pour into Buenos Aires every day, a multitude of tousle-haired dark-skinned provincials, workers and servant girls who are sucked into the city's mouth and are promptly devoured. During the week Buenos Aires chews them up; on Sundays it spits out the pieces.

At the feet of the arrogant Moloch, great peaks of cement, Evita is paralyzed by a panic that only lets her clasp her hands, red and cold, and weep. Then she dries her tears, clenches her teeth, takes a firm grip of her cardboard valise, and buries herself in the city.

(311 and 417)

1935: Buenos Aires
Alfonsina

The ovaries of a woman who thinks dry up. Woman is born to produce milk and tears, not ideas; not to live life but to spy on it through slatted venetian blinds. A thousand times they have explained it to her but Alfonsina Storni never believed them, and her best-known verses protest against the macho jailer.

When she came to Buenos Aires from the provinces, all Alfonsina had were some down-at-heel shoes and, in her belly, a child with no legal father. In this city she worked at whatever she could get and stole blank telegram forms to write her sorrows. As she polished her words, verse by verse, night by night, she crossed her fingers and kissed the cards that announced journeys, inheritances, and loves.

Time has passed, almost a quarter of a century, and fate has given her no presents. But somehow Alfonsina has made her way in the male world. Her face, like a mischievous mouse, is never missing from group photos of Argentina's most illustrious writers.

This year, this summer, she finds she has cancer. So now she writes of the embrace of the sea and of the home that awaits her in the depths, on the avenue of Corals.

(310)

1935: Medellín
Gardel

Each time he sings, in that voice of many colors, he sings as never before. He makes dark notes, his opaque lyrics shine. He's the Magician, the Greatest, Carlos Gardel.

The shadow of a sombrero over his eyes, a perpetual and perfect smile forever young, he looks like a winner who has never been defeated. His origin is a mystery; his life, an enigma. Tragedy had no choice but to save him from explanation and decay. His worshippers would not have forgiven him for old age. The plane in which he is traveling takes off from Medellín airport and blows up in flight.

1936: Buenos Aires
Patoruzú

For ten years the Patoruzú comic strip, the work of Dante Quintero, has been published in the Buenos Aires dailies. Now, a monthly magazine appears wholly devoted to the character. Patoruzú is a big landlord, the owner of half of Patagonia, who lives in five-star hotels in Buenos Aires, squanders millions with both hands, and passionately believes in private property and the consumer civilization. Dante Quintero explains that Patoruzú is a typical Argentine Indian.

(446 and 456)

1936: Rio de Janeiro
Olga and He

With his rebel army Luis Carlos Prestes has crossed the immensity of Brazil on foot, end to end, there and back, southern prairies to northeastern deserts, the whole breadth of the Amazon jungle. In three years the Prestes Column has battled the coffee and sugar barons to a standstill, without a single defeat. So that Olga Benário imagined him as some devastating giant of a man, and is amazed when he turns out to be a fragile little fellow who blushes when she looks him in the eye.

She, toughened in the revolutionary struggles of Germany, a militant without frontiers, loves and sustains this rebel who has never known a woman. In time, both are taken prisoner. They are taken to different prisons.

From Germany, Hitler demands Olga, that Jew and Communist—vile blood, vile ideas—and Brazilian president Getulio Vargas turns her over. When soldiers come for her the prisoners riot. Olga stops them, seeing no point in useless slaughter, and lets herself be taken. Through the bars of his cell the novelist Graciliano Ramos sees her pass, handcuffed, with her pregnant belly.

At the docks a ship flying the swastika sits waiting for her; the captain has orders to head straight for Hamburg. There, Olga will be deposited in a concentration camp, asphyxiated in a gas chamber, carbonized in an oven.

(263, 302, and 364)

1936: Madrid
The Spanish War

The rising against the Spanish republic has been incubated in barracks, sacristies, and palaces. Generals, monks, lackeys of the king, and feudal lords of the gallows and the knife are its murky protagonists. The Chilean poet Pablo Neruda curses them, invoking the bullets that will one day find a home in their hearts. In Granada the fascists have just shot his beloved brother Federico García Lorca, the poet of Andalusía, *the ever-free flash of lightning,* for being or seeming to be homosexual and red.

Neruda roams the Spanish earth so soaked in blood and is transformed. The poet, distracted by politics, asks of poetry that it make itself useful like metal or flour, that it get ready to stain its face with coal dust and fight body to body.

(313 and 314)

1936: San Salvador
Martínez

At the head of the rebellion, Francisco Franco proclaims himself Generalisimo and Spanish Chief of State. The first diplomatic recognition comes to the city of Burgos from the remote Caribbean. General Maximiliano Hernández Martínez, dictator of El Salvador, congratulates the newly born dictatorship of his colleague.

Martínez, the kindly grandfather who murdered thirty thousand Salvadorans, believes killing ants more criminal than killing people; because ants, he says, cannot be reincarnated. Every Sunday Maestro Martínez speaks to the country on the radio about the international political situation, intestinal parasites, the reincarnation of souls, and the Communist peril. He routinely cures the ills of his ministers and officials with colored waters kept in big bottles on the patio of the presidential palace, and when the smallpox epidemic strikes he scares it off by wrapping the street lights in red cellophane.

To uncover conspiracies, he hangs a clock pendulum over steaming soup. For the gravest problems he resorts to President Roosevelt, communicating directly with the White House by telepathy.

(250)

1936: San Salvador
Miguel at Thirty-One

Miguel, just released from jail—almost two years handcuffed in solitary—wanders the roads, a ragged pariah with nothing. He has no party, because his Communist Party comrades suspect he made a deal with dictator Martínez. He has no work, because dictator Martínez sees to it that he can't get any. He has no wife, because she has left him and taken the children with her; no house either, or food, or shoes, or even a name. It has been officially established that Miguel Mármol does not exist, because he was executed in 1932.

He decides to put an end to it, once and for all. Enough of these thoughts. A single machete blow will open his veins. He is just raising the machete when a boy on a burro appears in the road. The boy greets him with a sweep of his enormous straw sombrero, asks to borrow the machete to split a coconut, then offers half the split nut, water to drink, coconut meat to eat. Miguel drinks and eats as if this unknown lad had invited him to a feast, and gets up and walks away from death.

And thus occurs the eighth birth of Miguel Mármol, at thirty-one years of age.

(126)

1936: Guatemala City
Ubico

Martínez has beaten him to it by a few hours, but Ubico is the second to recognize Franco. Ten days before Hitler and Mussolini, Ubico puts a stamp of legitimacy on the rising against Spanish democracy.

General Jorge Ubico, Chief of State of Guatemala, governs surrounded by effigies of Napoleon Bonaparte, whom he resembles, he says, like a twin. But Ubico rides motorcycles and the war he is waging has nothing to do with the conquest of Europe. His is a war against bad thoughts.

Against bad thoughts, military discipline. Ubico militarizes the post office employees, the symphony orchestra musicians, and the schoolchildren. Since a full belly is the mother of bad thoughts, he has United Fruit's plantation wages cut by half. He scourges idleness, father of bad thoughts, by forcing those guilty of it to work his lands for nothing. To expel the bad thoughts from the minds of revolutionaries, he invents a steel crown that squeezes their heads in police dungeons.

Ubico has imposed on the Indians a compulsory contribution of five centavos a month to raise a great monument to Ubico. Hand in jacket, he poses for the sculptor.

(250)

1936: Trujillo City

In the Year Six of the Trujillo Era

the name of the Dominican Republic's capital is corrected. Santo Domingo, so baptized by its founders, becomes Trujillo City. The port is now called Trujillo, as are many towns, plazas, markets, and avenues. From Trujillo City, Generalísimo Rafael Leónidas Trujillo sends Generalísimo Francisco Franco his most ardent support.

Trujillo, tireless bane of reds and heretics, was, like Anastasio Somoza, born of a U.S. military occupation. His natural modesty does not prevent him from allowing his name to appear on all automobile license plates and his likeness on all postage stamps, nor does he oppose the conferring of the rank of colonel on his three-year-old son Ramfis, as an act of simple justice. His sense of responsibility obliges him to appoint personally all ministers, porters, bishops, and beauty queens. To stimulate the spirit of enterprise, Trujillo grants the salt, tobacco, oil, cement, flour, and match monopolies to Trujillo. In defense of public health, Trujillo closes down businesses that do not sell meat from the Trujillo slaughterhouses or milk from his dairy farms; and for the sake of public security he makes obligatory the purchase of insurance policies sold by Trujillo. Firmly grasping the helm of progress, Trujillo releases the Trujillo enterprises from taxes, while providing his estates with irrigation and roads and his factories with customers. By order of Trujillo, shoe manufacturer, anyone caught barefoot on the streets of town or city goes to jail.

The all-powerful has a voice like a whistle, with which there is no discussion. At supper, he clinks glasses with a governor or deputy who will be off to the cemetery after coffee. When a piece of land interests him, he doesn't buy it: he occupies it. When a woman appeals to him, he doesn't seduce her; he points at her.

(89, 101, and 177)

Procedure Against Rain

What the Dominican Republic needs when torrential rains drown crops is a proper supplicant who can walk in the rain without getting wet to send up urgent pleas to God and the Blessed Saint Barbara. Twins are especially good at leashing rain and scaring off thunder.

In the Dominican region of Salcedo they use another method. They look for two big oval stones, the kind that get polished by the river; they tie them firmly to a rope, one at each end, and hang them from the bough of a tree. Giving the stone eggs a hard squeeze and a sharp tug, they pray to God, who lets out a yell and moves on somewhere else with his black clouds.

(251)

Procedure Against Disobedience

A woman of daily Masses and continual prayer and penitence, the mother of María la O skinned her knees imploring God for the miracle of making her daughter obedient and good, and begging pardon for the brazen girl's insolences.

One Good Friday evening, María la O went down to the river. Her mother tried in vain to stop her: *"Just think, they're killing Our Lord Jesus Christ . . ."*

God's wrath leaves forever stuck together those who make love on Good Friday, and though María la O was not going to meet a lover, she did commit a sin. She swam naked in the river, and when the water tickled the prohibited recesses of her body, she trembled with pleasure.

Afterward she tried to get out of the river and couldn't because she was covered with scales and had a flipper where her feet had been.

And in the waters of Dominican rivers María la O swims to this day: she was never forgiven.

(251)

1937: Dajabón

Procedure Against the Black Menace

The condemned are Haitian blacks who work in the Dominican Republic. This military exorcism, planned to the last detail by General Trujillo, lasts a day and a half. In the sugar region, the soldiers shut up Haitian day-laborers in corrals—herds of men, women, and children—and finish them off then and there with machetes; or bind their hands and feet and drive them at bayonet point into the sea.

Trujillo, who powders his face several times a day, wants the Dominician Republic white.

(101, 177, and 286)

1937: Washington

Newsreel

Two weeks later, the government of Haiti conveys to the government of the Dominican Republic its *concern about the recent events at the border*. The government of the Dominican Republic promises *an exhaustive investigation*.

In the name of continental security, the government of the United States proposes to President Trujillo that he pay an indemnity to avoid possible friction in the zone. After prolonged negotiation Trujillo recognizes the death of eighteen thousand Haitians on Dominican territory. According to him, the figure of twenty-five thousand victims, put forward by some sources, reflects the intention to manipulate the events dishonestly. Trujillo agrees to pay the government of Haiti, by way of indemnity, $522,000, or twenty-nine dollars for every officially recognized death.

The White House congratulates itself on an agreement reached within the framework of established inter-American treaties and procedures. Secretary of State Cordell Hull declares in Washington that

President Trujillo is one of the greatest men in Central America and in most of South America.

The indemnity duly paid in cash, the presidents of the Dominican Republic and Haiti embrace each other at the border.

(101)

1937: Rio de Janeiro

Procedure Against the Red Menace

The president of Brazil, Getulio Vargas, has no alternative but to set up a dictatorship. A drumroll of press and radio reports discloses the sinister Cohen Plan, obliging Vargas to suppress Parliament and the electoral process. The Fatherland is not about to sit back and succumb to the advance of Moscow's hordes. The Cohen Plan, which the government has discovered in some cellar, gives the full details—tactics *and* strategy—of the Communist plot against Brazil.

The plan is called "Cohen" due to a stenographic error. The originator of the plan, Captain Olympio Mourão Filho, actually baptized it the Kun Plan, having based it on documents from the brief Hungarian revolution headed by Béla Kun.

But the name is secondary. Captain Mourão Filho gets a well-earned promotion to major.

(43)

1937: Cariri Valley

The Crime of Community

From planes, they bomb and machinegun them. On the ground, they cut their throats, burn them alive, crucify them. Forty years after it wiped out the community of Canudos, the Brazilian army does the same to Caldeirão, verdant island in the northeast, and for the same crime—denying the principle of private property.

In Caldeirão nothing belonged to anyone: neither textile looms, nor brick ovens, nor the sea of cornfields around the village, nor the snowy immensity of cotton fields beyond. The owners were everyone and no one, and there were no naked or hungry. The needy had formed this community at the call of the Holy Cross of the Desert, which saintly José Lourenço, desert pilgrim, had carried there on his shoulder. The Virgin Mary had chosen both the spot for the cross and the holy man to bring it. Where he stuck in the cross, water flowed continuously.

According to the newspapers of distant cities, this squalid holy man is the prosperous sultan of a harem of eleven thousand virgins; and if that were not enough, also an agent of Moscow with a concealed arsenal in his granaries.

Of the community of Caldeirão nothing and no one is left. The colt Trancelim, which only the holy man mounted, flees into the stony mountains. In vain it seeks some shrub offering shade under this infernal sun.

(3)

1937: Rio de Janeiro
Monteiro Lobato

The censors ban *The Oil Scandal* by Monteiro Lobato. The book offends the oil trust and its technicians, hired or purchased, who claim that Brazil has no oil.

The author has ruined himself trying to create a Brazilian oil company. Before that, he failed in the publishing business, when he had the crazy idea of selling books not only in bookstores, but also in pharmacies, bazaars, and newsstands.

Monteiro Lobato was born not to publish books but to write them. His forte is telling tales to children. On the Benteveo Amarillo farm a pig of small intelligence is the Marquis of Rabicó and an ear of corn becomes a distinguished viscount who can read the Bible in Latin and talk in English to Leghorn chickens. The Marquis casts a warm eye on Emilia, the rag doll, who chatters on nonstop, because she started so late in life and has so much chatter stored up.

(252)

1937: Madrid
Hemingway

The reports of Ernest Hemingway describe the war that is raging a step from his hotel in this capital besieged by Franco's soldiers and Hitler's airplanes.

Why has Hemingway gone to lonely Spain? He is not exactly a militant like the ones who have come from all parts of the world to join the International Brigades. What Hemingway reveals in his writings is something else—the desperate search for dignity among men. And dignity is the only thing that is not rationed in these trenches of the Spanish republic.

(220 and 312)

1937: Mexico City

The Bolero

Mexico's Ministry of Public Education prohibits the boleros of Agustín Lara in schools, because *their obscene, immoral, and degenerate lyrics* might corrupt children.

Lara exalts the Lost Woman, in whose eyes are seen sun-drunk palm trees; he beseeches love from the Decadent One, in whose pupils boredom spreads like a peacock's tail; he dreams of the sumptuous bed of the silky-skinned Courtesan; with sublime ecstasy he deposits roses at the feet of the Sinful One, and covers the Shameful Whore with incense and jewels in exchange for the honey of her mouth.

(299)

1937: Mexico City

Cantinflas

For laughter, the people flock into the suburban tents, poor little makeshift theaters, where all the footlights shine on Cantinflas.

"There are moments in life that are truly momentary," says Cantinflas, with his pencil mustache and baggy pants, reeling off his spiel at top speed. His fusillade of nonsense apes the rhetoric of half-baked intellectuals and politicians, doctors of verbal diarrhea who say nothing, who pursue a point with endless phrases, never catching up to it. In these lands, the economy suffers from monetary inflation; politics and culture from verbal inflation.

(205)

1937: Mexico City
Cárdenas

Mexico does not wash its hands of the war in Spain. Lázaro Cárdenas—rare president, friend of silence and enemy of verbosity—not only proclaims his solidarity, but practices it, sending arms to the republican front across the sea, and receiving orphaned children by the shipload.

Cárdenas listens as he governs. He gets around and listens. From town to town he goes, hearing complaints with infinite patience, and never promising more than is possible. A man of his word, he talks little. Until Cárdenas, the art of governing in Mexico consisted of moving the tongue; but when he says yes or no, people believe it. Last summer he announced an agrarian reform program and since then has not stopped allocating lands to native communities.

He is cordially hated by those for whom the revolution is a business. They say that Cárdenas keeps quiet because, spending so much time among the Indians, he has forgotten Spanish, and that one of these days he will appear in a loincloth and feathers.

(45, 78, and 201)

1938: Anenecuilco
Nicolás, Son of Zapata

Earlier than anyone else, harder than anyone else, the campesinos of Anenecuilco have fought for the land; but after so much time and bloodshed, little has changed in the community where Emiliano Zapata was born and rose in rebellion.

A bunch of papers, eaten by moths and centuries, lie at the heart of the struggle. These documents, with the seal of the viceroy on them, prove that this community is the owner of its own land. Emiliano Zapata left them in the hands of one of his soldiers, Pancho Franco: *"If you lose them, compadre, you'll dry up hanging from a branch."*

And, indeed, on several occasions, Pancho Franco has saved the papers and his life by a hair.

Anenecuilco's best friend is President Lázaro Cárdenas, who has visited, listened to the campesinos, and recognized and amplified their rights. Its worst enemy is deputy Nicolás Zapata, Emiliano's eldest son, who has taken possession of the richest lands and aims to get the rest too.

(468)

1938: Mexico City
The Nationalization of Oil

North of Tampico, Mexico's petroleum belongs to Standard Oil; to the south, Shell. Mexico pays dearly for its own oil, which Europe and the United States buy cheap. These companies have been looting the subsoil and robbing Mexico of taxes and salaries for thirty years—until one fine day Cárdenas decides that Mexico is the owner of Mexican oil.

Since that day, nobody can sleep a wink. The challenge wakes up the country. In never-ending demonstrations, enormous crowds stream into the streets carrying coffins for Standard and Shell on their backs. To a marimba beat and the tolling of bells, workers occupy wells and refineries. But the companies reply in kind: all the foreign technicians, those masters of mystery, are withdrawn. No one is left to tend the indecipherable instrument panels of management. The national flag flutters over silent towers. The drills are halted, the pipelines emptied, the fires extinguished. It is war: war against the Latin American tradition of impotence, the colonial custom of *don't know, no can do.*

(45, 201, 234, and 321)

1938: Mexico City
Showdown

Standard Oil demands an immediate invasion of Mexico.

If a single soldier shows up at the border, Cárdenas warns, he will order the wells set on fire. President Roosevelt whistles and looks the other way, but the British Crown, adopting the fury of Shell, announces it will not buy one more drop of Mexican oil. France concurs. Other countries join the blockade. Mexico can't find anyone to sell it a spare part, and the ships disappear from its ports.

Still, Cárdenas won't get off the mule. He looks for customers

in the prohibited areas—Red Russia, Nazi Germany, Fascist Italy—
while the abandoned installations revive bit by bit. The Mexican
workers mend, improvise, invent, getting by on pure enthusiasm,
and so the magic of creation begins to make dignity possible.

(45, 201, 234, and 321)

1938: Coyoacán

Trotsky

Every morning he is surprised to find himself alive. Although his
house has guardtowers and electrified wire fences, Leon Trotsky knows
it to be a futile fortress. The creator of the Red Army is grateful to
Mexico for giving him refuge, but even more grateful to fate. *"See,
Natasha?"* he says to his wife each morning. *"Last night they didn't
kill us, and yet you're complaining."*

Since Lenin's death, Stalin has liquidated, one after another, the
men who had made the Russian revolution—to save it, says Stalin;
to take it over, says Trotsky, a man marked for death.

Stubbornly, Trotsky continues to believe in socialism, fouled as
it is by human mud; for when all is said, who can deny that Christianity
is much more than the Inquisition?

(132)

1938: The Hinterland

The *Cangaceiros*

operate on a modest scale and never without motive. They don't rob
towns with more than two churches, and kill only by specific order
or for a vengeance sworn by kissing a dagger. They work in the burned
lands of the desert, far from the sea and the salty breath of its dragons.
They cross the lonely stretches of northeast Brazil, on horse or on
foot, their half-moon sombreros dripping with decorations. They rarely
linger anywhere. They neither raise their children nor bury their
parents. They have made a pact with Heaven and Hell not to shelter
their bodies from bullets or knives simply for the sake of dying a
natural death; and sooner or later these hazardous, hazarded lives, a
thousand times lauded in the couplets of blind singers, come to very
bad ends: *God will say, God will give, high road, long road*—the

epic of wandering bandits who go from fight to fight, without time for their sweat to go cold.

(136, 348, and 353)

1938: Angico
The *Cangaceiro* Hunters

To throw their enemies off the scent, the *cangaceiros* imitate the noises and tracks of animals or use trick soles with heel and toe reversed. But those who know, know. A good tracker recognizes the passage of humans through this dying landscape from what he sees, a broken branch or a stone out of place, and what he smells. The *cangaceiros* are crazy about perfume. They douse themselves by the liter, and this weakness betrays them.

Following tracks and scents, the hunters reach the hideout of Chief Lampião; and behind them the troops, so close they hear Lampião arguing with his wife. Seated on a stone at the entrance to a cave, María Bonita curses him, while smoking one cigarette after another; from within, he makes sad replies. The soldiers mount their machineguns and await the command to fire.

A light drizzle falls.

(52, 348, 352, and 353)

1939: São Salvador de Bahia
The Women of the Gods

Ruth Landes, North American anthropologist, comes to Brazil to learn about the lives of blacks in a country without racism. In Rio de Janeiro, Minister Osvaldo Aranha receives her. He explains that the government proposes to clean up the Brazilian race, soiled as it is by black blood, because black blood is to blame for national backwardness.

From Rio, Ruth goes to Bahia. In this city, where the sugar- and slave-rich viceroy once had his throne, blacks are an ample majority, and whether it's religion, music, or food, black is what is worthwhile here. Nevertheless, all Bahians, including blacks, think white skin is proof of good quality. No, not everyone. Ruth discovers pride of blackness in the women of the African temples.

There it is nearly always women, black priestesses, who receive in their bodies the gods from Africa. Resplendent and round as cannonballs, they offer their capacious bodies as homes where it is pleasant to visit, to linger. While the gods enter them, dance in them, from the hands of these possessed priestesses the people get encouragement and solace, and from their mouths hear the voices of fate.

The black priestesses of Bahia accept lovers, not husbands. What matrimony gives in prestige, it takes away in freedom and happiness. None of them is interested in formal marriage before priest or judge. None wants to be a handcuffed wife, a Mrs. Someone-or-other. Heads erect, with languid swings, the priestesses move like queens of Creation, condemning their men to the incomparable torment of jealousy of the gods.

(253)

Exú

An earthquake of drums disturbs Rio de Janeiro's sleep. From the backwoods, by firelight, Exú mocks the rich, sending against them his deadly curses. Perfidious avenger of the have-nots, he lights up the night and darkens the day. If he throws a stone into a thicket, the thicket bleeds.

The god of the poor is also a devil. He has two heads: one, Jesus of Nazareth; the other, Satan of Hell. In Bahia he is a pesky messenger from the other world, a little second-class god; but in the slums of Rio he is the powerful master of midnight. Capable of caress or crime, Exú can save or kill, sometimes both at once.

He comes from the bowels of the earth, entering violently, destructively, through the soles of unshod feet. He is lent body and voice by men and women who dance with rats in shacks perilously suspended over the void, people whom Exú redeems with such craziness that they roll on the ground laughing themselves to death.

(255)

María Padilha

She is both Exú and one of his women, mirror and lover: María Padilha, the most whorish of the female devils with whom Exú likes to roll in the bonfires.

She is not hard to recognize when she enters the body. María Padilha shrieks, howls insults, laughs crudely, and at the end of a trance demands expensive drinks and imported cigarettes. She has to be treated like a great lady and passionately implored before she will deign to use her well-known influence with the most important gods and devils.

María Padilha doesn't enter just any body. To manifest herself in this world, she chooses the women of the Rio slums who make a livelihood selling themselves for small change. Thus do the despised become worthy of devotion. Hired flesh mounts to the center of the altar. The garbage of the night shines brighter than the sun.

1939: Rio de Janeiro

The Samba

Brazil is Brazilian and so is God, proclaims Ari Barroso in the very patriotic and danceable music that is becoming the heart of Rio's carnival.

But the tastier samba lyrics offered at the carnival, far from exalting the virtues of this tropical paradise, perversely eulogize the bohemian life and the misdeeds of free souls, damn poverty and the police, and scorn work. Work is for idiots, because anyone can see that the bricklayer can never enter what his hands erect.

The samba, black rhythm, offspring of the chants that convoke the black gods of the slums, now dominates the carnivals, even if in respectable homes it is still scorned. It invites distrust because it is black and poor and born in the refuges of people hunted by the police. But the samba quickens the feet and caresses the soul and there is no disregarding it once it strikes up. The universe breathes to the rhythms of the samba until Ash Wednesday in a fiesta that turns every proletarian into a king, every paralytic into an athlete, and every bore into a beautiful madman.

(74 and 285)

1939: Rio de Janeiro

The Scoundrel

most feared in Rio is called Madame Satan.

When the child was seven, the mother swapped it for a horse. Since then, it has passed from hand to hand, master to master, until it ended up in a brothel where it learned the craft of cooking and the pleasures of the bed. There it became a professional tough, protector of whores, male and female, and of all defenseless bohemians. Beaten often enough and hard enough by the police to send several men to the cemetery, this fierce black never gets past hospital or jail.

Madame Satan is a he from Monday to Friday, a panama-hatted devil who with fist and razor dominates the night in the Lapa barrio, where he strolls about whistling a samba and marking time with a box of matches; but on the weekends he is a she, the very harpy who has just won the carnival fancy-dress contest with the campiest golden-bat cape, who wears a ring on every finger and moves her hips like her friend Carmen Miranda.

(146)

1939: Rio de Janeiro

Cartola

On the Mangueira knoll, Cartola is the soul of samba, and of practically everything else.

Often he passes by in a flash, waving his pants like a flag, pursued by some intolerant husband. Between his sprees and flights, melodies and protestations of love float up inside him, to be hummed and quickly forgotten.

Cartola sells his sambas to anyone who comes along and for whatever pittance he can get. He is always amazed that there are people who will pay anything at all for them.

(428)

1939: Montserrat

Vallejo

Mortally wounded, the Spanish republic staggers its final few steps. Little breath remains to it as Franco's exterminating army pushes on.

In the abbey of Montserrat, by way of farewell, the militias publish verses that two Latin Americans have written in homage to Spain and its tragedy. The poems of the Chilean Pablo Neruda and the Peruvian Vallejo are printed on paper made from rags of uniforms, enemy flags, and bandages.

César Vallejo has just died, hurt and alone, like Spain. He died in Paris, a day he had foreseen and recorded, and his last poems, written between four menacing walls, were for Spain. Vallejo sang of the heroism of the Spanish people in arms, of Spain's independent spirit, its beloved sun, beloved shade; and Spain was the last word he spoke in his death agony, this American poet, this most American of poets.

(457)

1939: Washington

Roosevelt

When Franklin Delano Roosevelt became president, the United States had fifteen million workless workers looking around with the eyes of lost children, raising a thumb on the highways as they wandered from city to city, barefoot or with cardboard tops on leaky soles, using public urinals and railroad stations for hotels.

To save his nation, Roosevelt's first act was to put money in a cage: He closed all the banks until the way ahead was clear. Since then he has governed the economy without letting it govern him, and has consolidated a democracy threatened by the crisis.

With Latin American dictators, however, he gets along fine. Roosevelt protects them, as he protects Ford automobiles, Kelvinator refrigerators, and other products of the United States.

(276 and 304)

1939: Washington

In the Year Nine of the Trujillo Era

a twenty-one-gun salute welcomes him to West Point, where Trujillo cools himself with a perfumed ivory fan and salutes the cadets with flutters of his ostrich-plume hat. A plump delegation of bishops, generals, and courtiers accompanies him, as well as a doctor and a sorcerer, both specializing in eye problems, not to speak of Brigadier General Ramfis Trujillo, age nine, dragging a sword longer than himself.

General George Marshall offers Trujillo a banquet on board the *Mayflower* and President Roosevelt receives him in the White House. Legislators, governors, and journalists shower this exemplary statesman with praise. Trujillo, who pays cash for murders, acquires his eulogies likewise, and lists the disbursements under the heading "Birdseed" in the executive budget of the Dominican Republic.

(60 and 177)

1939: Washington

Somoza

Before the Marines made him a general and the supreme boss of Nicaragua, Anastasio Tacho Somoza had pursued a successful career forging gold coins and cheating at poker and love.

Now that all power is his, Sandino's murderer has turned the national budget into his private bank account and has personally taken over the country's richest lands. He has liquidated his lukewarm enemies by firing National Bank loans at them, while his warmer enemies have providentially ended up in accidents or ambushes.

Somoza's visit to the United States is no less triumphant than Trujillo's. President Roosevelt and several cabinet members appear at Union Station to welcome him. A military band plays the anthems of both countries, and a rumble of guns and speeches follows. Somoza announces that the main avenue of Managua, which crosses the city from lake to lake, will be renamed Roosevelt Avenue.

(102)

1939: New York

Superman

Action Comics celebrates the first anniversary of the successful launch of Superman.

This Hercules of our time guards private property in the universe. From a place called Metropolis, flying faster than the speed of light and breaking time barriers, he travels to other epochs and galaxies. Wherever he goes, in this world or others, Superman restores order more efficiently and quickly than the whole Marine Corps put together. With a glance he melts steel, with a kick he fells a forest of trees, with a punch he perforates mountain chains.

In his other personality, Superman is timid Clark Kent, as meek as any of his readers.

(147)

1941: New York

Portrait of an Opinion Maker

At first, few theaters dare to show *Citizen Kane*, the movie in which Orson Welles tells the story of a man sick with power fever, a man who too closely resembles William Randolph Hearst.

Hearst owns eighteen newspapers, nine magazines, seven castles, and quite a few people. He is expert at stirring up public opinion. In his long life he has provoked wars and bankruptcies, made and destroyed fortunes, created idols and demolished reputations. Among his best inventions are the scandal campaign and the gossip column, so good for what he likes to do best—land a solid punch well below the belt.

The most powerful fabricator of opinion in the United States thinks that the white race is the only really human race; believes in the necessary victory of the strongest; is convinced that Communists are to blame for alcohol consumption among the young; and that Japanese are born traitors.

When Japan bombs the naval base at Pearl Harbor, Hearst's newspapers have already been beating a steady warning rhythm for half a century about the Yellow Peril. The United States enters the World War.

(130 and 441)

1942: New York

The Red Cross Doesn't Accept Black Blood

U.S. soldiers embark for the war fronts. Many are black under the command of white officers.

Those who survive will return home. The blacks will enter by the back door, and, in the Southern states, continue to live, work, and die apart, and even then will lie in separate graves. Hooded Ku Klux Klansmen will still insure that blacks do not intrude into the white world, and above all into the bedrooms of white women.

The war accepts blacks, thousands and thousands of them, but not the Red Cross. The Red Cross bans black blood in the plasma banks, so as to avoid the possibility that races might mix by tranfusion.

The research of Charles Drew, inventor of life, has finally made it possible to save blood. Thanks to him, plasma banks are reviving thousands of dying men on the battlefields of Europe.

When the Red Cross decides to reject the blood of blacks, Drew, director of the Red Cross plasma service, resigns. Drew is black.

(51, 218, and 262)

1942: Oxford, Mississippi

Faulkner

Seated on a rocker, on the columned porch of a decaying mansion, William Faulkner smokes his pipe and listens to the whispered confidences of ghosts.

The plantation masters tell Faulkner of their glories and their dreads. Nothing horrifies them like miscegenation. A drop of black blood, even one tiny drop, curses a whole life and ensures, after death, the fires of hell. The old Southern dynasties, born of crime and condemned to crime, watch anxiously over the pale splendor of their own twilight, affronted by the shadow of blackness, the slightest hint of blackness. These gentlemen would love to believe that purity

of lineage will not die out, though its memory may fade and the
trumpets of the horsemen defeated by Lincoln echo no more.

(163 and 247)

1942: Hollywood

Brecht

Hollywood manufactures films to turn the frightful vigil of humanity,
on the point of annihilation, into sweet dreams. Bertolt Brecht, exiled
from Hitler's Germany, is employed in this sleeping-pill industry.
Founder of a theater that sought to open eyes wide, he earns his
living at the United Artists studios, just one more writer who works
office hours for Hollywood, competing to produce the biggest daily
ration of idiocies.

On one of these days, Brecht buys a little God of Luck for forty
cents in a Chinese store and puts it on his desk. Brecht has been told
that the God of Luck licks his lips each time they make him take
poison.

(66)

1942: Hollywood

The Good Neighbors to the South

accompany the United States into the World War. It is the time of
democratic prices: Latin American countries supply cheap raw materials, cheap food, and a soldier or two.

The movies glorify the common cause. Rarely missing from a
film is the South American number, sung and danced in Spanish or
Portuguese. Donald Duck acquires a Brazilian sidekick, the little
parrot José Carioca. On Pacific islands or in the fields of Europe,
Hollywood Adonises wipe out Japanese and Germans by the heap.
And how many Adonises have at their sides a simpatico, indolent,
somewhat stupid Latin, who admires his blond northern brother and
serves as his echo and shadow, faithful henchman, merry minstrel,
messenger, and cook?

(467)

1942: María Barzola Pampa

A Latin American Method for Reducing Production Costs

Bolivia—subsisting, as ever, on hunger rations—is one of the countries that pays for the World War by selling its tin at a tenth of the normal price.

The mine workers finance this bargain price. Their wages go from almost nothing to nothing at all. And when a government decree calls for forced labor at gunpoint, the strikes begin. Another decree bans the strikes, but fails to stop them. So the president, Enrique Peñaranda, orders the army to take *severe and energetic* action. Patiño, king of the mines, issues his own orders: *Proceed without vacillation.* His viceroys, Aramayo and Hochschild, approve. The machineguns spit fire for hours and leave the ground strewn with people.

Patiño Mines pays for some coffins, but saves on indemnities. Death by machinegun is not an occupational hazard.

(97 and 474)

1943: Sans-Souci

Carpentier

Alejo Carpentier discovers the kingdom of Henri Christophe. The Cuban writer roams these majestic ruins, this memorial to the delirium of a slave cook who became monarch of Haiti and killed himself with the gold bullet that always hung around his neck. Ceremonial hymns and magic drums of invocation rise up to meet Carpentier as he visits the palace that King Christophe copied from Versailles, and walks around his invulnerable fortress, an immense bulk whose stones, cemented by the blood of bulls sacrificed to the gods, have resisted lightning and earthquakes.

In Haiti, Carpentier learns that there is no magic more prodigious and delightful than the voyage that leads through experience, through the body, to the depths of America. In Europe, magicians have become bureaucrats, and wonder, exhausted, has dwindled to a conjuring trick. But in America, surrealism is as natural as rain or madness.

(85)

1943: Port-au-Prince
Hands That Don't Lie

Dewitt Peters founds an open workshop and from it suddenly explodes Haitian art. Everybody paints everything: cloth, cardboard, cans, wooden boards, walls, whatever presents itself. They paint in a great outburst of splendor, with the seven souls of the rainbow. Everyone: the shoe repairman and fisherman, river washerwoman and market-stall holder. In America's poorest country, wrung out by Europe, invaded by the United States, torn apart by wars and dictatorships, the people shout colors and no one can shut them up.

(122, 142, and 385)

1943: Mount Rouis
A Little Grain of Salt

In a bar, surrounded by kids with bloated bellies and skeletal dogs, Hector Hyppolite paints gods with a brush of hens' feathers. Saint John the Baptist turns up in the evenings and helps him.

Hyppolite portrays the gods who paint through his hand. These Haitian gods, painted and painters, live simultaneously on earth and in heaven and hell: Capable of good and evil, they offer their children vengeance and solace.

Not all have come from Africa. Some were born here, like Baron Samedi, god of solemn stride, master of poisons and graves, his black-ness enhanced by top hat and cane. That poison should kill and the dead rest in peace depends upon Baron Samedi. He turns many dead into zombies and condemns them to slave labor.

Zombies—dead people who walk or live ones who have lost their souls—have a look of hopeless stupidity. But in no time they can escape and recover their lost lives, their stolen souls. One little grain of salt is enough to awaken them. And how could salt be lacking in the home of the slaves who defeated Napoleon and founded freedom in America?

(146, 233, and 295)

1944: New York

Learning to See

It is noon and James Baldwin is walking with a friend through the streets of downtown Manhattan. A red light stops them.

"Look," says the friend, pointing at the ground.

Baldwin looks. He sees nothing.

"Look, look."

Nothing. There is nothing to look at but a filthy little pool of water against the curb.

His friend insists: *"See? Are you seeing?"*

And then Baldwin takes a good look and this time he sees, sees a spot of oil spreading in the pool. Then, in the spot of oil, a rainbow, and even deeper down in the pool, the street moving, and people moving in the street: the shipwrecked, the madmen, the magicians, the whole world moving, an astounding world full of worlds that glow in the world. Baldwin sees. For the first time in his life, he sees.

(152)

1945: The Guatemala–El Salvador Border

Miguel at Forty

He sleeps in caves and cemeteries. Condemned by hunger to constant hiccups, he competes with the magpies for scraps. His sister, who meets him from time to time, says: *"God has given you many talents, but he has punished you by making you a Communist."*

Since Miguel recovered his party's confidence, the running and suffering have only increased. Now the party has decided that its most sacrificed member must go into exile in Guatemala.

Miguel manages to cross the border after a thousand hassles and dangers. It is deepest night. He stretches out, exhausted, under a tree. At daybreak, an enormous yellow cow wakens him by licking his feet.

"Good morning," Miguel says, and the cow, frightened, runs off

at full tilt, into the forest, lowing. From the forest promptly emerge five vengeful bulls. There is no escape. Behind Miguel is an abyss and the tree at his back has a smooth trunk. The bulls charge, then stop dead and stand staring, panting, breathing fire and smoke, tossing their horns and pawing the ground, tearing up undergrowth and raising the dust.

Miguel trembles in a cold sweat. Tongue-tied with panic, he stammers an explanation. The bulls stare at him, a little man half hunger and half fear, and look at each other. He commends himself to Marx and Saint Francis of Assisi as the bulls slowly turn their backs on him and wander off, heads shaking.

And so occurs the ninth birth of Miguel Mármol, at forty years of age.

(126)

1945: Hiroshima and Nagasaki
A Sun of Fire,

a violent light never before seen in the world, rises slowly, cracks the sky open, and collapses. Three days later, a second sun of suns bursts over Japan. Beneath remain the cinders of two cities, a desert of rubble, tens of thousands dead and more thousands condemned to die little by little for years to come.

The war was nearly over, Hitler and Mussolini gone, when President Harry Truman gave the order to drop atomic bombs on the populations of Hiroshima and Nagasaki. In the United States, it is the culmination of a national clamor for the prompt annihilation of the Yellow Peril. It is high time to finish off once and for all the imperial conceits of this arrogant Asian country, never colonized by anyone. The only good one is a dead one, says the press of these treacherous little monkeys.

Now all doubt is dispelled. There is one great conqueror among the conquerors. The United States emerges from the war intact and more powerful than ever. It acts as if the whole world were its trophy.

(140 and 276)

1945: Princeton
Einstein

Albert Einstein feels as if his own hand had pressed the button. Although he didn't make it, the atomic bomb would not have been possible without his discoveries about the liberation of energy. Now Einstein would like to have been someone else, to have devoted himself to some inoffensive task like fixing drains or building walls instead of investigating the secrets of life that others now use to destroy it.

When he was a boy, a professor said to him: *"You'll never amount to anything."*

Daydreaming, with the expression of someone on the moon, he wondered how light would look to a person able to ride on a beam. When he became a man, he found the answer in the theory of relativity, won a Nobel Prize, and deserved many more for his answers to other questions born in his mind of the mysterious link between Mozart's sonatas and the theorem of Pythagoras, or of the defiant arabesques that the smoke from his extra-long pipe drew in the air.

Einstein believed that science was a way of revealing the beauty of the universe. The most famous of sages has the saddest eyes in human history.

(150 and 228)

1945: Buenos Aires
Perón

General MacArthur takes charge of the Japanese, and Spruille Braden of the Argentines. To lead Argentina down the good road to Democracy, U.S. ambassador Braden brings together all the parties, Conservative to Communist, in a united front against Juan Domingo Perón. According to the State Department, Colonel Perón, the government's minister of labor, is the chief of a gang of Nazis. *Look* magazine calls him a pervert who keeps photos of nude Patagonian Indian women in his desk drawer along with pictures of Hitler and Mussolini.

Nonetheless, Perón flies swiftly along the road to the presidency with Evita, the radio actress with the feverish eyes and enticing voice;

and when he gets tired, or doubtful, or scared, it is she who takes the bit in her teeth. Perón now attracts more people than all the parties put together. When they call him "agitator," he accepts the epithet as an honor. VIPs and the fashionably chic chant the name of Ambassador Braden on the street corners of Buenos Aires, waving hats and handkerchiefs; but in worker barrios, the shirtless shout the name Perón. These laboring people, exiles in their own land, dumb from so much shutting up, find both a fatherland and a voice in this unusual minister who always takes their side.

Perón's popularity climbs and climbs as he shakes the dust off forgotten social laws or creates new ones. His is the law that compels respect for the rights of those who break their backs on estancias and plantations. The law does not merely remain on paper; thus the country peon, almost a thing, becomes a rural worker complete with a trade union.

(311 and 327)

1945: The Fields of Tucumán
The Familiar

flies into a rage over these novelties that disturb his dominions. Workers' unions infuriate and scare him more than the hilt of a knife.

On the sugarcane plantations of northern Argentina, the Familiar is responsible for the obedience of the peons. If one answers back or acts impertinently, the Familiar devours him in a single gulp. He moves with a clank of chains and stinks of sulphur, but no one knows if he is the devil in person or just an official. Only his victims have seen him, and no one seems able to add up the accounts. It is rumored that at night the Familiar turns into an enormous snake and patrols the sheds where the peons sleep, or that he crouches in wait on the roads in the form of a dog with flaming eyes, all black, with huge teeth and claws.

(103 and 328)

A Wake for a Little Angel

In the northern provinces of Argentina, they don't weep for the death of small children. One less mouth on earth, one more angel in heaven. Death is drunk and dances from the first cock-crow, sucking in long draughts of carob-bean liquor and *chicha* to the rhythm of bass drum and guitar. While the dancers whirl and stomp their feet, the child is passed from arm to arm. Once the child has been well rocked and fully celebrated, everyone breaks into song to start it on its flight to Paradise. There goes the little traveler, clothed in its Sunday best, as the song swells; and they bid it farewell, setting off fireworks, taking great care not to burn its wings.

(104)

1945: The Fields of Tucumán
Yupanqui

He has the stony face of an Indian who stares impassively at the mountain that stares back at him, but he comes from the plains of the south, from the echoless pampa that hides nothing, this gaucho singer of the mysteries of the Argentine north. He comes on a horse, stopping anyplace, with anyone, at the whim of the road. To continue his journey he sings, singing what he has traveled, Atahualpa Yupanqui. And he sings to keep history going, because the history of the poor is either sung or lost as well he knows, he who is left-handed on the guitar and in his thinking about the world.

(202, 270, and 472)

1946: La Paz
The *Rosca*

At the summit there are three; at the foot of the mountain three million. The mountain is tin and is called Bolivia.

The three at the summit form the *rosca*: Simón Patiño in the center; on one side, Carlos Aramayo; on the other, Mauricio Hochschild. Half a century ago, Patiño was a down-and-out miner, but a fairy touched him with her magic wand and turned him into one of the world's richest men. Now he wears a vest with a gold chain, and kings and presidents sit at his table. Aramayo comes from the local aristocracy, Hochschild, from the airplane that brought him to Bolivia. Each of them has more money than the state.

All that the tin earns remains outside Bolivia. To avoid taxes, Patiño's headquarters are in the United States, Aramayo's in Switzerland, and Hochschild's in Chile. Patiño pays Bolivia fifty dollars a year in income tax, Aramayo twenty-two, Hochschild nothing. Of every two children born at the *rosca*'s mines, one doesn't survive.

Each member of the *rosca* has at his disposal a newspaper and various ministers and legislators. It is traditional for the foreign minister to receive a monthly salary from Patiño Mines. But now that President Gualberto Villarroel suggests the *rosca* pay taxes and salaries that are not merely symbolic, what is there to do but hatch a plot?

(97)

1946: La Paz

Villarroel

President Villarroel does not defend himself. He abandons himself to fate—as if it were a matter of fate.

He is attacked by paid gunmen followed by a great motley crowd of godly women and students. Brandishing torches, black flags, and bloody sheets, the insurgents invade the government palace, throw Villarroel off a balcony, then hang what's left of him, naked, from a lamppost.

Besides defying the *rosca*, Villarroel had wanted to give equal rights to whites and Indians, wives and lovers, legitimate and illegitimate children.

The world cheers the crime. The leaders of democracy commend the liquidation of a tyrant in the pay of Hitler, who with unpardonable insolence sought to raise the rock-bottom price of tin. And in Bolivia, a country that never stops toiling for its own misfortune, the fall of what is and the restoration of what was is wildly celebrated: happy days for the League of Morality, the Association of Mothers of Priests, the War Widows, the U.S. embassy, every complexion of rightist, nearly all of the left—left of the left of the moon!—and the *rosca*.

(97)

1946: Hollywood

Carmen Miranda

Sequined and dripping with necklaces, crowned by a tower of bananas, Carmen Miranda undulates against a cardboard tropical backdrop.

Born in Portugal, daughter of a penurious barber who crossed the ocean, Carmen is the chief export of Brazil. Next comes coffee.

This diminutive hussy has little voice, and what she has is out of tune, but she sings with her hands and with her gleaming eyes, and that is more than enough. She is one of the best-paid performers in Hollywood. She has ten houses and eight oil wells.

But Fox refuses to renew her contract. Senator Joseph McCarthy has called her obscene, because at the peak of one of her production numbers, a photographer revealed intolerable glimpses of bare flesh and who knows what else under her flying skirt. And the press has disclosed that in her tenderest infancy Carmen recited lines before King Albert of Belgium, accompanying them with wiggles and winks that scandalized the nuns and gave the king prolonged insomnia.

(401)

1948: Bogotá

On the Eve

In placid Bogotá, home of monks and jurists, General Marshall sits down with the foreign ministers of Latin America.

What gifts does he bring in his saddlebags, this Wise King of the Occident who irrigates with dollars the European lands devastated by the war? General Marshall, impassive, microphones stuck to his chest, resists the downpour of speeches. Without moving so much as an eyelid, he endures the protracted professions of democratic faith offered by many Latin American delegates anxious to sell themselves for the price of a dead rooster; while John McCloy, head of the World Bank, warns: *"I'm sorry, gentlemen, but I didn't bring my checkbook in my suitcase."*

Beyond the salons of the Ninth Pan-American Conference, even more florid speeches shower down throughout the length and breadth of the host country. Learned liberals announce that they will bring peace to Colombia *as the goddess Pallas Athena made the olive branch blossom on the hills of Athens*, and erudite conservatives promise *to draw unknown forces into the sunshine, and light up with the dark fire that is the entrails of the globe the timid votive light of the candelabra that is lit on the eve of treachery in the night of darkness.*

While foreign ministers clamor, proclaim, and declaim, reality persists. In the Colombian countryside the war between conservatives and liberals is fought with guns. Politicians provide the words, campesinos provide the corpses. And already the violence is filtering into Bogotá, knocking at the capital's doors and threatening its time-honored routines—always the same sins, always the same metaphors. At the bullfights last Sunday, the desperate crowd poured into the arena and tore to pieces a wretched bull that refused to fight.

(7)

1948: Bogotá

Gaitán

The political country, says Jorge Eliécer Gaitán, *has nothing to do with the national country.* Gaitán, head of the Liberal Party, is also its black sheep. Poor people of all persuasions adore him. *What is the difference between liberal hunger and conservative hunger? Malaria is neither conservative nor liberal!*

Gaitán's voice unbinds the poor who cry out through his mouth. He turns fear on its back. They come from everywhere to hear him—to hear themselves—the ragged ones, trekking through the jungle, spurring their horses down the roads. They say that when Gaitán speaks the fog splits in Bogotá; and that even in heaven Saint Peter listens and forbids the rain to fall on the gigantic crowds gathered by torchlight.

This dignified leader, with the austere face of a statue, does not hesitate to denounce the oligarchy and the imperial ventriloquist on whose knee the oligarchs sit without life of their own or words of their own. He calls for agrarian reform and articulates other truths to put an end to the long lie.

If they don't kill him, Gaitán will be Colombia's next president. He cannot be bought. To what temptation would he succumb, this man who scorns pleasure, sleeps alone, eats little, drinks nothing, and even refuses anesthesia when he has a tooth pulled?

(7)

1948: Bogotá
The *Bogotazo*

At 2:00 P.M. of this ninth of April, Gaitán has a date with one of the Latin American students who are gathering in Bogotá on the fringes of General Marshall's Pan-American ceremony.

At half past one, the student leaves his hotel, intending to stroll to Gaitán's office. But after a few steps a noise like an earthquake stops him, a human avalanche engulfs him. The people, pouring out of the barrios, streaming down from the hills, are rushing madly past him, a hurricane of pain and anger flooding the city, smashing store windows, overturning streetcars, setting buildings afire.

They've killed him! They've killed him!

It was done in the streets, with three bullets. Gaitán's watch stopped at 1:05 P.M.

The student, a corpulent Cuban named Fidel Castro, shoves his cap on his head and lets himself be blown along by the wind of people.

(7)

1948: Bogotá
Flames

Indian ponchos and workers' sandals invade the center of Bogotá, hands toughened by earth or stone, hands stained with machine oil or shoe polish, a tornado of porters, students, and waiters, washer-women and market women, Jills of all beds and Jacks of all trades, ambulance chasers and fortune hunters. From the tornado a woman detaches herself, wearing four fur coats, clumsy and happy as a bear in love; running like a rabbit is a man with several pearl necklaces around his throat; walking like a tortoise, another with a refrigerator on his back.

At street corners, ragged kids direct traffic. Prisoners burst the bars of their cells. Someone cuts the fire hoses with a machete. Bogotá is an immense bonfire, the sky a vault of red; from the balconies of burning ministries typewriters plummet; from burning belltowers bullets rain. The police hide themselves or cross their arms before the fury.

At the presidential palace, a river of people is seen approaching. Machineguns have already repelled two of these attacks, although the crowd did succeed in hurling against the palace doors the disemboweled body of the puppet who killed Gaitán.

Doña Bertha, the first lady, sticks a revolver in her waistband and calls her confessor on the telephone: *"Father, be so good as to take my son to the American embassy."*

On another phone the president, Mariano Ospina Pérez, sees to the protection of General Marshall's house and dictates orders against the rebellious rabble. Then he sits and waits. The tumult grows in the streets.

Three tanks head the attack on the presidential palace. The tanks are swarming with people waving flags and yelling Gaitán's name, and behind them surges a multitude bristling with machetes, axes, and clubs. When they reach the palace the tanks halt. Their turrets turn slowly, aim to the rear, and commence mowing people down.

(7)

1948: Bogotá
Ashes

Someone wanders in search of a shoe. A woman howls, a dead child in her arms. The city smolders. Walk carefully or you'll step on bodies. A dismembered mannequin hangs on the streetcar cables. From the stairway of a burned monastery a naked, blackened Christ gazes skyward, arms outstretched. At the foot of that stairway, a beggar sits and drinks. The archbishop's mitre covers his head and a purple velvet curtain envelops his body. He further defends himself from the cold by sipping French cognac from a gold chalice, and offers drinks to passersby in a silver goblet. An army bullet ends the party.

The last shots ring out. The city, devastated by fire, regains order. After three days of vengeance and madness, a disarmed people returns to the old purgatory of work and woe.

General Marshall has no doubts. The *bogotazo* was the work of

Moscow. The government of Colombia breaks relations with the Soviet Union.

(7)

1948: Upar Valley
The *Vallenato*

"I want to let out a yell and they won't let me . . ."

The government of Colombia prohibits the "Vagabond Yell." Whoever sings it risks jail or a bullet. Along the Magdalena River, though, they keep singing.

The people of the Colombian coast defend themselves by making music. The "Vagabond Yell" is a *vallenato* rhythm, one of the cowboy songs that tell the story of the region and, incidentally, fill the air with joy.

Accordion to breast, the troubadours prance and navigate. Accordion on thigh, they receive the first drinks at all parties and challenge each other to a duel of couplets.

The *vallenato* verses born of accordions thrust back and forth like knives, like fusillades in daring musical battles that last for days and nights in markets and cockfight rings. The singers' most fearsome rival is Lucifer, that great musician, who gets bored in hell and comes to America at the drop of a hat, disguised, looking for fun.

(359)

1948: Wroclaw
Picasso

This painter embodies the best painters of all times. They cohabit in him, if rather uncomfortably. It is no easy task to assimilate such intractable folk, ancient and modern, who spend so much time in conflict with one another that the painter hasn't a free moment to listen to speeches, much less make them.

But for the first and only time in his life, Pablo Picasso makes a speech. This unheard-of event occurs in the Polish city of Wroclaw, at a world congress of intellectuals for peace: *"I have a friend who ought to be here . . ."*

Picasso pays homage to *the greatest poet of the Spanish language*

*and one of the greatest poets on earth, who has always taken the side
of the unfortunate: Pablo Neruda, persecuted by the police in Chile,
cornered like a dog . . .*

(442)

1948: Somewhere in Chile
Neruda

The main headline in the daily *El Imparcial* reads: *Neruda Sought
Throughout the Country*; and below: *Investigators locating his where-
abouts will be rewarded.*

The poet goes from hideout to hideout, traveling by night. Neruda is one of many suffering persecution for being red or for being
decent or for just being, and he doesn't complain of this fate, which
he has chosen. Nor does he regret the solitude: He enjoys and celebrates this fighting passion, whatever trouble it brings him, as he
enjoys and celebrates church bells, wine, eel broth, and flying comets
with wings spreads wide.

(313 and 442)

1948: San José de Costa Rica
Figueres

After six weeks of civil war, and two thousand dead, the rural middle
class comes to power in Costa Rica.

The head of the new government, José Figueres, outlaws the
Communist Party and promises *unconditional support to the struggle
of the free world against Russian imperialism.* But in an undertone
he also promises to continue to expand the social reforms the Communists have promoted in recent years.

Under the protection of President Rafael Calderón, friend of the
Communists, unions and cooperatives have multiplied in Costa Rica;
small landowners have won land from the great estates; health has
been improved and education extended.

The anticommunist Figueres does not touch the lands of the
United Fruit Company, that most powerful mistress, but nationalizes
the banks and dissolves the army, so that money will not speculate,

nor arms conspire. Costa Rica wants out of the ferocious turbulence of Central America.

(42, 243, 414, and 438)

1949: Washington
The Chinese Revolution

Between yesterday and tomorrow, an abyss. The Chinese revolution springs into the air and leaps the gap.

The news from Peking provokes anger and fear in Washington. After their long march of armed poverty, Mao's reds have triumphed. General Chiang Kai-shek flees. The United States enthrones him on the island of Formosa.

The parks in China had been forbidden to dogs and the poor, and beggars still froze to death in the early mornings, as in the old days of the mandarins; but it was not from Peking that the orders came. It was not the Chinese who named their ministers and generals, wrote their laws and decrees, and fixed their tariffs and salaries. By a geographical error, China was not in the Caribbean.

(156 and 291)

1949: Havana
Radio Theater

"Don't kill me," pleads the actor to the author.

Onelio Jorge Cardoso had had it in mind to polish off Captain Hook in the next episode; but if the character dies of a sword-thrust on the pirate ship, the actor dies of hunger in the street. The author, a good friend of the actor, promises him eternal life.

Onelio devises breathtaking adventures, but his radio plays enjoy little success.

He doesn't pour it on thick enough, he doesn't know how to wring hearts out like laundry—to the last drop. José Sánchez Arcilla, by contrast, touches the most intimate fibers. In his serial "The Necklace of Tears," the characters struggle against perverse destiny in nine hundred and sixty-five episodes that bathe the audience in tears.

But the greatest success of all time is "The Right to Be Born," by Felix B. Caignet. Nothing like it has ever been heard in Cuba or anywhere else. At the scheduled nighttime hour, it alone gets a hearing, a unanimous Mass. Movies are interrupted, streets empty, lovers suspend their dalliances, cocks quit fighting, and even flies alight for the duration.

For seventy-four episodes, all Cuba has been waiting for Don Rafael del Junco to speak. This character possesses The Secret. But not only is he totally paralyzed, he lost his voice in episode 197. We've now made it to episode 271 and Don Rafael still can only clear his throat. When will he manage to reveal The Truth to the good woman who sinned but once, succumbing to Mad Passion's call? When will he have the voice to tell her that Albertico Limonta, her doctor, is really the fruit of that same illicit love, the baby she abandoned soon after birth into the hands of a black woman with a white soul? When, oh, when?

The public, dying of suspense, does not know that Don Rafael is on a silence strike. This cruel silence will continue until the actor who plays Don Rafael del Junco gets the raise he has been demanding for two and a half months.

(266)

1950: Rio de Janeiro
Obdulio

Although the dice are loaded against him, Obdulio steps firmly and kicks. The captain of the Uruguayans, this commanding, muscular black man does not lose heart. The more the hostile multitude roars from the stands, the more Obdulio grows.

Surprise and sorrow in Maracaná Stadium: Brazil, the great, pulverizing, goal-scoring machine, the favorite all along, loses this last match at the last minute. Uruguay, playing for its life, wins the world football championship.

That night Obdulio Varela flees from his hotel, besieged by journalists, fans, and the curious. Preferring to celebrate alone, he goes looking for a drink in some remote dive or other, but everywhere meets weeping Brazilians.

"Obedulio is giving us the game," they were chanting in the stadium just hours ago, midway through the match. Now, bathed in tears, the same people cry, *"It was all Obedulio's fault."*

And Obdulio, having so recently disliked them, is stunned to see them individually. The victory begins to weigh on him. He has ruined the party of these good folk and begins to wonder if he shouldn't beg their pardon for the tremendous sin of winning. So he keeps on wandering the Rio streets, from bar to bar. Dawn finds him still drinking, embracing the vanquished.

(131 and 191)

1950: Hollywood

Rita

Changing her name, weight, age, voice, lips, and eyebrows, she conquered Hollywood. Her hair was transformed from dull black into flaming red. To broaden her brow, they removed hair after hair by painful electrolysis. Over her eyes they put lashes like petals.

Rita Hayworth disguised herself as a goddess, and perhaps was one—for the forties, anyway. Now, the fifties demand something new.

(249)

1950: Hollywood

Marilyn

Like Rita, this girl has been improved. She had thick eyelashes and a double chin, a nose round at the tip, and large teeth. Hollywood reduced the fat, suppressed the cartilage, filed the teeth, and turned the mousy chestnut hair into a cascade of gleaming gold. Then the technicians baptized her Marilyn Monroe and invented a pathetic childhood story for her to tell the journalists.

This new Venus manufactured in Hollywood no longer needs to climb into strange beds seeking contracts for second-rate roles in third-rate films. She no longer lives on hot dogs and coffee, or suffers the cold of winter. Now she is a star; or rather a small personage in a mask who would like to remember, but cannot, that moment when she simply wanted to be saved from loneliness.

(214 and 274)

1951: Mexico City
Buñuel

Stones rain upon Luis Buñuel. Most of the newspapers and press syndicates insist that Mexico expel this Spanish ingrate who repays favors with infamy. The film that arouses national indignation, *Los Olvidados*, depicts the slums of Mexico City. Adolescents who live hand to mouth in this horrendous underworld eat whatever they find, including each other, with garbage heaps for their playground. They peck each other to pieces, bit by bit, these baby vultures, and so fulfill the dark destiny their city has chosen for them.

A mysterious resonance, a strange force, echoes in Buñuel's films. Some long, deep roll of drums, perhaps the drums of his infancy in Calanda, make the earth tremble, even if the sound track registers no noise, and the world simulates silence and forgiveness.

(70 and 71)

1952: San Fernando Hill
Sick unto Death

is Colombia since Gaitán was murdered on that Bogotá street. In mountains and plains, frozen prairies and steamy valleys—everywhere—campesinos kill each other, poor against poor, all against all. A tornado of vendettas and vengeance allows Blackblood, the Claw, Tarzan, Tough Luck, the Roach, and other artists of butchery to excel at their chosen trade, but more ferocious crimes are committed by the forces of order. The Tolima Battalion kills fifteen hundred, not counting rapes or mutilations, in its sweep of the area from Pantamillo to San Fernando Hill. To leave no seed from which the future might grow, soldiers toss children aloft and run them through with bayonet or machete.

"Don't bring me stories," say those who give the orders, *"bring me ears."*

Campesinos who manage to escape seek protection deep in the mountains, leaving their smoking shacks in cinders behind them. Before leaving, in a sad ceremony they kill the dog, because he makes noise.

(217, 227, and 408)

1952: La Paz

El Illimani

Though you can't see him, he watches you. Hide where you like, he watches over you. No cranny escapes him. The capital of Bolivia belongs to him, although they don't know it, the gentlemen who till last night thought themselves masters of these houses, these people.

El Illimani, proud king, washes himself with mist. At his feet, the city begins its day. Campfires die out, the last machinegun volleys are heard. The yellow hats of miners overwhelm the military caps. An army that has never won against those outside nor lost against those within, collapses. People dance on any street corner. Handkerchiefs flutter, braids and multilayered skirts undulate to the beat of the *cueca*.

In the absolute blueness of the sky gleams El Illimani's crown of three peaks: From the snowy summits the gods contemplate the happiness of their children in arms, at the end of this endless footby-foot struggle through the back streets.

(17, 172, and 473)

1952: La Paz

Drum of the People

that beats and rolls and rolls again, vengeance of the Indian who sleeps in the yard like a dog and greets the master with bended knee: The army of the underdogs fought with homemade bombs and sticks of dynamite until, finally, the arsenal of the military fell into their hands.

Víctor Paz Estenssoro promises that from this day Bolivia will be for all Bolivians. By the mines the workers fly the national flag at half-mast, where it will stay until the new president fulfills his promise to nationalize tin. In London they see it coming: As if by magic, the price of tin falls by two-thirds.

On the Pairumani estate, Indians roast on a grill the prize bulls Patiño imported from Holland.

Aramayo's tennis courts, surfaced with brick dust from England, are turned into mule corrals.

(17, 172, and 473)

A Woman of the Bolivian Mines Gives the Recipe for a Homemade Bomb

Look for a little milk can. Put the dynamite right in the middle, a capsule. Then, bits of iron, slag, a little dirt. Add glass and small nails. Then cover it up good. Like this, see? You light it right there and—shsss!—throw it. If you have a sling you can throw it farther. My husband can throw from here to six blocks away. For that you put in a longer wick.

(268)

1952: Cochabamba

Cries of Mockery and Grievance

All over the Bolivian countryside times are changing: a vast insurgency against the large estates and against fear. In the Cochabamba valley, the women too hurl their defiance, singing and dancing.

At ceremonies of homage to the Christ of the Holy Cross, Quechua campesinos from the whole valley light candles, drink *chicha*, sing ballads, and cavort to the sound of accordions and charangos, around the Crucified One.

The young girls implore Christ for a husband who won't make them cry, for a mule loaded with corn, a white sheep and a black sheep, a sewing machine, or as many rings as their hands have fingers. Afterward they sing stridently, always in the Indian language, their protest. To Christ, to father, to boyfriend and to husband they promise love and service, at table as well as in bed, but they don't want to be battered beasts of burden anymore.

Singing, they shoot bullets of mockery at the bull's eye of the naked macho, well ravaged by years and insects, who sleeps or pretends to sleep on the cross.

(5)

Shameless Verses Sung by Indian Women
of Cochabamba to Jesus Christ

Little Father, to your flock,
"Daughter, daughter," you keep saying.
But how could you have fathered me
When you haven't got a cock?

"Lazy, lazy," you're reproving,
Little Father, Holy Cross,
But limp and lazy—look at you:
Standing up there, never moving.

Little fox with tail all curls,
Beady eyes on women spying,
Little old man with mousey face
And your nose so full of holes.

You won't put up with me unwed,
You condemn me to bear kids,
Dress and feed them while alive,
Bury them proper when they're dead.

Will you send to me a mate
Who would give me blows and kicks?
Why must every budding rose
Suffer the same wilted fate?

(5)

1952: Buenos Aires

The Argentine People Feel Naked
Without Her

Long live cancer! wrote some hand on a wall in Buenos Aires. They
hated her, they hate her, the well-fed—for being poor, a woman, and
presumptuous. She challenged them in talk and offended them in
life. Born to be a servant, or at best an actress in cheap melodramas,
Evita refused to memorize her part.

They loved her, they love her, the unloved—through her mouth they spoke their minds and their curses. Evita was the blonde fairy who embraced the leprous and ragged and gave peace to the despairing, a bottomless spring that gushed jobs and mattresses, shoes and sewing machines, false teeth and bridal trousseaux. The poor received these charities at a side door, while Evita wore stunning jewelry and mink coats in midsummer. Not that they begrudged her the luxury: They celebrated it. They felt not humiliated but avenged by her queenly attire.

Before the body of Evita, surrounded by white carnations, people file by, weeping. Day after day, night after night, the line of torches: a procession two weeks long.

Bankers, businessmen, and landowners sigh with relief. With Evita dead, President Perón is a knife without a cutting edge.

(311 and 417)

1952: On the High Seas
Wanted: Charlie the Tramp

Charles Chaplin sails for London. On the second day at sea, news reaches the ship that he won't be able to return to the United States. The attorney general applies to his case a law aimed at foreigners suspected of communism, depravity, or insanity.

Some years earlier Chaplin had been interrogated by officials of the FBI and the Immigration and Naturalization Service:

Are you of Jewish origin?

Are you a Communist?

Have you ever committed adultery?

Senator Richard Nixon and the gossip columnist Hedda Hopper agree: *Chaplin is a menace to our institutions.* Outside theaters showing his films, the Legion of Decency and the American Legion picket with signs demanding: *Chaplin, go to Russia.*

The FBI has for nearly thirty years been seeking proof that Chaplin is really a Jew named Israel Thonstein and that he works as a spy for Moscow. Their suspicions were aroused in 1923 when *Pravda* printed the comment: *Chaplin is an actor of undoubted talent.*

(121 and 383)

1952: London

An Admirable Ghost

named Buster Keaton has returned to the screen after long years of oblivion, thanks to Chaplin. *Limelight* opens in London, and in it for a few precious minutes Keaton teams up with Chaplin in an absurd double act that steals the show.

This is the first time Keaton and Chaplin have worked together. They appear gray-haired and wrinkled, though with the same charm as in those moments long ago, when they made silence wittier than words.

Chaplin and Keaton are still the best. They know that there is nothing more serious than laughter, an art demanding infinite work, and that as long as the world revolves, making others laugh is the most splendid of activities.

(382 and 383)

1953: Washington

Newsreel

The United States explodes the first H-bomb at Eniwetok.

President Eisenhower names Charles Wilson secretary of defense. Wilson, an executive of General Motors, has recently declared: *What's good for General Motors is good for America.*

After a long trial, Ethel and Julius Rosenberg are executed in the electric chair. The Rosenbergs, accused of spying for the Russians, deny guilt to the end.

The American city of Moscow exhorts its Russian namesake to change its name. The authorities of this small city in Idaho claim the exclusive right to call themselves Muscovites, and ask that the Soviet capital be rebaptized *to avoid any embarrassing associations.*

Half the citizens of the United States decisively support Senator McCarthy's campaign against the Communist infiltration of democracy, according to opinion polls.

One of the suspects McCarthy plans to interrogate, engineer Raymond Kaplan, commits suicide by throwing himself under a truck.

The scientist Albert Einstein appeals to intellectuals to refuse to testify before the House Un-American Activities Committee and to be prepared for jail or economic ruin. Failing this, believes Einstein, *the intellectuals deserve nothing better than the slavery which is intended for them.*

(45)

1953: Washington
The Witch Hunt

Incorrigible Albert Einstein, according to Senator McCarthy's list, is America's foremost *fellow traveler*. To get on the list, all you need to do is have black friends or oppose sending U.S. troops to Korea; but the case of Einstein is a much weightier one. McCarthy has proof to spare that this ungrateful Jew has a heart that tilts left and pumps red blood.

The hearing room, where the fires of this Inquisition burn, becomes a celebrity circus. Einstein's is not the only famous name that echoes here. For some time the Un-American Activities Committee has had its eye on Hollywood. The Committee demands names, and Hollywood names cause scandal. Those who won't talk lose their jobs and find their careers ruined; or go to jail, like Dashiell Hammett; or lose their passports, like Lillian Hellman and Paul Robeson; or are expelled from the country, like Cedric Belfrage. Ronald Reagan, a minor leading man, brands the reds and pinks who don't deserve to be saved from the furies of Armageddon. Another leading man, Robert Taylor, publicly repents having acted in a film in which Russians smile. Playwright Clifford Odets begs pardon for his ideas and betrays his old comrades. Actor José Ferrer and director Elia Kazan point their fingers at colleagues. To dissociate himself clearly from Communists, Kazan makes a film about the Mexican leader Emiliano Zapata in which Zapata is not the silent campesino who championed agrarian reform, but a charlatan who shoots off bullets and speeches in an unceasing diarrhea.

(41, 219, and 467)

1953: Washington
Portrait of a Witch Hunter

His raw material is collective fear. He rolls up his sleeves and goes to work. Skillful molder of this clay, Joseph McCarthy turns fear into panic and panic into hysteria.

Feverishly he exhorts them to betray. He swears not to shut his mouth as long as his country is infected by the Marxist plague. For him all ambiguity has the ring of cowardice. First he accuses, then he investigates. He sells certainties to the vacillating and lashes out, knee to groin or knife to belly, at anyone who questions the right of private property or opposes war and business as usual.

(395)

1953: Seattle
Robeson

They bar him from traveling to Canada, or anywhere else. When some Canadians invite him to perform, Paul Robeson sings to them by telephone from Seattle, and by telephone he swears that he will stand firm as long as there is breath in his body.

Robeson, grandson of slaves, believes that Africa is a source of pride and not a zoo run by Tarzan. A black with red ideas, friend of the yellows who are resisting the white invasion in Korea, he sings in the name of his insulted people and of all insulted peoples who by singing lift their heads; and he sings with a voice full of thundering heaven and quaking earth.

(381)

1953: Santiago de Cuba
Fidel

At dawn on July 26, a handful of youths attack the Moncada barracks. Armed with dignity and Cuban bravura and a few bird guns, they assault the dictatorship of Fulgencio Batista and half a century of colonization masquerading as a republic.

A few die in battle, but more than seventy are finished off by the army after a week of torture. The torturers tear out the eyes of Abel Santamaría, among others.

The rebel leader, taken prisoner, offers his defense plea. Fidel Castro has the look of a man who gives all of himself without asking anything in return. The judges listen to him in astonishment, missing not a word. His words are not, however, for the ones kissed by the gods; he speaks for the ones pissed on by the devils, and for them, and in their name, he explains what he has done.

Fidel Castro claims the ancient right of rebellion against despotism: *"This island will sink in the ocean before we will consent to be anybody's slaves . . ."*

He tosses his head like a tree, accuses Batista and his officers of exchanging their uniforms for butchers' aprons, and sets forth a program of revolution. In Cuba there could be food and work for all, and more to spare.

"No, that is not inconceivable."

(90, 392, and 422)

1953: Santiago de Cuba

The Accused Turns Prosecutor and Announces: "History Will Absolve Me"

What is inconceivable is that there should be men going to bed hungry while an inch of land remains unsown; what is inconceivable is that there should be children who die without medical care; that thirty percent of our campesinos cannot sign their names and ninety-nine percent don't know the history of Cuba; that most families in our countryside should be living in worse conditions than the Indians Columbus found when he discovered the most beautiful land human eyes had ever seen . . .

From such wretchedness it is only possible to free oneself by death; and in that the state does help them: to die. Ninety percent of rural children are devoured by parasites that enter from the soil through the toenails of their unshod feet.

More than half of the best cultivated production lands are in foreign hands. In Oriente, the largest province, the lands of the United Fruit Company and the West Indian Company extend from the north coast to the south coast . . .

Cuba continues to be a factory producing raw materials. Sugar

*is exported to import candies; leather exported to import shoes; iron
exported to import plows . . .*

(90)

1953: Boston
United Fruit

Throne of bananas, crown of bananas, a banana held like a scepter:
Sam Zemurray, master of the lands and seas of the banana kingdom,
did not believe it possible that his Guatemalan vassals could give him
a headache. *"The Indians are too ignorant for Marxism,"* he used to
say, and was applauded by his court at his royal palace in Boston,
Massachusetts.

Thanks to the successive decrees of Manuel Estrada Cabrera,
who governed surrounded by sycophants and spies, seas of slobber,
forests of familiars; and of Jorge Ubico, who thought he was Napoleon
but wasn't, Guatemala has remained part of United Fruit's vast do-
minion for half a century. In Guatemala United Fruit can seize whatever land it wants—enormous unused tracts—and owns the railroad,
the telephone, the telegraph, the ports, and the ships, not to speak
of soldiers, politicians, and journalists.

Sam Zemurray's troubles began when president Juan Jośe Arévalo forced the company to respect the union and its right to strike.
From bad to worse: A new president, Jacobo Arbenz, introduces
agrarian reform, seizes United Fruit's uncultivated lands, begins
dividing them among a hundred thousand families, and acts as if
Guatemala were ruled by the landless, the letterless, the breadless,
the *less*.

(50 and 288)

1953: Guatemala City
Arbenz

President Truman howled when workers on Guatemala's banana plantations started to behave like people. Now President Eisenhower spits
lightning over the expropriation of United Fruit.

The government of the United States considers it an outrage that
the government of Guatemala should take United Fruit's account

books seriously. Arbenz proposes to pay as indemnity only the value that the company itself had placed on its lands to defraud the tax laws. John Foster Dulles, the secretary of state, demands twenty-five times that.

Jacobo Arbenz, accused of conspiring with Communists, draws his inspiration not from Lenin but from Abraham Lincoln. His agrarian reform, an attempt to modernize Guatemalan capitalism, is less radical than the North American rural laws of almost a century ago.

(81 and 416)

1953: San Salvador

Dictator Wanted

Guatemalan General Miguel Ydígoras Fuentes, distinguished killer of Indians, has lived in exile since the fall of dictator Ubico. Now, Walter Turnbull comes to San Salvador to offer him a deal. Turnbull, representative of both United Fruit and the CIA, proposes that Ydígoras take charge of Guatemala. There is money available for such a project, if he promises to destroy the unions, restore United Fruit's lands and privileges, and repay this loan to the last cent within a reasonable period. Ydígoras asks time to think it over, while making it clear he considers the conditions abusive.

In no time word gets around that a position is vacant. Guatemalan exiles, military and civilian, fly to Washington to offer their services; others knock at the doors of U.S. embassies. José Luis Arenas, "friend" of Vice-President Nixon, offers to overthrow President Arbenz for two hundred thousand dollars. General Federico Ponce says he has a ten-thousand-man army ready to attack the National Palace. His price would be quite modest, although he prefers not to talk figures yet. Just a small advance . . .

Throat cancer rules out United Fruit's preference, Juan Córdova Cerna. On his deathbed, however, Doctor Córdova rasps out the name of his own candidate: Colonel Carlos Castillo Armas, trained at Fort Leavenworth, Kansas, a cheap, obedient burro.

(416 and 471)

1954: Washington

The Deciding Machine, Piece by Piece

Dwight Eisenhower   President of the United States. Overthrew the government of Mohammed Mossadegh in Iran because it nationalized oil. Has now given orders to overthrow the government of Jacobo Arbenz in Guatemala.

Sam Zemurray   Principal stockholder in United Fruit. All his concerns automatically turn into U.S. government declarations, and ultimately into rifles, mortars, machineguns, and CIA airplanes.

John Foster Dulles   U.S. Secretary of State. Former lawyer for United Fruit.

Allen Dulles   Director of the CIA. Brother of John Foster Dulles. Like him, has done legal work for United Fruit. Together they organize "Operation Guatemala."

John Moors Cabot   Secretary of State for Inter-American Affairs. Brother of Thomas Cabot, the president of United Fruit.

Walter Bedell Smith   Under Secretary of State. Serves as liaison in Operation Guatemala. Future member of the board of United Fruit.

Henry Cabot Lodge   Senator, U.S. representative to the United Nations. United Fruit shareholder. Has on various occasions received money from this company for speeches in the Senate.

Anne Whitman   Personal secretary to President Eisenhower. Married to United Fruit public relations chief.

Spruille Braden   Former U.S. ambassador to several Latin American countries. Has received a salary from United Fruit since 1948. Is widely reported in the press to have exhorted Eisenhower *to suppress communism by force in Guatemala.*

Robert Hill   U.S. ambassador to Costa Rica. Collaborates on "Operation Guatemala." Future board member of United Fruit.

John Peurifoy   U.S. ambassador to Guatemala. Known as *the butcher of Greece* for his past diplomatic service in Athens. Speaks no Spanish. Political background: the U.S. Senate, Washington, D.C., where he once worked as an elevator operator.

(416, 420, and 465)

1954: Boston

The Lie Machine, Piece by Piece

The Motor   The executioner becomes the victim; the victim, the executioner. Those who prepare the invasion of Guatemala from Honduras attribute to Guatemala the intention to invade Honduras and all Central America. *The tentacles of the Kremlin are plain to see*, says John Moors Cabot from the White House. Ambassador Peurifoy warns in Guatemala: *We cannot permit a Soviet republic to be established from Texas to the Panama Canal.* Behind this scandal lies a cargo of arms shipped from Czechoslovakia. The United States has forbidden the sale of arms to Guatemala.

Gear I   News and articles, declarations, pamphlets, photographs, films, and comic strips about Communist atrocities in Guatemala bombard the public. This educational material, whose origin is undisclosed, comes from the offices of United Fruit in Boston and from government offices in Washington.

Gear II   The Archbishop of Guatemala, Mariano Rossell Arellano, exhorts the populace to rise *against communism, enemy of God and the Fatherland.* Thirty CIA planes rain down his pastoral message over the whole country. The archbishop has the image of the popular Christ of Esquipulas, which will be named Captain General of the Liberating Brigade, brought to the capital.

Gear III   At the Pan-American Conference, John Foster Dulles pounds the table with his fist and gets the blessing of the Organization of American States for the projected invasion. At the United Nations, Henry Cabot Lodge blocks Jacobo Arbenz's demands for help. U.S. diplomacy is mobilized throughout the world. The complicity of England and France is obtained in exchange for a U.S. commitment to silence over the delicate matters of the Suez Canal, Cyprus, and Indochina.

Gear IV   The dictators of Nicaragua, Honduras, Venezuela, and the Dominican Republic not only lend training camps, radio transmitters, and airports to "Operation Guatemala," they also make a contribution to the propaganda campaign. Somoza I calls together the international press in Managua and displays some pistols with hammers and sickles stamped on them. They are, he says, from a Russian submarine intercepted en route to Guatemala.

(416, 420, and 447)

1954: Guatemala City

The Reconquest of Guatemala

Guatemala has neither planes nor antiaircraft installations, so U.S. pilots in U.S. planes bomb the country with the greatest of ease.

A powerful CIA transmitter, installed on the roof of the U.S. embassy, spreads confusion and panic: the Lie Machine informs the world that this is the rebel radio, the Voice of Liberation, transmitting the triumphal march of Colonel Castillo Armas from the jungles of Guatemala. Meanwhile, Castillo Armas, encamped on a United Fruit plantation in Honduras, awaits orders from the Deciding Machine.

Arbenz's government, paralyzed, attends the ceremony of its own collapse. The aerial bombings reach the capital and blow up the fuel deposits. The government confines itself to burying the dead. The mercenary army, *God, Fatherland, Liberty*, crosses the border. It meets no resistance. Is it money or fear that explains how Guatemala's military chiefs could surrender their troops without firing a shot? An Argentine doctor in his early twenties, Ernesto Guevara, tries in vain to organize popular defense of the capital: he doesn't know how or with what. Improvised militias wander the streets unarmed. When Arbenz finally orders the arsenals opened, army officers refuse to obey. On one of these dark ignoble days, Guevara has an attack of asthma and indignation; on another, one midnight after two weeks of bombings, President Arbenz slowly descends the steps of the National Palace, crosses the street, and seeks asylum in the Mexican embassy.

(81, 416, 420, and 447)

1954: Mazatenango

Miguel at Forty-Nine

As soon as the birds started singing, before first light, they sharpened their machetes, and now they reach Mazatenango at a gallop, in search of Miguel. The executioners are making crosses on a long list of those marked to die, while the army of Castillo Armas takes over Guatemala. Miguel is number five on the most-wanted list, condemned for being a red and a foreign troublemaker. Since his arrival on the run from El Salvador, he has not stopped for an instant his work of labor agitation.

They sic dogs on him. They aim to parade his body hanging from a horse along the roads, his throat slit by a machete. But Miguel, one very experienced and knowing animal, loses himself in the scrub.

And so occurs the tenth birth of Miguel Mármol, at forty-nine years of age.

(222)

1954: Guatemala City
Newsreel

The archbishop of Guatemala declares: *"I admire the sincere and ardent patriotism of President Castillo Armas."* Amid a formidable display of gibberish, Castillo Armas receives the blessing of the papal nuncio, Monsignor Genaro Verrolino.

President Eisenhower congratulates the CIA chiefs at the White House: *"Thanks to all of you. You've averted a Soviet beachhead in our hemisphere."*

The head of the CIA, Allen Dulles, assigns to a *Time* journalist the job of framing Guatemala's new constitution.

Time publishes a poem by the wife of the U.S. ambassador to Guatemala. The poem says that Mr. and Mrs. Peurifoy are *optimistic* because Guatemala is no longer *communistic.*

At his first meeting with the ambassador after the victory, President Castillo Armas expresses his concern at the insufficiency of local jails and the lack of necessary cells for all the Communists. According to lists sent from Washington by the State Department, Guatemala's Communists total seventy-two thousand.

The embassy throws a party. Four hundred Guatemalan guests sing in unison "The Star-Spangled Banner."

(416 and 420)

1954: Rio de Janeiro
Getulio

He wants to erase the memory of his own dictatorship, those bad old police-state days, and so in his final years governs Brazil as no one ever has before.

He takes the side of the wage earner. Immediately the profit-makers declare war.

To stop Brazil from being a colander, he corks up the hemorrhage of wealth. Immediately foreign capital takes to economic sabotage.

He recovers for Brazil its own oil and energy, which are as national a patrimony as anthem and flag. The offended monopolies immediately respond with a fierce counteroffensive.

He defends the price of coffee instead of burning half the crop, as was customary. The United States immediately cuts its purchases in half.

In Brazil, journalists and politicians of all colors and areas join the scandalized chorus.

Getulio Vargas has governed with dignity. When he is forced to bow down, he chooses the dignity of death. He raises the revolver, aims at his own heart, and fires.

(427, 429, and 432)

1955: Medellín
Nostalgia

It is almost twenty years since Carlos Gardel burned to death, and the Colombian city of Medellín, where the tragedy occurred, has become a place of pilgrimage and the focus of a cult.

The devotees of Gardel are known by their tilted hats, striped pants, and swaying walk. They slick down their hair, look out of the corners of their eyes, and have twisted smiles. They bow and sweep, as if in a constant dance, when shaking hands, lighting a cigarette, or chalking a billiard cue. They spend the night leaning against some suburban lamp-post, whistling or humming tangos which explain that all women are whores except mother, that sainted old lady whom God has taken to his glory.

Some local devotees, and certain visiting cultists from Buenos

Aires, sell relics of the idol. One offers genuine Gardel teeth, acquired on the spot when the plane blew up. He has sold more than thirteen hundred at an average of twelve dollars apiece. It was some years ago that he found his first buyer, a tourist from New York, a member of the Gardel Fan Club. On seeing the souvenir, how could the customer help but burst into tears?

(184)

1955: Asunción
Withdrawal Symptoms

When he commits the unforgivable sin of promulgating a divorce law, the Church makes the missing sign of the cross over him, and the military begin to conspire, in full daylight, to overthrow him.

The news is celebrated in drawing rooms and mourned in kitchens; Perón has fallen. Offering no resistance, he leaves Argentina, for Paraguay and exile.

In Asunción, his days are sad. He feels beaten, old, alone. He claims that by his act of renunciation a million deaths have been avoided. But he also says that the people didn't know how to defend what he gave them, that the ingrates deserve whatever misfortunes befall them, that they think with their bellies, not with their heads or hearts.

One morning Perón is confiding his bitterness to his host, Ricardo Gayol, when suddenly he half-closes his eyes and whispers: *"My smile used to drive them crazy. My smile . . ."*

He raises his arms and smiles as if he were on the palace balcony, greeting a plaza filled with cheering people. *"Would you like my smile?"*

His host looks at him, stupefied.

"Take it, it's yours," says Perón. He takes it out of his mouth and puts it in his host's hand—his false teeth.

(327)

1955: Guatemala City

One Year after the Reconquest of Guatemala,

Richard Nixon visits this occupied land. The union of United Fruit workers and five hundred and thirty-two other unions have been banned by the new government. The new penal code punishes with death anyone who calls a strike. Political parties are outlawed. The books of Dostoyevsky and other Soviet writers have been thrown onto the bonfire.

The banana kingdom has been saved from agrarian reform. The vice-president of the United States congratulates President Castillo Armas. For the first time in history, says Nixon, a Communist government has been replaced by a free one.

(416 and 420)

1956: Buenos Aires

The Government Decides That Peronism Doesn't Exist

While shooting workers on garbage dumps, the Argentine military decrees the nonexistence of Perón, Evita, and Peronism. It is forbidden to mention their names or their deeds. Possessing images of them is a crime. The presidential residence is demolished to the last stone, as though the disease were contagious.

But what about the embalmed body of Evita? She is the most dangerous symbol of the arrogance of the rabble who have sauntered the corridors of power as if in their own homes. The generals dump the body in a box labeled "Radio Equipment" and send it into exile. Just where is a secret. To Europe, rumor has it, or maybe to an island in mid-ocean. Evita becomes a wandering body traveling secretly through remote cemeteries, expelled from the country by generals who don't know—or don't want to know—that she lies within the people.

(311 and 327)

1956: León

Son of Somoza

Santa Marta, Santa Marta has a train, sing the musicmakers, dance the dancers, *Santa Marta has a train but has no tram*; and in the middle of the song and the fiesta, Rigoberto López Pérez, poet, owner of nothing, fells the owner of everything with four bullets.

A North American plane carries off the dying Anastasio Somoza to a North American hospital in the North American Panama Canal Zone, and he dies in a North American bed. They bury him in Nicaragua, with the honors of a prince of the Church.

Somoza I held power for twenty years. Every six years he lifted his state of siege for one day and held the elections that kept him on the throne. Luis, eldest son and heir, is now the richest and most powerful man in Central America. From Washington, President Eisenhower congratulates him.

Luis Somoza bows before the statue of his father, the bronze hero who gallops motionlessly in the very center of Managua. In the shadow of the horse's hoofs he seeks advice from the founder of the dynasty, guide to good government, proliferator of jails and businesses, then covers the monumental tomb with flowers.

Evading the vigilance of an honor guard, the hand of somebody, anybody, everybody, has hurriedly scrawled this epitaph on the marble tomb: *Here lies Somoza, a bit rottener than in life.*

(10, 102, and 460)

1956: Santo Domingo

In the Year Twenty-Six of the Trujillo Era

his likeness is sold in the markets, among the little engravings of the Virgin Mary, Saint George, and other miracle workers.

"Saints, cheap saints!"

Nothing Dominican is beyond his grasp. All belongs to him: the first night of the virgins, the last wish of the dying, the people and the cows, the air fleet and the chain of brothels, the sugar and wheat mills, the beer factory and the virility-potion bottling plant.

For twenty-six years Trujillo has occupied God's vice-presidency.

Every four years, this formula has been blessed by democratic elections: *God and Trujillo*, proclaim all walls.

In her work *Moral Meditations*, which earns her the title of First Lady of Caribbean Letters, Doña María de Trujillo compares her husband to El Cid and Napoleon Bonaparte. Plump Doña María, who practices usury during the week and mysticism on Sundays, has in turn been compared with Saint Teresa de Jesus by local critics.

With El Cid's sword or Napoleon's hat, Trujillo poses for statues. Statues multiply him in bronze and marble, with a chin he doesn't have and without the double chin he does. Thousands of statues: From high on their pedestals, Trujillo straddles the most remote corner of every city or village, watching. In this country not a fly shits without his permission.

(63 and 101)

1956: Havana

Newsreel

The Cuban army has thwarted an armed expedition from Mexico, surrounding the invaders, machinegunning and bombing them at a place called Alegría de Pío in Oriente province. Among the many dead are Fidel Castro, leader of the gang, and an Argentine Communist agitator, Ernesto Guevara.

After enjoying a long stay in the city of New York, Dr. Ernesto Sarrá and his very attractive and elegant wife, Loló, figures of the highest rank in this capital's social circles, have returned to Havana.

Also arriving from New York is Bing Crosby, the popular singer who, without removing his topcoat or beaver hat, declared at the airport: *"I have come to Cuba to play golf."*

A young Havanan, on the point of winning the grand prize in the "TV School Contest," fails to answer the next to last question. The final question, which remained unasked, was: *What is the name of the river that crosses Paris?*

An exceptional lineup will run tomorrow at the Marianao Racecourse.

(98)

1956: At the Foot of the Sierra Maestra

Twelve Lunatics

They go a week without sleep, huddled together like sardines in a can, vomiting, while the north wind toys playfully with the little boat *Granma*. After much seesawing in the Gulf of Mexico, they disembark in the wrong place, and a few steps ashore are swept by machinegun fire or burned alive by incendiary bombs, a slaughter in which almost all of them fall. The survivors consult the sky for directions but get the stars mixed up. The swamps swallow their backpacks and their arms. They have no food except sugarcane, and they leave its betraying refuse strewn along the trail. They lose their condensed milk by carrying the cans holes down. In a careless moment they mix their little remaining fresh water with sea water. They get lost and search aimlessly for one another. Finally, one small group discovers another small group on these slopes, by chance, and so the twelve saved from annihilation join together.

These men, or shadows of men, have a total of seven rifles, a little damp ammunition, and uncounted sores and wounds. Since the invasion began there is hardly a mistake they haven't made. But on this starless night they breathe fresher, cleaner air, and Fidel says, standing before the foothills of the Sierra Maestra: *"We've already won the war. Batista is fucked!"*

(98 and 209)

1957: Benidorm

Marked Cards

Between liberals and conservatives, a conjugal agreement. On a beach in the Mediterranean, Colombia's politicians sign the compromise that puts an end to ten years of mutual extermination. The two main parties offer each other an amnesty. From now on, they will alternate the presidency and divvy up the other jobs. Colombians will be able to vote, but not elect. Liberals and conservatives are to take turns in power, to guarantee the property and inheritance rights over the country that their families have brought or received as gifts.

In this pact among the wealthy there is no good news for the poor.

(8, 217, and 408)

1957: Majagual

Colombia's Sainted Egg

Burning towns and killing Indians, leveling forests and erecting wire fences, the masters of the land have pushed the campesinos right up against the river banks in this coastal region of Colombia. Many campesinos have nonetheless refused to serve as slaves on the haciendas and have instead become fishermen—artists at gritting their teeth and living on what they can find. Eating so much turtle, they learn from him: The turtle never lets go what he catches in his mouth and knows how to bury himself on the beaches in the dry season when the seagulls threaten. With that and God's help they get by.

Few monks remain in these hot regions. Here on the coast no one takes the Mass seriously. Whoever isn't paralyzed runs from marriage and work, and, the better to enjoy the seven deadly sins, indulges in endless siestas in endless hammocks. Here God is a good fellow, not a grouchy, carping police chief.

The boring Christ of Jegua is dead—a broken doll that neither sweats nor bleeds nor performs miracles. No one has even wiped the bat shit off him since the priest fled with all the silver. But very much alive, sweating and bleeding and miracle-working, is Our Little Black Lord, the dark Christ of San Benito Abad, giving counsel to anyone who will stroke him affectionately. Alive, too, and wagging their tails, are the frisky saints who appear on the Colombian coast at the drop of a hat and stick around.

One stormy night, some fishermen discover God's face, agleam in lightning flashes, on a stone the shape of an egg. Since then they celebrate the miracles of Saint Egg, dancing the *cumbia* and drinking to his health.

The parish priest of Majagual announces that he will go up river at the head of a battalion of crusaders, throw the sacrilegious stone to the bottom of the waters, and set fire to their little palm-frond chapel.

In the tiny chapel, where Masses are celebrated with lively music, the fishermen stand guard around Saint Egg. Ax in hand, day and night.

(159)

1957: Sucre
Saint Lucío

While the Majagual priest declares war on Saint Egg, the priest of Sucre expels Saint Lucía from his church, because a female saint with a penis is unheard of.

At first it looked like a cyst, or a bump on the neck; but it kept moving lower and lower, and growing, bulging beneath the sacred tunic that shortened every day. Everyone pretended not to notice, until one day a child suddenly blurted out: "*Saint Lucía has a dick!*"

Exiled, Saint Lucío finds refuge in a hut not far from the little temple of Saint Egg. In time, the fishermen put up an altar to him, because Saint Lucío is a fun-loving, trustworthy guy who joins the binges of his devotees, listens to their secrets, and is happy when summer comes and the fish begin to rise.

This he, who used to be she, doesn't figure among the saints listed in the Bristol Almanac, nor has Saint Egg been canonized by the Pope of Rome. Neither has Saint Board, unhinged from the box of soap in which a laundrywoman found the Virgin Mary; or Saint Kidney, the humble kidney of a cow in which a slaughterer saw Christ's crown of thorns. Nor Saint Domingo Vidal . . .

(159)

1957: *The Sinú River Banks*
Saint Domingo Vidal

He had been a dwarf and a paralytic. The people had named him a saint, Saint Domingo Vidal, because with his prophetic hunches he had known just where on this Colombian coast a lost horse had strayed, and which cock would win the next fight, and because he had asked nothing for teaching the poor how to read and defend themselves from locusts and omnivorous landlords.

Son of Lucifer, the Church called him. A priest hauled him out of his grave inside the chapel of Chimá and broke his bones with an ax and hammer. His shattered remains ended up in a corner of the plaza, and another priest wanted to throw them in the garbage. The first priest died a writhing death, his hands turning into claws; the other suffocated, wallowing in his own excrement.

Like Saint Egg, Saint Lucío, and many of their local colleagues, Saint Domingo Vidal remains happily alive in the fervor of all those hereabouts who love—either in or out of wedlock—and in the noisy throng of people who share the grim battle for land and the joys of its fruits.

Saint Domingo Vidal protects the ancient custom of the Sinú River villagers, who visit each other bearing gifts of food. The people of one village bear litters to another loaded with flowers and delicacies from the river and its banks: dorado or shad stews, slices of catfish, iguana eggs, riced coconut, cheese, sweet *mongomongo*; and while the recipients eat, the donors sing and dance around them.

(160)

1957: Pino del Agua

Crucito

Batista offers three hundred pesos and a cow with calf to anyone who brings him Fidel Castro, alive or dead.

On the other side of the crests of the Sierra Maestra, the guerrillas sweat and multiply. They quickly learn the rules of war in the brush: to mistrust, to move by night, never to sleep twice in the same place, and above all, to make friends with the local people.

When the twelve bedraggled survivors arrived in this sierra, they knew not a single campesino, and the River Yara only through the song that mentions it. A few months later there are a few campesinos in the rebel ranks, the kind of men who cut cane for a while at harvest time and then are left to starve in unknown territory; and now the guerrillas know these areas as if they had been born in them. They know the names of the places, and when they don't, they baptize them after their own fashion. They have given the Arroyo of Death its name because there a guerrilla deserted who had sworn to fight to the death.

Others die fighting, without having sworn anything.

While smoking his pipe during the rest periods, José de la Cruz— "Crucito"—sierra troubadour, composes in ten-verse *guajira* stanzas the entire history of the Cuban revolution. For lack of paper he commits it to memory, but has it taken from him by a bullet, on the heights of Pino del Agua during an ambush of army trucks.

(209)

1957: El Uvero
Almeida

Juan Almeida claims he has a joy inside him that keeps tickling, making him laugh and jump. A very stubborn joy if one considers that Almeida was born poor and black on this island of private beaches which are closed to the poor because they are poor and to blacks because they stain the water; and that, to make matters worse, he decided to be a bricklayer's helper and a poet; and that, as if those were not complications enough, he rolled his life into this crap game of the Cuban revolution, and as one of the Moncada assailants was sentenced to jail and exile, and was navigator of the *Granma* before becoming the guerrilla that he is now; and that he has just stopped two bullets—not mortal, but motherfuckers—one in the left leg and one in the shoulder, during the three-hour attack on the Uvero barracks, down by the shore.

(209)

1957: Santiago de Cuba
Portrait of an Imperial Ambassador

Earl Smith, ambassador of the United States, receives the keys to the city of Santiago de Cuba. As the ceremony proceeds and the speeches pour forth, a commotion is heard through the curtains. Discreetly, the ambassador peers out the window and observes a number of women approaching, clad in black, chanting the national anthem and shouting *"Liberty!"* The police club them down.

The next day, the ambassador visits the U.S. military base at Guantánamo. Then he tours the iron and nickel mines of the Freeport Sulphur Company, which, thanks to his efforts, have just been exempted from taxes.

The ambassador publicly expresses his disgust with the police beatings, although he recognizes that the government has a right to defend itself from Communist aggression. Advisers have explained to the ambassador that Fidel has been abnormal since childhood, from having fallen off a moving motorcycle.

The ambassador, who was a champion boxer in his student days, believes General Batista must be defended at any cost. With Batista in power, tourists can pick from photos handed them on the airplane their pretty mulatta for the weekend. Havana is a North American city, full of one-armed bandits from Nevada and mafia bosses from Chicago, and with plenty of telephones to order a nice hot supper to be brought on the next flight out of Miami.

(431)

1957: El Hombrito
Che

In the Hombrito Valley, the rebels have installed an oven for baking bread, a printshop consisting of an old mimeograph machine, and a clinic that functions in a one-room hut. The doctor is Ernesto Guevara, known as Che, who apart from his nickname has retained certain Argentine customs, like maté and irony. American pilgrim, he joined Fidel's forces in Mexico, where he settled after the fall of Guatemala to earn a living as a photographer at one peso per photo, and as a peddler of little engravings of the Virgin of Guadalupe.

In the Hombrito clinic, Che attends a series of children with bloated bellies, almost dwarfs, and aged girls worn out from too many births and too little food, and men as dry and empty as gourds, because poverty turns everyone into a living mummy.

Last year, when machineguns mowed down the newly landed guerrillas, Che had to choose between a case of bullets and a case of medicines. He couldn't carry both and decided on the bullets. Now he strokes his old Thompson rifle, the only surgical instrument he really believes in.

(209)

Old Chana, Campesina of the
Sierra Maestra, Remembers:

Poor dear Che! I always saw him with that curse of his asthma and said, "Ay, Holy Virgin!" With the asthma he would get all quiet, breathing low. Some folks with asthma get hysterical, cough and open their eyes and open their mouth. But Che tried to soften up the asthma. He would throw himself in a corner to rest the asthma.

He didn't like sympathy. If you said, "Poor guy," he gave you a quick look that didn't mean anything, and meant a lot.

I used to warm him up a bit of water to rub on his chest for relief. He, the big flatterer, would say, "Oh, my girlfriend." But he was such a rascal.

(338)

1958: Stockholm

Pelé

Brazilian football glows. It dances and makes one dance. At the World Cup in Sweden, Pelé and Garrincha are the heroes, proving wrong those who say blacks can't play in a cold climate.

Pelé, thin as a rake, almost a boy, puffs out his chest and raises his chin to make an impression. He plays football as God would play it, if God decided to devote himself seriously to the game. Pelé makes a date with the ball anywhere, any time, and she never stands him up. He sends her high in the air. She makes a full curve and returns to his foot, obedient, grateful, or perhaps tied by an invisible elastic band. Pelé lifts her up, puffs out his chest, and she rolls smoothly down his body. Without letting her touch the ground he flips her to the other foot as he flings himself, running like a hare, toward the goal. No one can catch him, with lasso or bullet, until he leaves the ball, shining, white, tight against the back of the net.

On and off the field, he takes care of himself. He never wastes a minute of his time, nor lets a penny fall from his pocket. Until recently he was shining shoes down at the docks. Pelé was born to rise; and he knows it.

(279)

1958: Stockholm
Garrincha

Garrincha plays havoc with the other teams, always threatening to break through. Half turn, full turn, he looks like he's coming, but he's going! He acts like he's going, but he's coming. Flabbergasted opponents fall on their asses as if Garrincha were scattering banana peels along the field. At the goal line, when he has eluded them all, including the goalie, he sits on the ball. Then he backs up and starts again. The fans are amused, but the managers go crazy. Garrincha, carefree bird with bandy legs, plays for laughs, not to win, and forgets the results. He still thinks soccer's a party, not a job or a business. He likes to play for nothing, or a few beers, on beaches or ragged little fields.

He has many children, his own and other people's. He drinks and eats as if for the last time. Openhanded, he gives everything away, loses the works. Garrincha was born to fall; and he doesn't know it.

(22)

1958: Sierra Maestra
The Revolution Is an Unstoppable Centipede

As the war reaches its height, beneath the bullets Fidel introduces agrarian reform in the Sierra Maestra. Campesinos get their first land, not to speak of their first doctor, their first teacher, even their first judge—which is said to be a less dangerous way to settle a dispute than the machete.

Batista's more than ten thousand soldiers can't seem to do anything but lose. The rebel army is infinitely smaller and still poorly armed, but under it, above it, within it, ahead of and behind it, are the people.

The future is now. Fidel launches a final offensive: Cuba from end to end. In two columns, one under the command of Che Guevara, the other under Camilo Cienfuegos, a hundred and sixty guerrillas descend from the mountains to conquer the plain.

(98 and 209)

1958: Yaguajay

Camilo

Magically eluding bombardment and ambush, the invading columns
strike for the island's gut, slicing Cuba in two as Camilo Cienfuegos
takes the Yaguajay barracks after eleven days of fighting and Che
enters the city of Santa Clara. Suddenly, half of Batista's island has
disappeared.

Camilo Cienfuegos, brave and greedy, fights at such close quarters that, killing an enemy soldier, he catches his rifle in mid-air
without its touching the ground. Several times the fatal bullet that
should have been his just barely wasn't, and once he nearly died from
gobbling down a whole kid after two days of eating nothing at all.

Camilo has the beard and mane of a biblical prophet, but where
a worry-creased face should be, there's only an ear-to-ear grin. The
feat he is most proud of is that time up in the mountains when he
fooled a light military plane by painting himself red with iodine and
lying still with his arms crossed.

(179 and 210)

1959: Havana

Cuba Wakes Up Without Batista

on the first day of the year. The dictator lands in Santo Domingo and
seeks refuge with his colleague Trujillo; back in Havana, for the former
hangmen, it's *sauve qui peut*, a stampede.

U.S. Ambassador Earl Smith is appalled. The streets have been
taken over by rabble and by a few dirty, hairy, barefoot guerrillas,
just a Latin Dillinger gang who dance the *guaguancó*, marking time
with rifle shots.

(98 and 431)

The Rumba

The *guaguancó* is a kind of rumba, and every self-respecting Cuban
has the rumba under his belt, in peace, war, and anything between.
Even when picking a fight, the Cuban rumbas, so now he joins the

dance of the bullets without a second thought, and the crowds surge behind the drums that summon them.

"I'm enjoying it. And if they get me, too bad. At least I'm enjoying it."

On any street or field the music lets loose. There's no stopping it—that rumba rhythm on drums and crates, or, if there are no drums or crates, on bodies, or just in the air. Even ears dance.

(86, 198, and 324)

1959: Havana
Portrait of a Caribbean Casanova

Porfirio Rubirosa, the Dominican ambassador, looks with dread on this horrifying spectacle. He has nothing for breakfast but a cup of coffee. The news has taken away his appetite. While servants by the dozen nail down boxes and close trunks and suitcases, Rubirosa nervously lights a cigarette and puts his favorite song, "Taste of Me," on the phonograph.

The sun, they say, never sets on his bed. Trujillo's man in Cuba is a famous enchanter of princesses, heiresses, and movie stars. Rubirosa beguiles them with flattery and plays the ukulele to them before loving or beating them.

Some say his tremendous energy derives from the milk of his infancy, which came from sirens' tits. Dominican patriots insist that his secret is a virility elixir Trujillo concocts from the *pega-palo* plant and exports to the United States.

Rubirosa's career began when Trujillo made him his son-in-law; continued when, as Dominican ambassador to Paris, he sold visas to Jews persecuted by Hitler; and was perfected in his marriages to multi-millionairesses Doris Duke and Barbara Hutton. It is the smell of money that excites the tropical Casanova, as the smell of blood excites sharks.

(100)

1959: Havana

"We have only won the right to begin,"

says Fidel, who rides into town on top of a tank, direct from the Sierra Maestra. To a surging crowd he explains that all this, while it might look like a conclusion, is no more than a beginning.

Half of Cuba's land is uncultivated. According to the statistics, last year was the most prosperous in the island's history; but the campesinos, who can't read statistics or anything else, haven't noticed. From now on, a different cock will crow, with agrarian reform and a literacy campaign, as in the sierra, the most urgent tasks. But before that, the dismantling of an army of butchers. The worst torturers go up against a wall. The aptly named "Bonebreaker" faints each time the firing squad takes aim. They have to bind him to a post.

(91)

1960: Brasília

A City, or Delirium in the Midst of Nothing

Brazil lifts the curtain on its new capital. Suddenly, Brasília is born at the center of a cross traced on the red dust of the desert, very far from the coast, very far from everything, out at the end of the world— or perhaps its beginning.

The city has been built at a dizzying speed. For three years this was an anthill where workers and technicians labored shoulder to shoulder, night and day, sharing jobs, food, and shelter. But when Brasília is finished, the fleeting illusion of brotherhood is finished, too. Doors slam: This city is not for servants. Brasília locks out those who raised it with their own hands. Their place is piled together in shacks that blossom by God's grace on the outskirts of town.

This is the government's city, house of power. No people in its plazas, no paths to walk on. Brasília is on the moon: white, luminous, floating way up, high above Brazil, shielded from its dirt and its follies.

Oscar Niemeyer, architect of its palaces, did not dream of it that way. When the great inaugural fiesta occurs, Niemeyer does not appear on the podium.

(69 and 315)

1960: Rio de Janeiro
Niemeyer

He hates right angles and capitalism. Against capitalism there's not much he can do; but against the right angle, that oppressor, constrictor of space, his architecture triumphs. It's free and sensual and light as clouds.

Niemeyer imagines human habitations in the form of a woman's body, a sinuous shoreline, or a tropical fruit. Also in the form of a mountain, if the mountain breaks up into beautiful curves against the sky, as do the mountains of Rio de Janeiro, designed by God on that day when God thought he was Niemeyer.

(315)

1960: Rio de Janeiro
Guimaraes Rosa

Daring and undulating, too, is the language of Guimaraes Rosa, who builds houses with words.

Works warm with passion are created by this formal gentleman, metronomically punctual, incapable of crossing a street against the light. Tragedy blows ferociously through the stories and novels of the smiling career diplomat. When he writes he violates all literary rules, this bourgeois conservative who dreams of entering the Academy.

1960: Artemisa
Thousands and Thousands of Machetes

wave in the air, brushing, rubbing, colliding, clashing, providing a background of battle-music for Fidel's speech—or, rather, for the song he is singing from the platform. Here, on the eastern end of the island, he explains to sugar workers why his government has expropriated Texaco Oil.

Cuba reacts to each successive blow with neither trepidation nor deference. The State Department refuses to accept the agrarian reform: Cuba divides the U.S.-owned estates among campesinos. Eisenhower sends planes to set fire to canefields and threatens not to

buy Cuban sugar: Cuba breaks the commercial monopoly and ex-
changes sugar for oil with the Soviet Union. U.S. oil companies refuse
to refine Soviet oil: Cuba nationalizes them.

Every discourse is a course. For hours and hours Fidel reasons
and asks, teaches and learns, defends and accuses, while Cuba gropes
forward, each step a search for the way.

(91)

1961: Santo Domingo

In the Year Thirty-One of the Trujillo Era

The paperweight on his desk, lying amid gilt cupids and dancing girls,
is a porcelain baseball glove. Surrounded by busts of Trujillo and
photos of Trujillo, Trujillo scans the latest lists of conspirators sub-
mitted by his spies. With a disdainful flick of the wrist he crosses out
names, men and women who will not wake up tomorrow, while his
torturers wrench new names from prisoners who scream in the Ozama
fortress.

The lists give Trujillo cause for sad reflection. Leading the
conspirators arrayed against him are the U.S. ambassador and the
archbishop primate of the Indies, who only yesterday shared his government. Now Empire and Church are repudiating their faithful son,
who has become unpresentable in the eyes of the world, and whose
prodigal hand they now reject. Such ingratitude from the authors of
capitalist development in the Dominican Republic hurts him deeply.
Nevertheless, among all the decorations that hang from his breast,
his belly, and the walls, Trujillo still loves best the Grand Cross
of the Order of Saint Gregory, which he received from the Vatican,
and the little medal which, many years ago, recognized his services
to the U.S. Marines.

Until death he will be the Sentinel of the West, despite all the
grief, this man who has dubbed himself Benefactor of the Fatherland,
Savior of the Fatherland, Father of the Fatherland, Restorer of Fi-
nancial Independence, Champion of World Peace, Protector of Culture, First Anticommunist of the Americas, Outstanding and Most
Illustrious Generalísimo.

(60, 63, and 101)

1961: Santo Domingo

The Defunctísimo

leaves as his bequest an entire country—in addition to nine thousand six hundred neckties, two thousand suits, three hundred and fifty uniforms, and six hundred pairs of shoes in his closets in Santo Domingo, and five hundred and thirty million dollars in his private Swiss bank accounts.

Rafael Leónidas Trujillo has fallen in an ambush, bullets tattooing his car. His son, Ramfis, flies in from Paris to take charge of the legacy, the burial, and vengeance.

Colleague and buddy of Porfirio Rubirosa, Ramfis Trujillo has acquired a certain notoriety since a recent cultural mission to Hollywood. There, he presented Mercedes Benzes and chinchilla coats to Kim Novak and Zsa Zsa Gabor in the name of the hungry but generous Dominican people.

(60, 63, and 101)

1961: Bay of Pigs

Against the Wind,

against death, moving ahead, never back, the Cuban revolution remains scandalously alive no more than eight minutes' flying time from Miami.

To put an end to this effrontery, the CIA organizes an invasion to be launched from the United States, Guatemala, and Nicaragua. Somoza II sees the expeditionary force off at the pier. In the Cuban Liberation Army, machine-tooled, oiled, and greased by the CIA, soldiers and policemen from the Batista dictatorship cohabit with displaced inheritors of sugar plantations, banks, newspapers, gambling casinos, brothels, and political parties.

"Bring me back some hairs from Castro's beard!" Somoza instructs them.

U.S. planes, camouflaged and decorated with the star of the Cuban Air Force, enter Cuban skies. These planes, flying low, strafe the people who greet them, then bomb the cities. After this softening-up operation, the invaders land haplessly in the swamps of the Bay of Pigs.

Meanwhile, President Kennedy golfs in Virginia. He has issued the invasion order, but it was Eisenhower who had set the plan in motion, Eisenhower who gave it the green light at the same desk where he approved the invasion of Guatemala. Allen Dulles, head of the CIA, assured him it would be as simple to do away with Fidel as it was with Arbenz. A matter of a couple of weeks, give or take a day or two; even the same CIA team to take charge of it. Same men, same bases. The landing of the liberators would unleash popular insurrection on this island under the boot of red tyranny. U.S. intelligence operatives report exactly that. The people of Cuba, fed up with forming queues, await the signal to rise.

(415 and 469)

1961: Playa Girón
The Second U.S. Military Defeat
in Latin America

It takes Cuba only three days to finish off the invaders. Among the dead are four U.S. pilots. The seven ships of the invasion fleet, escorted by the United States Navy, flee or sink in the Bay of Pigs.

President Kennedy assumes full responsibility for this CIA fiasco.

The Agency believed, as always, in the reports of its local spies, whom it paid to say what it was desperate to hear; and, as always, it confused geography with a military map unrelated to people or to history. The marshes the CIA chose for the landing had been the most miserable spot in all Cuba, a kingdom of crocodiles and mosquitos—that is, until the revolution. Then human enthusiasm had transformed these quagmires, peppering them with schools, hospitals, and roads.

The people here are the first to face the bullets of the invaders who have come to save them.

(88, 435, and 469)

1961: Havana

Portrait of the Past

The invaders—hangers-on and hangmen, young millionaires, veterans of a thousand crimes—answer the journalists' questions. No one assumes responsibility for Playa Girón; no one assumes responsibility for anything. They were all cooks.

Ramón Calvino, famous torturer of the Batista regime, suffers total amnesia when confronted by the women he had beaten, kicked and raped, who identify and revile him. Father Ismael de Lugo, chaplain of the assault brigade, seeks shelter beneath the Virgin's cloak. He had fought on Franco's side in the Spanish war—on the Virgin's advice, he says—and joined the invasion force to keep the Virgin from having to suffer any more the spectacle of communism. Father Lugo invokes the tycoon Virgin, owner of some bank or nationalized plantation, who thinks and feels like the other twelve hundred prisoners: that right is the right of property and inheritance; freedom, the freedom of enterprise; the model society, a business corporation; exemplary democracy, a shareholders' meeting.

All the invaders have been educated in the ethics of impunity. None admit to having killed anybody; but then, like them, poverty doesn't exactly sign its name to its crimes either. Some journalists question them about social injustice, but they wash their hands of it, the system washes its hands. After all, children in Cuba—in all of Latin America—who die soon after birth, die of gastroenteritis, not capitalism.

(397)

1961: Washington

Who Invaded Cuba? A Dialogue in the U.S. Senate

SENATOR CAPEHART: *How many [planes] did we have?*
ALLEN DULLES (director of the CIA): *How many did the Cubans have?*
SENATOR SPARKMAN: *No, the Americans had how many?*
DULLES: *Well, these are Cubans.*
SPARKMAN: *The rebels.*

DULLES: *We do not call them rebels.*
CAPEHART: *I mean, the revolutionary forces.*
SPARKMAN: *When he said how many did we have, that is what we are referring to, anti-Castro forces.*
RICHARD M. BISSELL (deputy director of the CIA): *We started out, sir, with sixteen B-26s . . .*

(108)

1961: Havana
María de la Cruz

Soon after the invasion, a vast crowd assembles in the plaza to hear Fidel announce that the prisoners will be exchanged for children's medicines. Then he gives out diplomas to forty thousand campesinos who have learned to read and write.

An old woman insists on mounting the platform, insists so energetically that finally they bring her up. She flaps vainly at the too-high microphone, until Fidel hands it down to her.

"I wanted to meet you, Fidel. I wanted to tell you . . ."

"Look, you'll make me blush."

But the old woman, all wrinkles and little bones, isn't about to be put off. She says she's finally learned to read and write at the age of a hundred and six. She introduces herself. Her Christian name is María de la Cruz, because she was born on the day that the Holy Cross was invented; her surname is Semanat, after the sugar plantation on which she was born a slave, the daughter of slaves, granddaughter of slaves. In those days the masters sent blacks who tried to get an education to the pillory, María de la Cruz explains, because blacks were supposed to be machines that went into action at the sound of a bell, to the rhythm of whips, and that was why she took so long to learn.

María de la Cruz takes over the platform. After speaking, she sings. After singing, she dances. It's been more than a century since María de la Cruz began dancing. Dancing she emerged from her mother's belly and dancing she journeyed through pain and horror until she arrived here, where she should have been long ago. Now no one can stop her.

(298)

1961: Punta del Este
Latrine Diplomacy

After the fiasco of the military landing in Cuba, the United States changes its tune, announcing a massive landing of dollars in Latin America.

To isolate Cuba's bearded ones, President Kennedy floods Latin America with a torrent of donations, loans, investments.

"Cuba is the hen that laid your golden eggs," Che Guevara tells the Pan-American Conference at Punta del Este, calling this proposed program of bribery an enormous joke on Latin America.

So that nothing should change, the rhetoric of change is unleashed. The conference's official reports run to half a million pages, not one of which neglects to mention "revolution," "agrarian reform," or "development." While the United States knocks down the prices of Latin American products, it promises latrines for the poor, for Indians, for blacks—no machinery, no equipment, just latrines.

"For the technical gentlemen," says Che, *"planning amounts to the planning of latrines. If we took them seriously, Cuba could be . . . a paradise of the latrine!"*

(213)

1961: Escuinapa
The Tale Spinner

Once he saddled and mounted a tiger, thinking it was a burro. Another time he belted his pants with a live snake—only noticing because it had no buckle. Everyone believes him when he explains that no plane can land unless grains of corn are thrown on the runway, or when he describes the terrible bloodbath the day the train went mad and started running sideways. *"I never lie,"* lies Wily Humbug.

Wily, a shrimp fisherman in the Escuinapa estuaries, is a typical loose tongue in this region. He is of that splendid Latin American breed of tale spinners, magicians of crackerbarrel talk that's always spoken, never written down.

At seventy, his eyes still dance. He even laughed at Death, who came one night to seek him out.

"Toc toc toc," Death knocked.

"Come in," Wily coaxed from his bed. *"I was expecting you."*
But when he tried to take her pants down, Death fled in panic.

(309)

1961: São Salvador de Bahia

Amado

While Wily Humbug scares off death in Mexico, in Brazil novelist Jorge Amado invents a captain who scares off solitude. According to Amado, this captain defies hurricanes and will-o'-the-wisps, bestrides seaquakes and black whirlpools, while treating his barrio neighbors to drinks prepared from the recipes of an old Hong Kong sea-wolf.

When the captain is shipwrecked off the coast of Peru, his neighbors are shipwrecked too. It wrings their hearts, timid retired officials that they are, sick with boredom and rheumatism, to see a mountain of ice advancing toward the ship, off the port bow, on the foggy North Sea; or the monsoon blowing furiously on the Sea of Bengal. All shiver with pleasure as the captain evokes once again the Arab beauty who bit juicy grapes as she danced on the sands of Alexandria, wearing nothing but a white flower in her navel.

The captain has never left Brazil, nor set foot on any kind of boat, because the sea makes him sick. He sits in the living room of his house and the house sails off, drifting farther than Marco Polo or Columbus or the astronauts ever dreamed.

(19)

1962: Cosalá

One Plus One Is One

Hitched to the same post, overloaded with dry wood, they look at each other. He, amorously; she, dizzily. As the male and the female burro consider and reconsider each other, devout women cross the plaza, heading toward church, wrapped up in prayer. Because it's Good Friday they chant mournful Masses for Our Lord Jesus Christ as they go by, all in black: black mantillas, black stockings, black gloves. They become frantic when the two burros, breaking their bonds, romp over to enjoy themselves right there, in the plaza, facing the church, rumps to city hall.

Screams resound across Mexico. The mayor of Cosalá, José Antonio Ochoa, emerges onto the balcony, lets out a shriek, and covers his eyes. He promptly orders the rebellious burros shot. They fall dead, hooked together in love.

(308 and 329)

1962: Villa de Jesús María
One Plus One Is All

In another mountain village not far away, the Cora Indians don masks and paint their naked bodies. As on every Good Friday, they give things new names while the fiesta lasts—passion of Christ, magic deer-hunt, murder of the god Sun, that crime from which human life on earth began.

"Let him die, let him kill, let him beget."

At the foot of the cross, dancing lovers offer themselves, embrace, enter one another, while the clown dancers skip about imitating them. Everyone joins in love-play, caressing, tickling, teasing. Everyone eats as they play: Fruits become projectiles, eggs bombs, and this great banquet ends in a war of hurled tortillas and showering honey. The Cora Indians enjoy themselves like lunatics, dancing, loving, eating in homage to the first agonies of the dying Christ. From the cross he smiles his thanks.

(46)

1963: Bayamo
Hurricane Flora

pounds Cuba for more than a week. The longest hurricane in the nation's history attacks, retreats, then returns as if realizing it had forgotten to smash a few last things. Everything spins around this giant, furious snake which twists and strikes suddenly, where least expected.

Useless to nail up doors and windows. The hurricane rips everything off, playing with houses and trees, flipping them into the air. The sky empties of panicky birds, while the sea floods the whole east of the island. From a base at Bayamo, brigades venture forth in launches and helicopters; volunteers come and go rescuing people and animals, vaccinating whatever they find alive and burying or burning the rest.

(18)

1963: Havana
Everyone a Jack-of-All-Trades

On this hurricane-devastated island, blockaded and harassed by the United States, getting through the day is a feat. Store windows display Vietnam solidarity posters but not shoes or shirts, and to buy the smallest thing, you wait hours in line. The occasional automobile runs on piston rings made of ox horns, and in art schools pencil graphite is ground up to approximate paint. In the factories, cobwebs cover some new machines, because a particular spare part has not yet completed its six-thousand-mile journey to get here. From remote Baltic ports come the oil and everything else Cuba needs, and a letter to Venezuela has to circle the globe before reaching its nearby destination.

And it's not only things that are lacking. Many know-it-alls have gone to Miami on the heels of the have-it-alls.

And now?

"Now we have to invent."

At eighteen, Ricardo Gutiérrez paraded into Havana, rifle held high, amid a tide of rifles, machetes, and palm-frond sombreros celebrating the end of Batista's dictatorship. On the following day he had to take charge of various enterprises abandoned by their owners. A women's underwear factory, among others, fell to his lot. Immediately the raw-material problems began. There was no latex foam for the brassieres. The workers discussed the matter at a meeting and decided to rip up pillows. It was a disaster. The pillow stuffing couldn't be washed because it never dried.

Ricardo was twenty when they put two pesos in his pocket and sent him to administer a sugar mill. He had never seen a sugar mill in his life, even from a distance. There he discovered that cane juice has a dark color. The previous administrator, a faithful servant with a half-century of experience, had disappeared over the horizon carrying under his arm the oil portrait of Julio Lobo, lord of these canefields which the revolution has expropriated.

Now the foreign minister sends for him. Raúl Roa sits on the floor before a big map of Spain spread over the carpet, and starts to draw little crosses. This is how Ricardo finds out, at twenty-two, that they have made him a consul.

"But I type with only two fingers," he stammers.

"I type with one and I'm a minister," says Roa, putting an end to the matter.

1963: Havana

Portrait of the Bureaucrat

A black time engenders a red time that will make possible a green time: Solidarity slowly replaces greed and fear. Because it is capable of invention, of creation and madness, the Cuban revolution is making out. But it has enemies to spare. Among those most to be feared is the bureaucrat, devastating as the hurricane, asphyxiating as imperialism. There is no revolution without this germ in its belly.

The bureaucrat is the wooden man, that bloodless error of the gods, neither decisive nor indecisive, an echo with no voice, a transmitter of orders, not ideas. He considers any doubt heresy, any contradiction treason; confuses unity with unanimity, and sees the people as an eternal child to be led by the ear.

It is highly improbable that the bureaucrat will put his life on the line. It is absolutely impossible that he'll put his job on the line.

1963: Havana

Bola de Nieve

"This is Yoruba-Marxism-Leninism," says Bola de Nieve, singer of Guanabacoa, son of Domingo the cook and Mama Inés. He says it in a sort of murmur, in his enormous little hoarse, fleshy voice. *Yoruba-Marxism-Leninism* is the name Bola de Nieve gives to the ardor and jubilation of these people who dance the Internationale with swaying hips, in this revolution born of the fierce embrace of Europe and Africa on the sands of America. In this place, gods made by men are crossed with men made by gods, the former descending to earth, the latter launched to conquer heaven; and Bola de Nieve celebrates it all with his salty songs.

1963: Río Coco

On His Shoulders He Carries
the Embrace of Sandino,

which time has not obliterated. Thirty years later, Colonel Santos López returns to war in the northern forests, so that Nicaragua may *be*.

A few years ago, the Sandinista Front was born. Carlos Fonseca Amador and Tomás Borge gave it birth along with Santos López and others who'd never known Sandino but wanted to perpetuate him.

The job will cost them blood, and they know it: "*So much filth can't be washed with water, no matter how holy,*" says Carlos Fonseca.

Lost, weaponless, drenched by the eternal rain, with nothing to eat—but eaten up, fucked over, and frustrated—the guerrillas wander the forest. There is no worse moment than sunset. Day is day and night is night, but dusk is the hour of agony, of frightful loneliness, and the Sandinistas are nothing yet, or nearly nothing.

(58 and 267)

1963: San Salvador

Miguel at Fifty-Eight

Miguel is living, as usual, from hand to mouth, unionizing campesinos and making mischief, when the police catch him in some little town and haul him, hands and feet bound, into the city of San Salvador.

Here he gets a protracted beating. For eight days they beat him hung up, and for eight nights they beat him on the floor. His bones creak, his flesh cries out, but he utters no sound as they torture him for his secrets. Yet when the captain insults the people he loves, the defiant old man heaves up his bleeding remains; the plucked rooster lifts his crest and crows.

Miguel orders the captain to shut his swinish trap. The captain buries a revolver barrel in his neck. Miguel defies him to shoot. The two remain face to face, ferocious, both gasping as if blowing on embers: the soldier, finger on trigger, eyes fixed on Miguel's; Miguel unblinking, counting the seconds, the centuries, as they pass, listening to the pounding of his heart as it rises into his head. Miguel gives himself up for dead now, really dead, when suddenly a shadow dims the furious glitter of the torturer's eyes, a weariness, or who knows what, and Miguel takes those eyes by storm. The torturer blinks, as if surprised to be where he is. Slowly, he lowers the gun, and with it, his eyes.

And so occurs the eleventh birth of Miguel Mármol, in his fifty-eighth year.

(222)

1963: Dallas

The Government Decides That Truth Doesn't Exist

At noon, on a street in Dallas, the president of the United States is assassinated. He is hardly dead when the official version is broadcast. In that version, which will be the definitive one, Lee Harvey Oswald alone has killed John Kennedy.

The weapon does not coincide with the bullet, nor the bullet with the holes. The accused does not coincide with the accusation: Oswald is an exceptionally bad shot of mediocre physique, but according to the official version, his acts were those of a champion marksman and Olympic sprinter. He has fired an old rifle with impossible speed and his magic bullet, turning and twisting acrobatically to penetrate Kennedy and John Connally, the governor of Texas, remains miraculously intact.

Oswald strenuously denies it. But no one knows, no one will ever know what he has to say. Two days later he collapses before the television cameras, the whole world witness to the spectacle, his mouth shut by Jack Ruby, a two-bit gangster and minor trafficker in women and drugs. Ruby says he has avenged Kennedy out of patriotism and pity for the poor widow.

(232)

1963: Santo Domingo

A Chronicle of Latin American Customs

From the sands of Sosúa, he used to swim out to sea, with a band playing to scare off the sharks.

Now, General Toni Imbert, potbellied and slack, rarely goes into the water; but he still returns to the beach of his childhood. He likes to sit on the waterfront, take aim, and shoot sharks. In Sosúa, the sharks compete with the poor for the leftovers from the slaughter-house. General Imbert is sorry for the poor. From the beach, he throws ten-dollar bills at them.

General Imbert greatly resembles his bosom friend, General Wessin y Wessin. Even with a cold, both can smell a Communist a mile off; and both have won many medals for getting up early and killing shackled people. When they say *"el presidente,"* both refer to the president of the United States.

Dominican graduates of the U.S. School of the Americas in Panama, Generals Imbert and Wessin y Wessin both fattened up under Trujillo's protection. Then both betrayed him. When, after Trujillo's death, elections were held and the people voted *en masse* for Juan Bosch, they could not stand still. Bosch refused to buy planes for the Air Force, announced agrarian reform, supported a divorce law, and raised wages.

The red lasted seven months. Imbert, Wessin y Wessin, and other generals of the nation have recovered power, that rich honeycomb, in an easy barracks revolt at dawn.

The United States loses no time recognizing the new government.

(61 and 281)

1964: Panama

Twenty-Three Boys Are Pumped Full of Lead

when they try to hoist the flag of Panama on Panamanian soil.

"We only used bird-shot," the commander of the North American occupation forces says defensively.

Another flag flies over the strip that slits Panama from sea to sea. Another law prevails, another police keep watch, another language is spoken. Panamanians may not enter the Canal Zone without permission, even to pick up fallen fruit from a mango tree, and they work here at second-class pay, like blacks and women.

The Canal Zone, North American colony, is both a business and a military base. The School of the Americas' courses are financed with the tolls ships pay. In the Canal Zone barracks, Pentagon officers teach anticommunist surgery to Latin American military men who will soon, in their own countries, occupy presidencies, ministries, commands, and embassies.

"They are the leaders of the future," explains Robert McNamara, secretary of defense of the United States.

Wary of the cancer that lies in wait for them, these military men will cut off the hands of anyone who dares to commit agrarian reform or nationalization, and tear out the tongues of the impudent or the inquisitive.

(248)

1964: Rio de Janeiro
"There are dark clouds,"

says Lincoln Gordon:
"Dark clouds are closing in on our economic interests in Brazil . . ."

President João Goulart has just introduced agrarian reform, the nationalization of oil refineries, and an end to the flight of capital. The indignant ambassador of the United States loudly attacks him. From the embassy, rivers of money flow to pollute public opinion, and the military prepare to seize power. A shrill call for a coup d'état is publicized by the media. Even the Lions Club signs it.

Ten years after Vargas's suicide the same furor erupts again, several times stronger. Politicians and journalists call for a uniformed Messiah who can put some order into the chaos. The TV broadcasts a film showing Berlin walls cutting Brazilian cities in two. Newspapers and radios exalt the virtues of private capital, which turns deserts into oases, and the merits of the armed forces, who keep Communists from stealing the water. Down the avenues of the chief cities the March of the Family with God for Liberty pleads to heaven for mercy.

Ambassador Lincoln Gordon excoriates the Communist plot: Goulart, estancia owner, is betraying his class at the moment of choice between devourers and devoured, between the makers and the objects of opinions, between the freedom of money and the freedom of people.

(115 and 141)

1964: Juiz de Fora
The Reconquest of Brazil

Almost thirty years after Captain Olympio Mourão Filho fabricated a Communist plot at the orders of President Vargas, General Mourão Filho buys a Communist plot fabricated by Ambassador Lincoln Gordon. The modest general confesses that in political matters he is just a uniformed ox, but he does understand about Communist conspiracies.

In the Juiz de Fora barracks he raises his sword: *"I'll snatch Brazil from the abyss!"*

Mourão has been awake since before dawn. While shaving he recites the psalm of David, the one that declares that all verdure will perish. Then he eats breakfast, congratulates his wife on being married to a hero, and at the head of his troops sets out to march on Rio de Janeiro.

The rest of the generals fall into line, and from the United States, already heading for Brazil, come one aircraft carrier, numerous planes and warships, and four fuel-supply ships. It's "Operation Brother Sam," to assist the rising.

João Goulart, irresolute, watches it happen. His colleague Lyndon Johnson sends warmest approval to the authors of the coup, even though Goulart still occupies the presidency; the State Department immediately offers generous loans to the new government. From the south, Leonel Brizola's attempt at resistance produces no echo. At last, Goulart heads into exile.

Some anonymous hand writes on a wall in Rio de Janeiro: *"No more middlemen! Lincoln Gordon for president!"*

But the triumphant generals choose Marshall Castelo Branco, a solemn military man without a sense of humor or a neck.

(115, 141, and 307)

1964: La Paz

Without Shame or Glory,

like the president of Brazil, President Víctor Paz Estenssoro boards a plane that will take him into exile.

He leaves behind him René Barrientos, babbling aviator, as dictator of Bolivia. Now the U.S. ambassador participates in cabinet meetings, seated among the ministers, and the manager of Gulf Oil draws up economic decrees.

Paz Estenssoro had been left devastatingly alone, and along with him falls the national revolution after twelve years in power. Bit by bit the revolution had turned around until it had shown its back to the workers, the better to suckle the new rich and the bureaucrats who squeezed it dry. Now, a slight puff suffices to blow it over.

Meanwhile, the divided workers fight among themselves, as if they were Laime and Jucumani tribesmen.

(16, 17, 26, and 473)

1964: North of Potosí

With Savage Fury

the Laime Indians fight the Jucumanis. The poorest of poor Bolivia, pariahs among pariahs, they devote themselves to killing one another on the frozen steppe north of Potosí. Five hundred from both tribes have died in the past ten years; the burned huts are beyond counting. Battles continue for weeks, without letup or mercy. The Indians cut one another to pieces to avenge petty grievances or disputes over scraps of sterile land in these lofty solitudes to which they were banished long, long ago.

Laimes and Jucumanis live on potatoes and barley, all the steppe with great effort will yield them. They sleep on sheepskins, accompanied by lice that welcome the warmth of their bodies.

For the ceremonies of mutual extermination they cover their heads with rawhide caps in the exact shape of the conquistadors' helmets.

(180)

Hats

in today's Bolivia are descended from Europe, brought by conquistadors and merchants; but they have been adapted to belong to this land and this people. Originally they were like cattle brands, compulsory disguises that helped each Spanish master recognize the Indians he owned. As time passed, communities began to deck out their headgear with their own stamps of pride, symbols of joy: stars and little moons of silver, colored feathers, glass beads, paper flowers, crowns of corn . . . Later, the English flooded Bolivia with bowlers and top hats: the black stovepipe hat of the Potosí Indian women, the white one of those of Cochabamba. By some mistake, the borsalino hat arrived from Italy and settled down on the heads of La Paz's Indian women.

The Bolivian Indian, man or woman, boy or girl, may go barefoot, but never hatless. The hat prolongs the head it protects; and when the soul falls, the hat picks it up off the ground.

(161)

1965: San Juan, Puerto Rico

Bosch

People stream into the streets of Santo Domingo, armed with whatever they can find, and pitch themselves against the tanks. "Thieves, get out!" they yell. "Come back, Juan Bosch, our president!"

The United States holds Bosch prisoner in Puerto Rico, preventing his return to his country in flames. A man of strong fiber, all tendon and tension, Bosch, alone in his anger, bites his fists, and his blue eyes pierce walls.

A journalist asks him over the phone if he is an enemy of the United States. No, he is only an enemy of U.S. imperialism.

"No one who has read Mark Twain," says Bosch, *"can be an enemy of the United States."*

(62 and 269)

1965: *Santo Domingo*

Caamaño

Into the melee pour students, soldiers, women in hair curlers. With barricades of barrels and overturned trucks, the rumbling advance of the tanks is stopped. Stones and bottles fly, while from the wingtips of swooping planes machinegun fire sweeps the Ozama River bridge and the thronged streets. The tide of people rises, and rising, separates the soldiers who had formerly served Trujillo: on one side, those commanded by Imbert and Wessin y Wessin, who are shooting people; on the other, the followers of Francisco Caamaño, who break open the arsenals and begin distributing rifles.

This morning, Colonel Caamaño set off the uprising for Bosch's return, believing it would be a matter of minutes. By midday, he realized it was a long job, that he would have to confront his comrades-in-arms, that blood was flowing; and had a horrifying presentiment of national tragedy. At nightfall he sought asylum in the Salvadoran embassy.

Collapsed in an armchair, Caamaño tries to sleep. He takes sedatives, his usual dose and more, but nothing works. Insomnia, teeth-grinding, nail-biting: Trujillo's legacy to him from the time when he was an officer in the dictator's army and performed, or saw performed, dark, sometimes atrocious deeds. Tonight it's worse than ever. He no sooner closes his eyes than he starts to dream. Dreaming, he is honest with himself; awakening he trembles, weeps, rages with shame for his fear.

Morning comes and his exile ends: It has lasted just one night. Colonel Caamaño wets his face and leaves the embassy. He walks staring at the ground, through the smoke of the fires, thick smoke that casts a shadow, and emerges into the shimmering light of day to return to his post at the head of the rebellion.

(223)

1965: Santo Domingo
The Invasion

Not by air, not by land, not by sea. General Wessin y Wessin's planes and General Imbert's tanks cannot still the free-for-all in the burning city any more than the ships that fire on the Government Palace, occupied by Caamaño, but kill housewives.

The United States embassy, which calls the rebels *Communist scum* and *a gang of thugs*, reports that there is no way to stop the disturbance and requests urgent aid from Washington. The Marines land.

Next day, the first invader dies: a boy from the mountains of northern New York State, shot from a roof, in a narrow street of this city whose name he had never heard in all his life. The first Dominican victim is a child of five. He dies on a balcony from a grenade explosion. The invaders had mistaken him for a sniper.

President Lyndon Johnson warns that he will not tolerate another Cuba in the Caribbean. More troops land. And more. Twenty thousand, thirty-five thousand, forty-two thousand. As U.S. soldiers tear up Dominicans, North American volunteers stitch them together in hospitals. Johnson exhorts his allies to join this Western Crusade. The military dictatorship of Brazil, the military dictatorship of Paraguay, the military dictatorship of Honduras, and the military dictatorship of Nicaragua all send troops to the Dominican Republic to save the democracy threatened by its people.

Trapped between river and sea, in the old barrio of Santo Domingo, its people resist.

José Mora Otero, secretary general of the Organization of American States, meets privately with Colonel Caamaño. He offers him six million dollars to leave the country, and is told to go to hell.

(62, 269, and 421)

1965: Santo Domingo
One Hundred Thirty-Two Nights

and this war of sticks and knives and carbines against mortars and machineguns still goes on. The city smells of gunpowder, garbage, and death.

Unable to force a surrender, the invaders, all-powerful as they are, have no alternative but agreement. The nobodies, the nothings have not let themselves be beaten. They have fought fierce battles by night, every night, house to house, body to body, yard by yard, until the moment the sun raised his flaming flag from the bottom of the sea, when they lowered themselves into darkness until the next night. And after so many nights of horror and glory, the invading troops do not succeed in installing General Imbert in power, nor General Wessin y Wessin, nor any other general.

(269 and 421)

1965: Havana

This Multiplier of Revolutions,

Spartan *guerrillero*, sets out for other lands. Fidel makes public Che Guevara's letter of farewell. *"Now nothing legal ties me to Cuba,"* says Che, *"only the bonds that cannot be broken."*

Che also writes to his parents and to his children. He asks his children to be able to feel in their deepest hearts any injustice committed against anyone in any part of the world.

Here in Cuba, asthma and all, Che has been the first to arrive and the last to go, in war and in peace, without the slightest weakening.

Everyone has fallen in love with him—the women, the men, the children, the dogs, and the plants.

(213)

Che Guevara Bids Farewell to His Parents

Once again I feel under my heels the ribs of Rocinante: I return to the road with shield on arm . . .

Many will call me an adventurer, and that I am; only of a different type—of those who risk their hides to demonstrate their truths. This may be the decisive one. I do not seek it but it is within the logical estimate of probabilities. If that's how it is, this is my last embrace.

I have loved you a lot, only haven't known how to express my affection; I am extremely rigid in my actions and I think you sometimes didn't understand me. It wasn't easy to understand me, but just believe me today.

Now the will that I have polished with the delight of an artist will sustain this flabby pair of legs and these weary lungs. I will do it. Think once in a while about this little twentieth-century condottiere.

(213)

1966: Patiocemento
"We know that hunger is mortal,"

said the priest Camilo Torres. *"And if we know that, does it make sense to waste time arguing whether the soul is immortal?"*

Camilo believed in Christianity as the practice of loving one's neighbor, and wanted that love to be effective. He had an obsession about effective love. That obsession made him take up arms, and because of it, he has died, in an unknown corner of Colombia, fighting with the guerrillas.

(448)

1967: Llallagua
The Feast of San Juan

Bolivian miners are sons of the Virgin and nephews of the Devil, but neither can save them from early death. They are buried in the bowels of the earth, an implacable rain of mine dust annihilating them: In just a moment, a few short years, their lungs turn to stone and their tracheas close. Even before the lungs forget to breathe, the nose forgets smells and the tongue forgets tastes, the legs become like lead and the mouth discharges nothing but insult and vengefulness.

When they emerge from the pit, the miners look for a party. While their short life lasts and their legs still move, they need to eat spicy stews and swallow strong drink and sing and dance by the light of the bonfires that warm the barren plain.

On this night of San Juan, as the greatest of all fiestas is in progress, the army crouches in the mountains. Almost nothing is known here about the guerrillas of the distant Ñancahuazú River, although the story goes that they are fighting for a revolution so beautiful that, like the ocean, it has never been seen. But General Barrientos believes that a sly terrorist is lurking within every miner.

Before dawn, just as the Feast of San Juan is ending, a hurricane of bullets slashes through the town of Llallagua.

(16, 17, and 458)

1967: Catavi

The Day After

The light of the new day is like a glitter of bones. Then the sun hides behind clouds as the outcasts of the earth count their dead and carry them off in little carts. The miners march down a narrow muddy road in Llallagua. The procession crosses the river, dirty saliva flowing among stones of ash, and threads onto the vast pampa heading toward Catavi cemetery.

The sky, immense roof of tin, has no sun, and the earth no bonfires to warm it. Never was this steppe so frozen.

Many graves have to be dug. Bodies of every size are lined up, stretched out, waiting.

From the top of the cemetery wall, a woman screams.

(458)

1967: Catavi

Domitila

cries out against the murderers from the top of the wall.

She lives in two rooms without latrine or running water with her miner husband and seven children. The eighth child is eager to be born. Every day Domitila cooks, washes, sweeps, weaves, sews, teaches what she knows, cures what she can, prepares a hundred meat pies, and roams the streets looking for buyers.

For insulting the Bolivian army, they arrest her. A soldier spits in her face.

(458)

The Interrogation of Domitila

He spat in my face. Then he kicked me. I wouldn't take it and I slapped him. He punched me again. I scratched his face. And he was hitting me, hitting me . . . He put his knee here on my belly. He squeezed my neck and I almost choked. It seemed like he wanted to make my belly burst. He tightened his hold more and more . . . Then, with my two hands, with all my two hands, with all my strength I pulled his hands down. And I don't remember how, but I had grabbed him with my fist and was biting him, biting . . . I was horribly disgusted tasting his blood in my mouth . . . Then, with all my fury— tchá—I spat his blood all over his face. A tremendous howling started. He grabbed me, kicked me, hollered at me . . . He called the soldiers and had me seized by four or more of them . . .

When I woke up as if from a dream, I'd been swallowing a piece of my tooth. I felt it here in my throat. Then I noticed that this monster had broken six of my teeth. The blood was pouring over me and I couldn't open my eyes or my nose . . .

Then, as if fate ordained it, I began to give birth. I started to feel pains, pains and pains, and sometimes the baby that was coming seemed too much for me . . . I couldn't stand it any more. And I went to kneel down in a corner. I supported myself and covered my face, because I couldn't muster even a bit of strength. My face felt as if it was going to burst. And in one of those moments it came. I saw that the baby's head was already out . . . And right there I fainted.

How long afterward I don't know: "Where am I? Where am I?"

I was completely wet. The blood and the liquid that comes when you give birth had soaked me all over. Then I made an effort and somehow I got hold of the baby's cord. And pulling up the cord, at the end of the cord I found my little baby, cold, frozen, there on the floor.

(458)

1967: Catavi

The God in the Stone

After the gale of bullets, a gale of wind sweeps through the mining town of Llallagua removing all the roofs. In the neighboring parish of Catavi, the same wind topples and breaks the statue of the Virgin.

Its stone pedestal, however, remains intact. The priest comes to pick off the floor the pieces of the Immaculate One.

Look, father, say the workers, and they show him how the pedestal has shrugged off the burdensome Virgin.

Inside this pedestal the conquered ancient gods still sleep, dream, breathe, care for petitioners, and remind the mine workers that the great day will come: *Our day, the one we're waiting for.*

From the day it was originally found and worshipped by the workers the priest had condemned the miracle-working stone. He had shut it up in a cement cage so that the workers couldn't parade it in processions; then he put the Virgin on top of it. The mason who caged the stone at the priest's order has been shaking with fever and squinting ever since that fateful day.

(268)

1967: On the Ñancahuazú River Banks

Seventeen Men March to Annihilation

Cardinal Maurer arrives in Bolivia. From Rome he brings the Pope's blessings and word that God unequivocally backs General Barrientos against the guerrillas.

Meanwhile, hungry and disoriented, the guerrillas twist and turn through the Ñancahuazú River scrub. There are few campesinos in these immense solitudes; and not one, not a single one, has joined the little troop of Che Guevara. His forces dwindle from ambush to ambush. Che does not weaken, won't let himself weaken, although he feels that his body is a stone among stones, a heavy stone he drags along at the head of the others; nor does he let himself be tempted by the idea of saving the group by abandoning the wounded. By Che's order they all move at the pace of those least able to move: Together they will all be saved or lost.

Lost. Eighteen hundred soldiers, led by U.S. Rangers, are treading on their shadow. A ring is drawing tighter and tighter. Finally, a couple of campesino informers and the radar of the U.S. National Security Agency reveal their exact location.

(212 and 455)

1967: Yuro Ravine
The Fall of Che

Machinegun bullets break his legs. Sitting, he fights until the rifle is blown from his hands.

The conquering soldiers fall to blows over his watch, his canteen, his belt, his pipe. Several officers interrogate him, one after another. Che keeps quiet as his blood flows. Vice Admiral Ugarteche, daring land-wolf, head of the navy in a country without an ocean, insults and threatens him. Che spits in his face.

From La Paz comes the order to finish off the prisoner. A burst of gunfire. Che dies from a treacherous bullet shortly before his fortieth birthday, the age at which Zapata and Sandino died, also from treacherous bullets.

In the little town of Higueras, General Barrientos exhibits his trophy to journalists. Che lies on a laundry sink. They shoot him a final time, with flashbulbs. This last face has accusing eyes and a melancholy smile.

(212 and 455)

1967: Higueras
Bells Toll for Him

Did he die in 1967 in Bolivia because he guessed wrong about the when and the where and the how? Or did he not die at all, not anywhere, because he wasn't wrong about what really matters despite all the whens and wheres and hows?

He believed that one must defend oneself from the traps of greed without ever letting down one's guard. When he was president of the National Bank of Cuba, he signed the banknotes "Che," in mockery of money. For love of people, he scorned things. Sick is the world, he thought, in which to have and to be mean the same thing. He never kept anything for himself, nor ever asked for anything.

Living is giving oneself, he thought; and he gave himself.

1967: La Paz

Portrait of a Supermacho

On the shoulders of Nene, his giant bodyguard, General Barrientos crosses the city of La Paz. From Nene's shoulders he greets those who applaud him. He enters the government palace. Seated at his desk, with Nene behind him, he signs decrees that sell at bargain prices the sky, the soil, and the subsoil of Bolivia.

Ten years ago, Barrientos was putting in time in a Washington, D.C., psychiatric clinic when the idea of being president of Bolivia entered his head. He'd already made a career for himself as an athlete. Disguising himself as a North American aviator, he laid siege to power; and now he exercises it, machinegunning workers and pulling down libraries and wages.

The killer of Che is a cock with a loud crow, a man with three balls, a hundred women, and a thousand children. No Bolivian has flown so high, made so many speeches, or stolen so much.

In Miami, the Cuban exiles elect him Man of the Year.

(16, 17, 337, and 474)

1967: Estoril

Society Notes

Pinned to the hostess's gleaming coiffure are some of the world's largest diamonds. The cross on her granddaughter's necklace displays one of the world's largest emeralds. The Patiños, inheritors of one of the world's largest fortunes, throw one of the world's largest parties.

To make a thousand people happy night and day for a week, the Patiños collect *all* the elegant flowers and fine drinks buyable in Portugal. The invitations have gone out well ahead, so that the fashion-designers and society reporters could do their jobs properly. Several times a day the ladies change their dresses, all exclusive designs, and when two similar gowns appear in one salon, someone observes that she will fry Yves Saint-Laurent in oil. The orchestras come by charter from New York. The guests come in yachts or private planes.

Europe's nobility is out in force. The late lamented Simón Patiño, the anthropophagous Bolivian, devourer of miners, bought top-quality alliances. He married his daughters to a count and a marquis, and his son to a king's first cousin.

(34)

1967: Houston
Ali

They called him Cassius Clay: He chooses to call himself Muhammad Ali.

They made him a Christian: He chooses to make himself a Muslim.

They made him defend himself: No one punches like Ali, so fierce and fast, light tank, bulldozing feather, indestructible possessor of the world crown.

They told him that a good boxer confines his fighting to the ring: He says the real ring is something else, where a triumphant black fights for defeated blacks, for those who eat leftovers in the kitchen.

They advised discretion: From then on he yells.

They tapped his phone: From then on he yells on the phone, too.

They put a uniform on him to send him to Vietnam: He pulls it off and yells that he isn't going, because he has nothing against the Vietnamese, who have done no harm to him or to any other black American.

They took away his world title, they stopped him from boxing, they sentenced him to jail and a fine: He yells his thanks for these compliments to his human dignity.

(14 and 149)

1968: Memphis
Portrait of a Dangerous Man

The Reverend Martin Luther King preaches against the Vietnam War. He protests that twice as many blacks as whites are dying there, cannon fodder for an imperial adventure comparable to the Nazi crimes. The poisoning of water and land, the destruction of people and harvests are part of a plan of extermination. Of the million Vietnamese dead, says the preacher, the majority are children. The United States, he claims, is suffering from an infection of the soul; and any autopsy would show that the name of that infection is Vietnam.

Six years ago the FBI put this man in Section A of the Reserved List, among those dangerous individuals who must be watched and jailed in case of emergency. Since then the police hound him, spying on him day and night, threatening and provoking him.

Martin Luther King collapses on the balcony of a Memphis hotel. A bullet full in the face puts an end to this nuisance.

(254)

1968: San Jose, California
The Chicanos

Judge Gerald Chargin passes sentence on a lad accused of incest, and while he's at it, advises the young man to commit suicide and tells him, *"You Chicanos are worse than animals, miserable, lousy, rotten people . . ."*

The Chicanos are the descendants of those who came across the border river from Mexico to harvest cotton, oranges, tomatoes, and potatoes at dirt-cheap wages, and who stayed on in these southwestern and western states, which until little more than a century ago were the north of Mexico. In these lands, no longer theirs, they are used and despised.

Of every ten North Americans killed in Vietnam, six are blacks or Hispanics. And to them they say:

If you're so tough and strong, you go to the front lines first.

(182, 282, 369, and 403)

1968: San Juan, Puerto Rico
Albizu

Puerto Ricans are also good at dying in Vietnam in the name of those who took away their country.

The island of Puerto Rico, North American colony, consumes what it doesn't produce and produces what it doesn't consume. On its abandoned lands not even the rice and beans of the national dish are grown. Washington teaches the Puerto Ricans to breathe refrigerated air, eat canned food, drive long, well-chromed cars, sink up to the neck in debt, and lose their souls watching television.

Pedro Albizu Campos died a while back after almost twenty years spent in U.S. jails for his unceasing activities as an agitator. To win back the fatherland, one should love it with one's soul and one's life, he thought, as if it were a woman; to make it breathe again, one should rescue it with bullets.

He always wore a black tie for the lost fatherland. He was more and more alone.

(87, 116, 199, and 275)

1968: Mexico City
The Students

invade the streets. Such demonstrations have never been seen before in Mexico, so huge, so joyous, everyone linked arm in arm, singing and laughing. The students cry out against President Díaz Ordaz and his ministerial mummies, and all the others who have taken over Zapata's and Pancho Villa's revolution.

In Tlatelolco, a plaza where Indians and conquistadors once fought to the death, a trap is sprung. The army blocks every exit with strategically placed tanks and machineguns. Inside the corral, readied for the sacrifice, the students are hopelessly jammed together. A continuous wall of rifles with fixed bayonets advances to seal the trap.

Flares, one green, one red, give the signal. Hours later, a woman searches for her child, her shoes leaving bloody tracks on the ground.

(299 and 347)

"There was much, much blood," says the mother of a student,

"so much that I felt it thick on my hands. There was also blood on the walls. I think the walls of Tlatelolco have their pores full of blood; all Tlatelolco breathes blood . . . The bodies lay on the concrete waiting to be removed. I counted many from the window, about sixty-eight. They were piling them up in the rain. I remembered that my

*son Carlitos was wearing a green corduroy jacket and I thought I
saw it on each body . . ."*

(347)

1968: Mexico City
Revueltas

He has been around for half a century, but repeats daily the crime
of being young. Always at the center of any uproar, José Revueltas
now denounces the owners of power in Mexico, who, out of incurable
hatred for all that pulses, grows, and changes, have murdered three
hundred students in Tlatelolco.

*"The gentlemen of the government are dead. For that they
kill us."*

In Mexico, power assimilates or annihilates, shoots deadly lightning with a hug or a slug, consigns to grave or prison the impudent
ones who will not be bought off with a sinecure. The incorrigible
Revueltas rarely sleeps outside a cell; and when he does, he spends
the night stretched out on some bench in a park, or on a desk at the
university. Hated by the police for being a revolutionary and by
dogmatists of all types for being free, he is condemned by pious leftists
for his predilection for cheap bars. Not long ago, his comrades provided him with a guardian angel to save him from temptation, but
the angel had to pawn his wings to pay for the sprees they enjoyed
together.

(373)

1968: Banks of the River Yaqui
The Mexican Revolution Isn't There Anymore

The Yaqui Indians, warriors for centuries, call upon Lázaro Cárdenas.
They meet him on a bright sunny prairie in northern Mexico, near
their ancestral river.

Standing in the shade of a leafy breadfruit tree, the chiefs of the
eight Yaqui tribes welcome him. On their heads gleam the plumes
reserved for great occasions.

"Remember, Tata?" Thirty years have passed and this is a great

occasion. The top chief speaks: *"Tata Lázaro, do you remember? You gave us back the lands. You gave us hospitals and schools."*

At the end of each sentence the chiefs beat the ground with their staves, and the dry echo reverberates across the prairie.

"You remember? We want you to know, the rich have taken back the lands. The hospitals have been turned into barracks. The schools are cantinas."

Cárdenas listens and says nothing.

(45)

1968: Mexico City
Rulfo

In the silence, the heartbeat of another Mexico. Juan Rulfo, teller of tales about the misadventures of the dead and the living, keeps silent. Fifteen years ago he said what he had to say, in a small novel and a few short stories, and since then he says nothing. Or rather, he made the deepest kind of love, and then went to sleep.

1969: Lima
Arguedas

splits his skull with a bullet. His story is the story of Peru: Sick with Peru, he kills himself.

The son of whites, José María Arguedas was raised by Indians and spoke Quechua throughout his childhood. At seventeen, he was torn away from the sierra and thrust into the coastal area—from the small communal towns to the proprietorial cities.

He learned the language of the victors and spoke and wrote it. He never wrote *about* the vanquished, rather *from* them. He knew how to express them; but his feat was his curse. He felt that everything about him was treachery or failure; he felt torn apart. He couldn't be Indian; he didn't want to be white. He couldn't endure both the scorning and the being scorned.

This lonely wayfarer walked at the edge of an abyss, between two enemy worlds that divided his soul. Many an avalanche of anguish swept down on him, worse than any landslide of mud and rocks, until finally he was overwhelmed.

(30 and 256)

1969: Sea of Tranquillity
The Discovery of the Earth

The space ship from Houston, Texas, puts down its long spider legs on the Moon. Astronauts Armstrong and Aldrin see the Earth as no one has seen it before, an Earth that is not the generous breast that gives us milk and poison to suck, but a handsome frozen stone rotating in the solitude of the universe. The Earth seems to be childless, uninhabited, perhaps even indifferent, as if it didn't feel a single tickle from the human passions that swarm on its soil.

Via television and radio, the astronauts send us preprogrammed words about the great step that humanity is taking, while they stick the flag of the United States of America into the stony Sea of Tranquillity.

1969: Bogotá
The Urchins

They have the street for a home. They are cats made for jumping and slapping, sparrows for flying, little cocks for fighting. They go about in packs, in gangs. They sleep in clusters, bunched together against the freezing dawns. They eat what they steal or the leftovers they beg or the garbage they find; they have grey teeth and faces burned by the cold.

Arturo Dueñas, of the Twenty-second Street gang, leaves his pack, fed up with offering his bottom to be spanked just because he's the smallest, the bedbug, the tick. He decides he'll fare better on his own.

One night, a night like any other, Arturo slips under a restaurant table, grabs a chicken leg, and brandishing it like a flag, scoots off down an alley. When he finds some obscure nook, he sits down to have supper. A little dog watches him and licks its chops. Several times Arturo pushes it away, but the dog returns. They examine each other: The two are equals, sons of nobody, beaten, pure bone and grime. Arturo resigns himself and shares.

Since then they've gone together on winged feet, sharing the danger, the booty, and the lice. Arturo, who has never talked to anybody, opens up, and the little dog sleeps curled up at his feet.

One accursed day the police catch Arturo robbing buns and haul him to the Fifth Precinct for a tremendous beating. When, in time, Arturo returns to the street, all battered, the little dog is nowhere to be seen. Arturo runs back and forth, searching wildly everywhere, but it doesn't appear. A lot of questions, and nothing. A lot of calling, and nothing. No one in the world is so alone as this child of seven who is alone on the streets of the city of Bogotá, hoarse from so much screaming.

(68 and 342)

1969: Any City
Someone

On a corner, by a red light, someone swallows fire, someone washes windshields, someone sells Kleenex, chewing gum, little flags, and dolls that make pee-pee. Someone listens to the horoscope on the radio, pleased that the stars are concerned about him. Walking between the tall buildings, someone would like to buy silence or air, but doesn't have the cash. In a filthy barrio, amid swarms of flies above and armies of rats below, someone hires a woman for three minutes. In a whorehouse cell the raped becomes the rapist, better than making it with a donkey in the river. Someone talks to no one on the phone, after hanging up the receiver. Someone talks to no one in front of the TV set. Someone talks to no one in front of a one-armed bandit. Someone waters a pot of plastic flowers. Someone climbs on an empty bus, at dawn, and the bus stays empty.

1969: Rio de Janeiro
Expulsion from the Slums

They refuse to go. They have been the poorest of the poor in the countryside and now they're the poorest in the city, always the last in line, people with cheap hands and dancing feet. Here, at least, they live near the places where they earn their bread. The inhabitants of Praia do Pinto and the other slums covering Rio de Janeiro's mountains have turned stubborn. But the military has long eyed these tracts, highly salable and resalable and well-suited for speculation, and so the problem will be solved by means of an opportune fire. The firemen never turn up. Dawn is the hour of tears and cinders. After fire destroys the houses made of garbage, they sweep up the people like garbage and take them far away for dumping.

(340)

1969: Baixo Grande

A Castle of Garbage

Old man Gabriel dos Santos does what his dreams tell him to do. He dreams the same crazy dreams in Brazil that Antonio Gaudí dreamed decades ago in Catalonia, in far-off Barcelona, although old Gabriel has never heard of Gaudí or seen his works.

As soon as he awakes, old Gabriel starts modeling with his hands the marvels he sees in his dreams, before they get away from him. Thus he has built the House of the Flower. In it he lives, on the slope of a hill beaten by the ocean wind. From dream to dream, through the years, old Gabriel's home keeps growing, this strange castle or beast of bright colors and sinuous forms, all made of garbage.

Old Gabriel, worker in the salt mines, never went to school, never watched television, never had money. He knows no rules, has no models. He plays around, in his own free style, with whatever leftovers the nearby city of Cabo Frío throws his way: fenders, headlights, splintered windows and smashed bottles, broken dishes, bits of old iron, chair legs, wheels . . .

(171)

1969: Arque Pass

The Last Stunt of Aviator Barrientos

Cardinal Maurer says that President Barrientos is like Saint Paul, because he roams the Bolivian countryside handing out truths. Barrientos also hands out money and soccer balls. He comes and goes, raining banknotes by helicopter. Gulf Oil gave the helicopter to Barrientos in exchange for the two billion dollars' worth of gas and one billion of petroleum that Barrientos gave Gulf Oil.

On this same helicopter, Barrientos paraded with Che Guevara's body tied to its skids through the skies of Bolivia. On this helicopter Barrientos arrives at Arque Pass on one of his incessant junkets, and as usual tosses money down on the campesinos; but on taking off, he collides with a wire fence and crashes against some rocks, burning himself alive. After burning so many pictures and books, fiery Barrientos dies cooked to a crisp in his helicopter, filled to the brim with banknotes that burn with him.

(16, 17, and 474)

1969: San Salvador and Tegucigalpa

Two Turbulent Soccer Matches

are played between Honduras and El Salvador. Ambulances remove the dead and wounded from the stands, while fans continue the stadium uproar in the streets.

Immediately, the two countries break relations. In Tegucigalpa, automobile windshields carry stickers that say: *Honduran—grab a stick, be a man, kill a Sal-va-dor-e-an.* In San Salvador, the newspapers urge the army to invade Honduras *to teach those barbarians a lesson.* Honduras expels Salvadoran campesinos, who are mostly unaware they are foreigners, having never seen an identity document. The Honduran government forces the Salvadorans to leave with nothing but what they have on, and then burns their shacks, describing the expulsion as "agrarian reform." The government of San Salvador considers all Hondurans who live there to be spies.

War soon breaks out. The army of El Salvador crosses into Honduras and advances, machinegunning border villages.

(84, 125, and 396)

1969: San Salvador and Tegucigalpa

The Soccer War

pits as enemies two fragments of Central America, shreds of what was a single republic a century and a half ago.

Honduras, a small agrarian country, is dominated by big landlords.

El Salvador, a small agrarian country, is dominated by big land-lords.

The campesinos of Honduras have neither land nor work.

The campesinos of El Salvador have neither land nor work.

In Honduras there is a military dictatorship born of a coup d'état.

In El Salvador there is a military dictatorship born of a coup d'état.

The general who governs Honduras was trained at the School of the Americas in Panama.

The general who governs El Salvador was trained at the School of the Americas in Panama.

From the United States come the weapons and advisers of the dictator of Honduras.

From the United States come the weapons and advisers of the dictator of El Salvador.

The dictator of Honduras accuses the dictator of El Salvador of being a Communist in the pay of Fidel Castro.

The dictator of El Salvador accuses the dictator of Honduras of being a Communist in the pay of Fidel Castro.

The war lasts one week. While war continues, the people of Honduras think their enemy is the people of El Salvador and the people of El Salvador think their enemy is the people of Honduras. They leave four thousand dead on the battlefields.

(84 and 125)

1969: Port-au-Prince

A Law Condemns to Death Anyone Who Says or Writes Red Words in Haiti

Article One: Communist activities are declared to be crimes against the security of the state, in whatsoever form: any profession of Communist faith, verbal or written, public or private, any propagation of Communist or anarchist doctrines through lectures, speeches, conversations, readings, public or private meetings, by way of pamphlets, posters, newspapers, magazines, books, and pictures; any oral or written correspondence with local or foreign associations, or with persons dedicated to the diffusion of Communist or anarchist ideas; and furthermore, the act of receiving, collecting, or giving funds directly or indirectly destined for the propagation of said ideas.

Article Two: The authors and accomplices of these crimes shall be sentenced to death. Their movable and immovable property shall be confiscated and sold for the benefit of the state.

> Dr. François Duvalier
> President-for-Life
> of the Republic of Haiti
> (351)

1970: Montevideo

Portrait of a Torture Trainer

The Tupamaro guerrillas execute Dan Anthony Mitrione, one of the North American instructors of the Uruguayan police.

The dead man gave his courses to officers in a soundproof basement. For his practical lessons he used beggars and prostitutes pulled off the street. He showed his pupils the effects of various electric voltages on the most sensitive parts of the human body, and how to apply emetics and other chemical substances efficaciously. In recent months three men and a woman died during these classes in the Technique of Interrogation.

Mitrione despised disorder and dirt. A torture chamber should be as aseptic as an operating room. And he detested incorrect language: *"Not balls, commissioner. Testicles."*

He also abominated useless expense, unnecessary movement, avoidable damage.

"It's an art, more than a technique," he said. *"The precise pain in the precise place, in the precise amount."*

(225)

1970: Managua

Rugama

A distinguished poet, a little man in a surplice who received Holy Communion standing up, shoots his last bullet and dies resisting a whole battalion of Somoza's troops.

Leonel Rugama was twenty.

Of friends, he preferred chess players.

Of chess players, those who lose because of the girl passing by.
Of those who pass by, the one who stays.
Of those who stay, the one who has yet to come.
Of heroes, he preferred those who don't say they are dying for their country.
Of countries, the one born of his death.

(399)

1970: Santiago de Chile
Landscape after Elections

In a display of unpardonably bad conduct, the Chilean people elect Salvador Allende president. Another president, of the International Telephone and Telegraph Corporation, offers a million dollars to whoever can put an end to this disgrace, while the president of the United States earmarks ten million for the affair. Richard Nixon instructs the CIA to prevent Allende from sitting in the presidential chair; or, should he sit, to see that the chair doesn't stay under him long.

General René Schneider, head of the army, rejects the call for a coup d'état and is struck down in an ambush: *"Those bullets were for me,"* says Allende.

Loans from the World Bank and all other official and private banks are suspended, except those for the military. The price of copper plummets.

From Washington, Secretary of State Henry Kissinger explains: *"I don't see why we should have to stand by and let a country go Communist due to the irresponsibility of its own people."*

(138, 181, and 278)

1971: Santiago de Chile
Donald Duck

and his nephews spread the virtues of consumer civilization among the savages of an underdeveloped country with picture-postcard landscapes. Donald's nephews offer soap bubbles to the stupid natives in exchange for nuggets of pure gold, while Uncle Donald fights outlaw revolutionaries who disturb order.

From Chile, Walt Disney's comic strips are distributed throughout South America and enter the souls of millions of children. Donald Duck does not come out against Allende and his red friends; he doesn't need to. The world of Disney is already the lovable zoo of capitalism: Ducks, mice, dogs, wolves, and piglets do business, buy, sell, respond to advertising, get credit, pay dues, collect dividends, dream of bequests, and compete among themselves to have more and get more.

(139 and 287)

1971: Santiago de Chile
"Shoot at Fidel,"

the CIA has ordered two of its agents. Certain TV cameras that appear to be busy filming Fidel Castro's visit to Chile conceal automatic pistols. The agents zoom in on Fidel, they have him in their sights— but neither shoots.

For many years now, specialists of the CIA's technical services division have been dreaming up attacks on Fidel. They've spent fortunes trying out cyanide capsules in chocolate malteds, and pills that dissolve in beer and rum and are untraceable in an autopsy. They've tried bazookas and telescopic rifles, a thirty-kilo plastic bomb that an agent was to put in a drain beneath a speaker's platform. Even poisoned cigars: They fixed up a special Havana for Fidel—supposed to kill the moment it touched his lips. But it didn't work, so they tried another guaranteed to produce nausea and, worse yet, a high-pitched voice—if they couldn't kill *him*, they hoped at least to kill his prestige. To this end also they tried spraying the microphone with a powder guaranteed to provoke in mid-speech an irresistible tendency to talk nonsense, and then, as the coup de grâce, concocted a depilatory potion to make his beard fall out, leaving him naked before the crowd.

(109, 137, and 350)

1972: Managua
Nicaragua, Inc.

The tourist arrives in Somoza's plane or ship and lodges in one of Somoza's hotels in the capital. Tired, he falls asleep on a bed and mattress manufactured by Somoza. On awaking, he drinks Presto coffee, property of Somoza, with milk from Somoza's cows and sugar harvested on a Somoza plantation and refined in a Somoza mill. He lights a match produced by Somoza's firm, Momotombo, and tries a cigarette from the Nicaraguan Tobacco Company, which Somoza owns in association with the British-American Tobacco Company.

The tourist goes out to change money at a Somoza bank and buys the Somoza daily *Novedades* on the corner. Reading *Novedades* is an impossible feat, so he throws the paper into the garbage which, tomorrow morning, will be collected by a Mercedes truck imported by Somoza.

The tourist climbs on one of Somoza's Condor buses, which will take him to the mouth of the Masaya volcano. Rolling toward the fiery crest, he sees through the window the barrios of tin cans and mud where live the dirt-cheap hands used by Somoza.

The tourist returns at nightfall. He drinks a rum distilled by Somoza, with ice from the Somoza Polar company, eats meat from one of his calves, butchered in one of his slaughterhouses, with rice from one of his farms and salad dressed with Corona oil, which belongs jointly to Somoza and United Brands.

Half past midnight, the earthquake explodes. Perhaps the tourist is one of the twelve thousand dead. If he doesn't end in some common grave, he will rest in peace in a coffin from Somoza's mortuary concern, wrapped in a shroud from El Porvenir textile mill, property of . . .

(10 and 102)

1972: *Managua*
Somoza's Other Son

The cathedral clock stops forever at the hour the earthquake lifts the city into the air. The quake shakes Managua and destroys it.

In the face of this catastrophe Tachito Somoza proves his virtues both as statesman and as businessman. He decrees that bricklayers shall work sixty hours a week without a centavo more in pay and declares: *"This is the revolution of opportunities."*

Tachito, son of Tacho Somoza, has displaced his brother Luis from the throne of Nicaragua. A graduate of West Point, he has sharper claws. At the head of a voracious band of second cousins and third uncles, he swoops down on the ruins. He didn't invent the earthquake, but he gets his out of it.

The tragedy of half a million homeless people is a splendid gift for this Somoza, who traffics outrageously in debris and lands; and, as if that weren't enough, he sells in the United States the blood donated to victims of the quake by the International Red Cross. Later, he extends this profitable scam: Showing more initiative and enterprising spirit than Count Dracula, Tachito Somoza founds a limited company to buy blood cheap in Nicaragua and sell it dear on the North American market.

(10 and 102)

Tachito Somoza's Pearl of Wisdom

I don't show off my money as a symbol of power, but as a symbol of job opportunities for Nicaraguans.

(434)

1972: Santiago de Chile
Chile Trying to Be Born

A million people parade through the streets of Santiago in support of Salvador Allende and against the embalmed bourgeoisie who pretend to be alive and Chilean.

A people on fire, a people breaking the custom of suffering: In search of itself, Chile recovers its copper, iron, nitrates, banks, foreign trade, and industrial monopolies. It also nationalizes the ITT telephone system, paying for it the small amount that ITT said it was worth in its tax returns.

(278 and 449)

1972: Santiago de Chile
Portrait of a Multinational Company

ITT has invented a night scope to detect guerrillas in the dark, but doesn't need it to find them in the government of Chile—just money, of which the company is spending plenty against President Allende.

Recent experience shows how worthwhile it is: The generals who now rule Brazil have repaid ITT several times over the dollars invested to overthrow President Goulart.

ITT, with its four hundred thousand workers and officials in seventy countries, earns much more than Chile. On its board of directors sit men who were previously directors of the CIA and the World Bank. ITT conducts multiple businesses on all the continents: It produces electronic equipment and sophisticated weapons, organizes national and international communication systems, participates in space flights, lends money, works out insurance deals, exploits forests, provides tourists with automobiles and hotels, and manufactures telephones and dictators.

(138 and 407)

1973: Santiago de Chile
The Trap

By diplomatic pouch come the dollars that finance strikes, sabotage, and lies. Businessmen paralyze Chile and deny it food. There is no other market than the black market. People have to form long lines for a pack of cigarettes or a kilo of sugar. Getting meat or oil requires a miracle of the Most Sainted Virgin Mary. The Christian Democrats and the newspaper El Mercurio abuse the government and openly demand a redemptory coup d'état, since the time has come to finish with this red tyranny. Newspapers, magazines, and radio and TV stations echo the cry. For the government it is tough to make any move whatsoever: judges and parliamentarians dig in their heels, while in the barracks key military men whom Allende believes loyal conspire against him.

In these difficult times, workers are discovering the secrets of the economy. They're learning it isn't impossible to produce without bosses or supply themselves without merchants. But they march without weapons, empty-handed, down this freedom road.

Across the horizon sail U.S. warships preparing to exhibit themselves off the Chilean coast. The military coup, so much heralded, occurs.

(181, 278, and 449)

1973: Santiago de Chile
Allende

He likes the good life. He has said many times that he doesn't have what it takes to be an apostle or a martyr. But he has also said that it's worthwhile to die for that without which it's not worthwhile to live.

The rebel generals demand his resignation. They offer him a plane to take him out of Chile. They warn him that the presidential palace will be bombarded.

Together with a handful of men, Salvador Allende listens to the news. The generals have taken over the country. Allende dons a helmet and readies his rifle. The first bombs fall with a shuddering crash. The president speaks on the radio for the last time:

"I am not going to resign . . ."

(449 and 466)

1973: Santiago de Chile
Great Avenues Will Open Up, Announces Salvador Allende in His Final Message

I am not going to resign. Placed in a critical moment of history, I will pay with my life for the loyalty of the people. And let me tell you that I am sure the seed we sowed in the dignified conscience of Chileans will definitely not be destroyed. They have the force. They might be able to overcome us, but social processes cannot be stopped with crime or force. History is ours and the people make it . . .

Workers of my country: I have faith in Chile and its destiny. Other men will surmount this gray and bitter moment when treason seeks to impose itself. Rest assured that, much sooner than later, great avenues will once again open up through which free mankind shall pass to build a better society. Long live Chile, long live the people, long live the workers! These are my last words. I am certain that my sacrifice will not be in vain.

1973: Santiago de Chile
The Reconquest of Chile

A great black cloud rises from the flaming palace. President Allende dies at his post as the generals kill Chileans by the thousands. The Civil Registry does not record the deaths, because the books don't have room enough for them, but General Tomás Opazo Santander offers assurances that the victims do not exceed .01 percent of the population, which is not, after all, a high social cost, and CIA director William Colby explains in Washington that, thanks to the executions, Chile is avoiding a civil war. Señora Pinochet declares that the tears of mothers will redeem the country.

Power, all power, is assumed by a military junta of four members, formed in the School of the Americas in Panama. Heading it is General Augusto Pinochet, professor of geopolitics. Martial music resounds against a background of explosions and machinegun fire. Radios broadcast decrees and proclamations which promise more bloodshed, while the price of copper suddenly rises on the world market.

The poet Pablo Neruda, dying, asks for news of the terror. At moments he manages to sleep, and raves in his sleep. The vigil and the dream are one great nightmare. Since he heard Salvador Allende's proud farewell on the radio, the poet has begun his death-throes.

(278, 442, and 449)

1973: Santiago de Chile
The Home of Allende

Before attacking the presidential palace, they bombarded Allende's house.

Afterward, the soldiers wiped out whatever remained. With bayonets they ripped up paintings by Matta, Guayasamín, and Portocarrero; with axes they smashed furniture.

A week has passed. The house is a garbage heap. Arms and legs from the suits of armor that adorned the staircase are littered everywhere. In the bedroom a soldier snores, sleeping off a hangover, his legs flung apart, surrounded by empty bottles.

From the living room comes a moaning and panting. There, in a big yellow armchair, torn apart but still standing, the Allendes' bitch is giving birth. The puppies, still blind, grope for her warmth and milk. She licks them.

(345)

1973: Santiago de Chile
The Home of Neruda

Amid the devastation, in a home likewise chopped to bits, lies Neruda, dead from cancer, dead from sorrow. His death isn't enough, though, Neruda being a man of many lives, so the military must kill his possessions. They splinter his happy bed and happy table, they disembowel his mattress and burn his books, smash his lamps and his colored bottles, his pots, his paintings, his seashells. They tear the pendulum and the hands off his wall clock; and with a bayonet gouge out the eye of the portrait of his wife.

From his devastated home, flooded with water and mud, the poet leaves for the cemetery. A cortege of intimate friends escorts him, led by Matilde Urrutia. (He once said to her: *It was so beautiful to live when you were living.*)

Block by block, the cortege grows. On every street corner it is joined by people who fall into step despite the military trucks bristling with machineguns and the carabineros and soldiers who come and go on motorcycles and in armored cars, exuding noise and fear. Behind some window, a hand salutes. High on some balcony a handkerchief waves. This is the twelfth day since the coup, twelve days of shutting up and dying, and for the first time the Internationale is heard in Chile—the Internationale hummed, groaned, wept, but not sung until the cortege becomes a procession and the procession a demonstration, and the people, marching against fear, break into song in the streets of Santiago, at the top of their lungs, with all their voices, to accompany in a fitting way Neruda, the poet, their poet, on his last journey.

(314 and 442)

1973: Miami

Sacred Consumerism Against
the Dragon of Communism

The bloodbath in Chile inspires fear and disgust everywhere, but not in Miami: A jubilant demonstration of exiled Cubans celebrates the murder of Allende and all the others.

Miami now has the greatest concentration of Cubans in the world, Havana excepted. Eighth Street is the Cuba that was. The dreams of bringing down Fidel have faded, but walking down Eighth Street one returns to the good old lost days.

Bankers and mafiosi run the show here; anyone who thinks is crazy or a dangerous Communist, and blacks still know their place. Even the silence is strident. Plastic souls and flesh-and-blood automobiles are manufactured. In the supermarkets, things buy people.

(207)

1973: Recife

Eulogy of Humiliation

In the capital of northeast Brazil, Gilberto Freyre attends the opening of a restaurant named for his famous book, *Great House and Slave Quarters*. Here, the writer celebrates the fortieth anniversary of the book's first edition.

The waiters serving the tables are dressed as slaves. Atmosphere is created by whips, shackles, pillories, chains, and iron collars hanging from the walls. The guests feel they have returned to a superior age when black served white without any joking, as the son served the father, the woman her husband, the civilian the soldier, and the colony the motherland.

The dictatorship of Brazil is doing everything possible to further this end. Gilberto Freyre applauds it.

(170 and 306)

1974: Brasília
Ten Years after the Reconquest of Brazil

the economy is doing very well. The people, very badly. According to official statistics, the military dictatorship has made Brazil an economic power, with a high growth index for its gross national product. They also show that the number of undernourished Brazilians has risen from twenty-seven million to seventy-two million, of whom thirteen million are so weakened by hunger that they can no longer run.

(371, 377, and 378)

1974: Rio de Janeiro
Chico

This dictatorship hurts people and decomposes music. Chico Buarque, made of music and people, sings against it.

Of every three songs he writes, the censor bans or mutilates two. Almost daily, the political police make him undergo long interrogations. As he enters their offices, they search his clothing. As he leaves, Chico searches his innards to see if the police have put a censor in his soul or, in an unguarded moment, confiscated his joy.

1974: Guatemala City
Twenty Years after the Reconquest of Guatemala

In towns and cities chalk crosses appear on doors, and by the roadsides heads are stuck on stakes. As a lesson and a warning, crime is turned into a public spectacle. The victims are stripped of name and history, then thrown into the mouth of a volcano or to the bottom of the sea, or buried in a common grave under the inscription *NN*, which means *non nato*, which means not born. For the most part this state terrorism functions without uniform. It is called the Hand, the Shadow, the Lightning Flash, the Secret Anticommunist Army, the Order of Death, the Squadron of Death.

General Kjell Laugerud, newly come to the presidency after

faked elections, commits himself to a continued application in Guatemala of the techniques pioneered by the Pentagon in Vietnam. Guatemala is the first Latin American laboratory for dirty war.

(450)

1974: Forests of Guatemala
The Quetzal

was always the joy of the air in Guatemala. The most resplendent of birds continues to be the symbol of this country, although now rarely if ever seen in the high forests where it once flourished. The quetzal is dying out while vultures are multiplying. The vulture, who has a good nose for death from afar, completes the work of the army, following the executioners from village to village, circling anxiously.

Will the vulture, shame of the sky, replace the quetzal on banknotes, in the national anthem, on the flag?

1974: Ixcán
A Political Education Class in Guatemala

Full of worms and uncertainties, the guerrillas cross the forest. These famished shadows have been walking in the dark for many days beneath a roof of trees, shut off from the sun. For a clock, they use the voices of the thicket: The nightjar sings from the river announcing dawn; at dusk the parrots and macaws begin their scandalous chatter; when night falls the badgers scream and the coatis cough. On this occasion, for the first time in months, the guerrillas hear a cock crow. A village is close by.

In this village on this sierra, a landlord known as the Tiger of Ixcán is boss. Like the other masters of this land, he is exempted from the law and criminal responsibility. On his farms are gallows, whips, and pillories. When the local labor force is insufficient, the army sends him Indians by helicopter, to cut down trees or pick coffee for nothing.

Few have seen the Tiger of Ixcán. All fear him. He has killed many, has had many killed.

The guerrillas bring the Indians together and show them. The Tiger, dead, looks like an empty costume.

(336)

1974: Yoro

Rain

In Chile he has seen a lot of dying, his dearest friends shot, beaten, or kicked to death. Juan Bustos, one of President Allende's advisers, has saved himself by a hair.

Exiled in Honduras, Juan drags out his days. Of those who died in Chile, how many died instead of him? From whom is he stealing the air he breathes? He has been this way for months, dragging himself from sorrow to sorrow, ashamed of surviving, when one evening his feet take him to a town called Yoro, in the central depths of Honduras.

He arrives in Yoro for no particular reason, and in Yoro spends the night under any old roof. He gets up very early and starts walking half-heartedly through the dirt streets, fearing melancholy, staring without seeing.

Suddenly, the rain hits him, so violent that Juan covers his head, though noticing right away that this prodigious rain isn't water or hail. Crazy silver lights bounce off the ground and jump through the air.

"It's raining fish!" cries Juan, slapping at the live fish that dive down from the clouds and leap and sparkle around him. Never again will it occur to him to curse the miracle of being alive, never again will he forget that he had the luck to be born in America.

"That's right," says a neighbor, quietly, as if it were nothing. *"Here in Yoro it rains fish."*

1975: San Salvador

Miguel at Seventy

Each day of life is an unrepeatable chord of a music that laughs at death. With the dangerous Miguel still alive, El Salvador's masters decide to hire an assassin to send his life and his music somewhere else.

The assassin has a dagger hidden beneath his shirt. Miguel sits talking to students at the university. He is telling them that young people must take the place of their jaded elders, that they must act, risk their necks, and do what must be done without cackling like hens each time they lay an egg. The assassin slowly slips through the audience until he's right behind Miguel. But as he raises the blade, a woman screams and Miguel automatically flings himself to the ground, just avoiding the blow.

And thus occurs the twelfth birth of Miguel Mármol, at seventy years of age.

(222)

1975: San Salvador
Roque

Roque Dalton, Miguel Mármol's pupil in the art of resurrection, has twice escaped death up against the wall. Once he was saved because the government fell; the second time because the wall itself fell, thanks to an opportune earthquake. He also escaped from the torturers, who left him in bad shape but alive, and from the police, who chased him with blazing guns. He even escaped from stone-throwing soccer fans, from the fury of a woman scorned, and from numerous husbands thirsting for revenge.

Profound yet playful, the poet Roque preferred to laugh at himself than take life too seriously, and so saved himself from grandiloquence, solemnity, and other ailments so gravely afflicting Latin American political poetry.

Only from his comrades can he not save himself. It is they who condemn him, for the crime of Difference of Opinion. This bullet, the only one that could find Roque, had to come from right beside him.

(127)

1975: Amazon River
Tropical Landscape

The ship chugs slowly up the Amazon on this endless voyage from Belém to Manaos. Now and then, some shack masked by tangled lianas comes into view, and a naked child waves his hand at the crew.

On the jammed deck someone reads the Bible aloud, sonorous praises to God, but most people prefer to laugh and sing as bottles and cigarettes pass from mouth to mouth. A tame cobra entwines itself on iron crossbeams, brushing against the skins of dead brothers drying in the air. The owner of the cobra, seated on the deck, challenges the other passengers to a game of cards.

A Swiss journalist traveling on this ship has for hours been watching a poor, bony old man embracing a large carton he never unclutches, even in his sleep. Stung by curiosity, the Swiss offers cigarettes, cookies, and conversation, but the old fellow is one without vices who isn't hungry and has nothing to say.

In the middle of the voyage, in mid-jungle, the old man disembarks. The Swiss, helping him take the big carton ashore, peeks through the half-open lid and sees inside, wrapped in cellophane, a plastic palm tree.

(264)

1975: Amazon River

This Is the Father of All Rivers,

the mightiest river in the world, and the jungle sprouting from its breath is the last lung of this planet. The adventurous and the avaricious have flocked to Amazonia since the first Europeans who came this way discovered Indians with reversed feet, who walked backward instead of forward over these lands promising prodigious fortunes.

Since then, all business in Amazonia starts with a massacre. At an air-conditioned desk in São Paulo or New York, a corporate executive signs a check which amounts to an extermination order, for the initial job of clearing the jungle begins with Indians and other wild beasts.

They give the Indians sugar or salt mixed with rat poison, or bomb them from the air, or hang them by the feet to bleed to death without bothering to skin them, because who would buy the hides?

The job is finished off by Dow Chemical's defoliants, which devastated Vietnam's forests and now Brazil's. Blind tortoises stumble about where trees used to be.

(55, 65, 67, and 375)

1975: Ribeirão Bonito

A Day of Justice

Large as countries are the lands of the cattle companies, conquerors of Amazonia. The Brazilian generals exempt them from taxes, open up roads for them, give them credits and permission to kill.

The companies use tattered campesinos from the northeast transplanted here by rivers and poverty. The campesinos kill Indians, and are killed in turn; they steal the Indians' lands, and are stolen from in turn. They drive off the Indians' cattle, whose flesh they will never taste.

When the highway reaches the village of Ribeirão Bonito, the police begin the expulsion. Campesinos who resist are persuaded in jail. Pulverizing them with clubs or sticking needles under their fingernails prove useful techniques. The priest João Bosco Burnier arrives in the village, enters the jail, asks for the torturers. A cop replies by blowing his head off with a bullet.

The next day, furious women—Carmesinha, Naide, Margarida—erect an enormous cross. Behind them, six hundred campesinos brandish axes, picks, sticks. The whole village joins the attack, singing in chorus, a magnificent voice of voices; and now, where the jail stood, a small pile of rubble remains.

(65 and 375)

1975: Huayanay

Another Day of Justice

For some years the community of Huayanay in the Peruvian Andes has had a terrible affliction: Matías Escobar. This scoundrel, thief of goats and women, arsonist and murderer, does much harm before the community catches, judges, sentences, and executes him. Matías dies of two hundred and thirty blows in the village Plaza de Armas: Each member of the community contributes one blow, and afterward two hundred and thirty thumbprints sign the confession.

No one has paid the slightest attention to General Velasco Alvarado's decree that made Quechua an official language. Quechua is not taught in the schools or accepted in the courts. In the incomprehensible Castilian tongue a judge interrogates various Huayanay Indians, jailed in Lima. He asks them, as if it wasn't known, who killed Matías Escobar.

(203)

1975: Cuzco
Condori Measures Time by Bread

He works as a mule. At cockcrow the first cargo is already loaded on his back at the market or the station, and until nightfall he is on the streets of Cuzco transporting whatever he can get in exchange for whatever he can get. Crushed beneath the weight of bundles and years, his clothing in shreds, a man in shreds, Gregorio Condori works and remembers as long as his back and his memory hold out.

Since his bones hardened as a boy, he has been shepherd and pilgrim, laborer and soldier. In Urcos he was jailed for nine months for accepting a little broth made from a stolen cow. In Sicuani he saw his first train, a black snake snorting fire out of its head, and years later he fell on his knees as a plane crossed the sky like a condor announcing with hoarse screams the end of the world.

Condori remembers the history of Peru in terms of loaves: *"When five big loaves of pure wheat bread cost one real, and three cost half a real, Odría took the presidency from Bustamante."*

And then someone else came along who seized power from Odría, and then someone else, and another, and another, until finally Velasco threw out Belaúnde. And now who'll throw out Velasco? Condori has heard that Velasco sides with the poor.

(111)

1975: Lima
Velasco

A rooster crows out of tune. Hungry birds peck at dry grains. Blackbirds flap their wings over others' nests. Not exactly thrown out, he leaves anyway. Sick, pecked to pieces, discouraged, General Juan Velasco Alvarado quits the presidency of Peru.

The Peru he leaves is less unjust than the one he found; he took on the imperial monopolies and the feudal lords, and tried to enable Indians to be something more than exiles in their own land.

The Indians, tough as esparto grass, keep hoping their day will come. By Velasco's decree the Quechua language now has the same rights as Spanish, and is equally official, though no official cares. The Academy of the Quechua Language gets a subsidy from the state— the equivalent of six dollars and seventy-five cents a year.

1975: Lima

The Altarpieces of Huamanga

In Lima painters and scholars are indignant; even the avant-garde registers shock. The National Art Prize has been given to Joaquín López Antay, altarpiece-maker of Huamanga. A scandal. Artisanship is okay, say the Peruvian artists, as long as it knows its place.

The altarpieces of Huamanga, first created as portable altars, have been changing their casts of characters with the passage of time. Saints and apostles have given way to sheep suckling their lambs with the condor watching over the world, laborers and shepherds, punitive bosses, hatmakers in their workshops, and singers mournfully caressing their charangos.

López Antay, intruder into Art Heaven, learned from his Indian grandmother how to make altarpieces. More than half a century ago she taught him to do saints, and now she watches him at work, from the peace of her grave.

(31 and 258)

The Molas of San Blas

The Cuna Indians, on Panama's San Blas islands, make molas to be shown off from back or breast. With needle and thread, talent and patience, they combine scraps of colored cloth in unrepeatable patterns. Sometimes they imitate reality; sometimes they invent it. And sometimes, wanting to copy, just copy, some bird they have seen, they cut and sew, stitch by stitch, and end up discovering a new creature more colorful and melodious and fleet than any bird that's ever soared in the sky.

The Bark Paintings of the Balsas River

Before the rains, in the season of the new moon, they strip off the bark of the amate tree. The stripped tree dies. On its skin the Mexican Indians of the Balsas River region paint flowers and fantasies, radiant mountain birds and monsters lying in wait, or they paint the daily round of events in communities which greet the Virgin in devout procession and summon the rain in secret ceremonies.

Before the European conquest, other Indians had painted on amate bark the codices that told of people's lives and of the stars. When the conquistadors imposed their paper and their images, amates disappeared. For more than four centuries no one in the land of Mexico painted on this forbidden paper. Not long ago, in the middle of our century, amates returned: *"All the people are painters. All. Everyone."*

Ancient life breathes through these amates, which come from afar, from so very far away, but never arrive tired.

(57)

The Arpilleras of Santiago

The children, sleeping three to a bed, stretch out their arms toward a flying cow. Santa Claus has a bag of bread, not toys, slung over his shoulder. At the foot of a tree a woman begs. Under the red sun a skeleton drives a garbage cart. On endless roads go men without faces. An enormous eye watches. At the center of the silence and the fear steams the communal stewpot.

Chile is this world of colored rags against a background of flour sacks. With scraps of wool and old cloth, women from Santiago's wretched slums embroider arpilleras. The arpilleras are sold in churches. That anyone buys them is incredible. The women are amazed: *"We embroider our problems, and our problems are ugly."*

This was first done by the wives of prisoners. Then others took it up—for money, which is a help, but not just for money. Embroidering arpilleras brings the women together, eases their loneliness and sadness, and for a few short hours breaks the routine of obedience to husband, father, macho son, and General Pinochet.

The Little Devils of Ocumicho

Like the Chilean arpilleras, the little clay devils of the Mexican village of Ocumicho are the creations of women. These devils make love, in pairs or in groups, go to school, drive motorcycles or airplanes, sneak into Noah's Ark, hide among the rays of the moon-loving sun, and intrude into Christmas nativity scenes. They lie in wait under the table at the Last Supper, while Jesus Christ, nailed to the cross, shares a meal of Patzcuaro lakefish with his Indian disciples. Eating, Christ laughs from ear to ear as if he had suddenly discovered that this world is more easily redeemed by pleasure than by pain.

In dark, windowless houses the Ocumicho potters model these luminous figures. Women tied to an endless chain of children, prisoners of drunken husbands who beat them, practice a new free-style art. Condemned to submission, destined for sadness, they create each day a new rebellion.

On Private Property and the Right of Creation

Buyers want the Ocumicho potters to sign their works, so they use stamps to engrave their names at the foot of their little devils. But often they forget, or use a neighbor's stamp if their own isn't handy, so that María comes out as the artist of a work by Nicolasa, or vice versa.

They don't understand this business of solitary glory. In their Tarascan Indian community, all are one when it comes to this sort of thing. Outside the community, like the tooth that falls from a mouth, one is nobody.

(183)

1975: Cabimas

Vargas

Oil, passing along the banks of Lake Maracaibo, has taken away the colors. In this Venezuelan garbage dump of sordid streets, dirty air, and oily waters, Rafael Vargas lives and paints.

Grass does not grow in Cabimas, dead city, emptied land, nor do fish remain in its waters, nor birds in its air, nor roosters in its dawns; but in Vargas's paintings the world is in fiesta, the earth breathes at the top of its lungs, the greenest of trees burst with fruit and flowers, and prodigious fish, birds, and roosters jostle one another like people.

Vargas hardly knows how to read or write. He does know how to earn a living as a carpenter, and how as a painter to earn the clean light of his days: His is the revenge, the prophecy of one who paints not the reality he knows but the reality he needs.

1975: Salta

Happy Colors of Change

As in a painting by the Venezuelan Vargas, in the Argentine province of Salta police patrol cars were painted yellow and orange. Instead of sirens, they had music, and instead of prisoners, children: Patrol cars rolled along filled with children who came and went from remote shacks to the city's schools. Punishment cells and torture chambers were demolished. The police withdrew from soccer games and demonstrations. The tortured went free and the torturers, officers who specialized in breaking bones with hammers, disappeared behind bars. Police dogs, which once had terrorized the poor, began giving acrobatic performances in the slums.

This happened a couple of years ago, when Rubén Fortuny was Salta's chief of police. Fortuny didn't last long. While he did what he did, though, other men like him were committing similar insanities throughout Argentina, as if the whole country were clasped in some euphoric embrace.

Sad epilogue to this newest Peronist episode: Perón, having returned to power, has died, and the hangmen are once again free and busy.

They kill Fortuny with a bullet in the heart. Then they kidnap the governor who appointed him, Miguel Ragone. All they leave of Ragone is a bloodstain and a shoe.

1975: Buenos Aires

Against the Children of Evita and Marx

But for Argentines the dangerous wind of change refuses to die down. The military see the threat of social revolution peeking out of every door and prepare to save the nation. They have been saving the nation for nearly half a century; and more recently, in courses in Panama, have found support in the Doctrine of National Security, which confirms for them that the enemy is within. Certain finishing touches are added to the next coup d'état. The program of national purification will be applied *by every means*: This is a war, a war against the children of Evita and Marx, and in war the only sin is inefficiency.

(106, 107, and 134)

1976: Madrid

Onetti

He doesn't expect to find any messages in any bottles in any sea. But the despairing Juan Carlos Onetti refuses to be alone. He would be alone, of course, if it weren't for the inhabitants of the town of Santa María, sad like himself, invented by him to keep him company.

Onetti has lived in Madrid since he came out of prison. The military rulers of Uruguay had jailed him because a story to which he had given a prize in a competition he was judging was not to their liking.

Hands clasped behind his neck, the exile contemplates the damp stains on the ceiling of his room in Santa María or Madrid or Montevideo or who knows where. From time to time he picks himself up and writes shouts that only seem like whispers.

1976: San José

A Country Stripped of Words

President Aparicio Méndez declares that *the Democratic Party of the United States and the Kennedy family are sedition's best partners in Uruguay*. A journalist tapes this sensational revelation, in the presence of the bishop of the city of San José and other witnesses.

Aparicio Méndez was chosen president in an election in which twenty-two citizens voted: fourteen generals, five brigadiers, and three admirals. The military have forbidden their president to talk to journalists, to anyone, in fact, except his wife. For this particular indiscretion they punish the newspaper that publishes his declaration with two days' suspension; and the journalist is fired.

Before silencing their president, the military took the reasonable precaution of silencing the rest of Uruguay. Every word that is not a lie is subversive. No one may mention any of the thousands of politicians, trade unionists, artists, and scientists who have been placed outside the law. The word *guerrilla* is officially banned; instead, one must say *lowlife, criminal, delinquent,* or *evildoer.* Carnival musicians, typically cheeky and disrespectful, may not sing the words *agrarian reform, sovereignty, hunger, clandestine, dove, green, summer,* or *contracanto.* Nor may they sing the word *pueblo,* even when it means a small city.

In the kingdom of silence the chief jail for political prisoners is called Liberty. The prisoners, held in isolation, invent codes to speak without voices, knocking on the walls from cell to cell to form letters and words so they can continue liking and teasing each other.

(124 and 235)

A Uruguayan Political Prisoner, Mauricio Rosencof, Says His Piece

It is like the struggle of a man who resists being turned into a cow. Because they put us in a cow-making machine and told us that instead of talking we should moo. And that is the question: How a prisoner can resist being animalized in such a situation. It is a battle for dignity . . . There was one compañero who got hold of a bit of sugarcane, bored a hole in it with his fingernail, and made a flute. And this clumsy, rudimentary thing stammers a sort of music . . .

(394)

1976: Liberty
Forbidden Birds

The Uruguayan political prisoners may not talk without permission, or whistle, smile, sing, walk fast, or greet other prisoners; nor may they make or receive drawings of pregnant women, couples, butterflies, stars, or birds.

One Sunday, Didaskó Pérez, school teacher, tortured and jailed *for having ideological ideas*, is visited by his daughter Milay, age five. She brings him a drawing of birds. The guards destroy it at the entrance to the jail.

On the following Sunday, Milay brings him a drawing of trees. Trees are not forbidden, and the drawing gets through. Didaskó praises her work and asks about the colored circles scattered in the treetops, many small circles half-hidden among the branches: *"Are they oranges? What fruit is it?"*

The child puts a finger on his mouth. *"Ssssshhh."*

And she whispers in his ear: *"Silly. Don't you see they're eyes? They're the eyes of the birds that I've smuggled in for you."*

(204 and 459)

1976: Montevideo
Seventy-Five Methods of Torture,

some copied, others invented thanks to the creativity of the Uruguayan military, punish solidarity. Anyone doubting property rights or the law of obedience ends up in jail, grave, or exile. The danger-meter classifies citizens in three categories, A, B, or C, according to whether they are "dangerous," "potentially dangerous," or "not dangerous." Trade unions become police stations, and wages are cut in half. Whoever thinks or has ever thought loses his or her job. In primary schools, high schools, even the university, speaking of José Artigas's agrarian reform program is prohibited. Who cares if it was the first in America? Nothing is allowed to contradict this order of the deaf and dumb. Obligatory new texts impose military pedagogy on the students.

(235)

1976: Montevideo

"One Must Obey," the New Official Texts
Teach Uruguayan Students

The existence of political parties is not essential for a democracy. We have the clear example of the Vatican, where political parties do not exist and nevertheless there is a real democracy . . .

The equality of women, badly interpreted, means stimulating her sex and her intellectuality, while postponing her mission as mother and wife. If from the juridical standpoint man and woman are evidently equal, such is not the case from the biological standpoint. The woman as such is subject to her husband and hence owes him obedience. It is necessary that in any society there be a head who serves as guide, and the family is a society . . .

It is necessary for some to obey in order that others may exercise command. If no one obeyed, it would be impossible to rule . . .

(76)

1976: Montevideo

The Head Shrinkers

Dedicated to the prohibition of reality and the arson of memory, the Uruguayan military have beaten the world record for newspaper closures.

The weekly *Marcha*, after a long life, has ceased to be. One of its editors, Julio Castro, has been tortured to death, then disappeared—a dead man without a corpse. The other editors have been sentenced to prison, exile, or silence.

One night Hugo Alfaro, a movie critic condemned to wordlessness, sees a film that excites him. As soon as it ends he runs home and types a few pages, in a big hurry because it's late and *Marcha* closes its entertainment pages in the early hours. As he pecks out the last period, Alfaro suddenly realizes that *Marcha* hasn't existed for two years. Ashamed, he drops his review in a desk drawer.

This review, written for no one, deals with a Joseph Losey film set during the Nazi occupation of France, a film which shows how the machinery of repression grinds up not just the persecuted but also those who think they are safe, those who know what is happening, and even those who prefer not to know.

Meanwhile, on the River Plata's other bank, the Argentine military make their own coup d'état. One of the heads of the new dictatorship, General Ibérico Saint-Jean, clarifies things: *"First we'll kill all the subversives. Then we'll kill the collaborators. Then the sympathizers. Then the undecided. And finally, we'll kill the indifferent."*

(13 and 106)

1976: La Perla
The Third World War

From the top of a hill, on a chestnut mount, an Argentine gaucho looks on. José Julián Solanille sees a long military caravan approaching. He recognizes General Menéndez dismounting from a Ford Falcon. Out of trucks, shoved by clubs, tumble men and women, hoods over their heads, hands tied behind their backs. The gaucho sees one of the hooded ones make a break for it. He hears the shots. The fugitive falls, gets up, and falls, several times before falling for the last time. When the fusillade begins, men and women collapse like rag dolls. The gaucho spurs his horse and takes off. Behind him black smoke rises.

This valley, in the first undulations of the Córdoba sierra, is one of the many dumps for corpses. When it rains, smoke drifts up from the pits because of the quicklime they throw on the bodies.

In this holy war, the victims *disappear.* Those not swallowed by the earth are devoured by fish at the bottoms of rivers or the sea. Many have committed no greater crimes than appearing on a list of phone numbers. They march into nothingness, into the fog, into death, after torture in the barracks. *No one is innocent,* says Monseñor Plaza, bishop of La Plata, and General Camps says it is right to liquidate a hundred suspects if only five of them turn out to be guilty. Guilty of terrorism.

Terrorists, explains General Videla, *are not only those who plant bombs, but also those who act with ideas contrary to our Western and Christian civilization.* This is vengeance for the defeat of the West in Vietnam:

"We are winning the Third World War," crows General Menéndez.

(100, 107, and 134)

1976: Buenos Aires

The Choice

One prisoner, pregnant, is offered the choice between rape or the
electric prod. She chooses the prod, but after an hour can no longer
endure the pain. They all rape her. As they rape her, they sing the
Wedding March.

"Well, this is war," says Monseñor Gracelli.

The men who burn breasts with blowtorches in the barracks wear
scapulars and take communion every Sunday.

"Above us all is God," says General Videla.

Monseñor Tortolo, president of the Episcopate, compares Gen-
eral Videla with Jesus Christ, and the military dictatorship with the
Easter Resurrection. In the name of the Holy Father, nuncio Pío
Laghi visits the extermination camps, exalts the military's love of God,
Fatherland, and Family, and justifies state terrorism on the grounds
that civilization has the right to defend itself.

(106, 107, and 134)

1976: La Plata

Bent over the Ruins, a Woman Looks

for something in her home that has not been destroyed. The forces
of order have shattered María Isabel de Mariani's home, and she
pokes through the remains in vain. What they have not stolen, they
have pulverized. Only one record, Verdi's *Requiem*, is intact.

María Isabel would like to find in the litter some memento of
her children and of her granddaughter, a photo or toy, book, ashtray,
anything. Her children, suspected of running a clandestine press,
have been gunned down. Her three-month-old granddaughter has
been given away or sold as war booty by the officers.

It is summer, and the smell of gunpowder mixes with the aroma
of flowering lindens. That aroma will forever be unbearable. María
Isabel has no one to be with. She is the mother of subversives. Seeing

her coming, her friends cross the street or avert their eyes. Her telephone is silent. No one tells her anything, even lies. Without help she proceeds to put the shreds of her destroyed home in boxes. Well after nightfall she pulls the boxes onto the sidewalk. Very early in the morning the garbage men collect the boxes, one by one, gently, without knocking them over. The garbage men treat the boxes with great care, as if aware they are full of the bits of a broken life. Silently peering through the remains of a venetian blind, María Isabel thanks them for this caress, the only one she has had since the sorrow began.

(317)

1976: Forest of Zinica
Carlos

He criticized you to your face, praised you behind your back.

He had the myopic, fanatical gaze of an angry rooster, sharp brown eyes from which he saw farther than others, a man of all or nothing; but moments of joy made him jump like a small child, and when he gave orders he seemed to be asking favors.

Carlos Fonseca Amador, leader of the Nicaraguan revolution, has died fighting in the jungle.

A colonel brings the news to the cell where Tomás Borge lies shattered.

Together they had traveled a long road, Carlos and Tomás, since the days when Carlos sold newspapers and candy in Matagalpa. Together they founded, in Tegucigalpa, the Sandinista Front.

"*He's dead,*" says the colonel.

"*You're wrong, colonel,*" says Tomás.

(58)

1977: Managua
Tomás

Bound to an iron ring, teeth chattering, drenched in shit, blood, and vomit, Tomás Borge is a pile of broken bones and stripped nerves, a scrap lying on the floor waiting for the next round of torture.

But this remnant of himself can still sail down secret rivers that take him beyond pain and madness. Letting himself go, he drifts into another Nicaragua. He sees it.

Through the hood that squeezes his face swollen by blows, he sees it: He counts the beds in each hospital, the windows in each school, the trees in each park, and sees the sleepers fluttering their eyelids, bewildered, those long dead from hunger and everything else that kills now being awakened by newly born suns.

(58)

1977: Solentiname Archipelago
Cardenal

The herons, looking at themselves in the shimmering mirror, lift their beaks. The fishermen's boats are already returning, and behind them swim the turtles that come here to give birth on the beach.

In a wooden cabin, Jesus is seated at the fishermen's table. He eats turtle eggs, fresh-caught *guapote*, and cassava. The forest, searching for him, slips its arms through the windows.

To the glory of this Jesus, Ernesto Cardenal, the poet-monk of Solentiname, writes. To his glory sings the trumpeter *zanate*, the homeless bird, always flying among the poor, that freshens its wings in the lake waters. And to his glory the fishermen paint. They paint brilliant pictures that announce Paradise—all brothers, no bosses, no peons—until one night the fishermen who paint Paradise decide to start making it, and cross the lake to attack the San Carlos barracks.

From the darkness, the owl promises trouble: *"Screwed . . . screwed . . ."*

The dictatorship kills many as these seekers of Paradise pass through the mountains and valleys and islands of Nicaragua. *The dough rises, the big loaf swells . . .*

(6 and 77)

Omar Cabezas Tells of the Mountain's Mourning for the Death of a Guerrilla in Nicaragua

I never forgave Tello for being killed with one bullet, just one bullet . . . I felt a great fear, and it was as if the mountain, too, felt fear. The wind dropped and the trees stopped swaying, not a leaf stirred, the birds stopped singing. Everything froze, awaiting that moment when they'd come and kill the lot of us.

And we set out. When we broke into a marching pace up the ravine, it was as if we were shaking the mountain, as if we were grabbing her and telling her: Who the hell does this bitch think she is?

Tello lived with the mountain. I'm convinced he had relations with her, she bore him sons; and when Tello died she felt that all was over, her commitment was gone, that all the rest was foolishness . . . But when she saw the will to fight of the men marching there over her, in her heart she realized that Tello was not the beginning and end of the world. Though Tello may have been her son, though he may have been her life, her secret lover, her brother, her creature, her stone, though Tello may have been her river . . . he was not the end of the world, and that after him came all of us who could still light a fire in her heart.

(73)

1977: Brasília

Scissors

Over a thousand Brazilian intellectuals sign a manifesto against censorship.

In July of last year, the military dictatorship stopped the weekly *Movimiento* from publishing the United States Declaration of Independence, because in it is said that the people have the right and the duty to abolish despotic governments. Since then the censorship has banned: the Bolshoi Ballet, because it is Russian; the erotic prints of Pablo Picasso, because they are erotic; and the *History of Surrealism*, because one of its chapters has the word *revolution* in its title ("Revolution in Poetry").

(371)

1977: Buenos Aires
Walsh

He mails a letter and several copies. The original letter, to the military junta that rules Argentina. The copies, to foreign press agencies. On the first anniversary of the coup d'état, he is sending a sort of statement of grievances, a record of the infamies committed by a regime that can only stagger in its dance of death. At the bottom he puts his signature and number (Rodolfo Walsh, I.D. 2845022). He is only steps from the post office when their bullets cut him down; and he is carried off wounded, not to be seen again.

His naked words were scandalous where such fear reigns, dangerous while the great masked ball continues.

(461)

1977: Río Cuarto
The Burned Books of Walsh and Other Authors Are Declared Nonexistent

IN VIEW OF *the measure taken by the ex–Military Intervention of this National University in fulfillment of express superior orders, with respect to withdrawing from the Library Area all reading material of an antisocial nature and whose contents exuded ideologies alien to the Argentine National Being, constituting a source of extreme Marxist and subversive indoctrination, and*
WHEREAS: *Said literature having been opportunely incinerated, it is fitting to strike it from the patrimony of this House of Advanced Studies, the Rector of the National University of Río Cuarto*
RESOLVES: *To strike from the patrimony of the National University of Río Cuarto (Library Area) all the bibliography listed below:* [Long list follows of books by Rodolfo Walsh, Bertrand Russell, Wilhelm Dilthey, Maurice Dobb, Karl Marx, Paulo Freire, and others].

(452)

1977: Buenos Aires

The Mothers of the Plaza de Mayo,

women born of their children, are the Greek chorus of this tragedy. Brandishing photos of their disappeared ones, they circle round and round the obelisk, before the Pink House of the government, as obstinately as they make pilgrimages to barracks, police stations, and sacristies, dried up from so much weeping, desperate from so much waiting for those who were and are no longer, or perhaps still are . . . who knows?

"I wake up believing he's alive," says one, say all. "I begin to disbelieve as the morning goes on. He dies on me again at noon. He revives in the evening, I begin to believe he'll come soon, and I set a place for him at the table, but he dies again and at night I fall asleep without hope. When I wake up, I feel he's alive . . ."

They call them *madwomen.* Normally no one speaks of them. With the situation normalized, the dollar is cheap and certain people, too. Mad poets go to their deaths, and normal poets kiss the sword while praising silence. With total normality the Minister of Finance hunts lions and giraffes in Africa and the generals hunt workers in the suburbs of Buenos Aires. New language rules make it compulsory to call the military dictatorship *Proceso de Reorganización Nacional.*

(106 and 107)

1977: Buenos Aires

Alicia Moreau

Sometimes she goes overboard in her faith, anticipating social revolution in a none too realistic way, or explodes publicly in tirades against military power and the Pope of Rome. But what would become of the Plaza de Mayo mothers without the enthusiasm of this sprite woman? She never lets them grow discouraged or feel defeated by so much indifference and jeering: *"One can always do something,"* she tells them. *"Together. Each one on her own, no. Let's—we have to—"*

She grasps her cane and is the first to move.

Alicia Moreau is nearly a hundred years old. She has been in the struggle since the days when socialists drank only water and sang only the Internationale. She has witnessed many marvels and betrayals, births and deaths, and whatever her momentary troubles, she keeps believing that it's worthwhile to believe. Alicia Moreau is as lively now as she was when the century began and she made speeches from soapboxes between red flags in the worker barrios of Buenos Aires, or crossed the Andes on muleback, hurrying the animal so as not to arrive late at a feminist congress.

(221)

1977: Buenos Aires
Portrait of a Croupier

The Minister of Finance of the Argentine dictatorship is a pious devotee of private enterprise. He thinks about it on Sundays, when he kneels at the Mass, and also on weekdays, when he gives courses at the Military School. Nevertheless, the minister correctly withdraws from the company he directs, generously ceding it to the state for ten times its worth.

The generals turn the country into a barracks. The minister turns it into a casino. Argentina is deluged with dollars and consumer goods. It is the time of the hangman, but also of the conman and the conjurer. The generals order the country to shut up and obey, while the minister orders it to speculate and consume. Anyone who works is a sucker, anyone who protests, a corpse. To cut wages in half and reduce rebellious workers to nothing, the minister slips sweet silver bribes to the middle class, who fly to Miami and return loaded with mountains of gadgets and gimmickry. In the face of the daily massacre, people shrug their shoulders: *"They must have done something. It's for a good reason."*

Or they whistle and look the other way: *"Don't get involved."*

(143)

1977: Caracas

The Exodus of the Intruders

The prophet spoke in a café on Caracas's Calle Real de Sabana Grande. An extraterrestrial with flaming eyes appeared for a moment and announced that on a certain August Sunday a furious ocean would split the mountains and wipe out the city.

Bishops, witches, astronomers, and astrologers repeatedly issued reassurances that there was nothing to worry about, but they couldn't stop the panic from growing, from rolling like a ball through the barrios of Caracas.

Yesterday was the Sunday in question. The president of the republic ordered the police to take charge of the city. More than a million Caracans stampeded, fled with their belongings on their backs. More automobiles than people remained in the city.

Today, Monday, the fugitives begin to return. The ocean is where it always was, the mountains too. In the valley, Caracas continues to exist. And so the oil capital recovers its terrified citizens. They reenter as if begging pardon, because they know now that they are superfluous, that this is a world of wheels, not legs. Caracas belongs to its prepotent automobiles, not to whoever dares cross its streets to the annoyance of the machines. What would become of these people, condemned to live in a city that doesn't belong to them, if María Lionza didn't protect them and José Gregorio didn't cure them?

(135)

María Lionza

Her breasts rise above the center of Caracas and reign, nakedly, over the frenzy. In Caracas, in all Venezuela, María Lionza is a goddess.

Her invisible palace is far from the capital on a mountain in the Sorte chain. The rocks scattered over this mountain were once María Lionza's lovers, men who paid for a night of embraces by being converted into breathing stones.

Simón Bolívar and Jesus of Nazareth work for her in the sanctuary. Also helping her are three secretaries: one black, one Indian, one white. They attend to the faithful, who come loaded with offerings of fruit, perfumes, and undergarments.

María Lionza, untamed woman, feared and desired by God and Satan, has the powers of heaven and hell. She can inspire happiness or unhappiness; she saves if she feels like saving, and thunders if she feels like thundering.

(190 and 346)

José Gregorio

He is chastest of the chaste, María Lionza's white secretary. Doctor José Gregorio Hernández has never yielded to the temptations of the flesh. All the insinuating women who approached him ended up in convents, repenting, bathed in tears. This virtuous Physician of the Poor, this Apostle of Medicine, ended his days in 1919, undefeated. His immaculate body was pitilessly crushed by one of the two or three automobiles that circulated in Caracas at a snail's pace in those happy days. After death, the miraculous hands of José Gregorio have continued prescribing remedies and operating on the sick.

In the sanctuary of María Lionza, José Gregorio busies himself with public health problems. He has never failed to turn up from the Great Beyond at the call of sufferers, the only saint ever in a necktie and hat.

(363)

1977: Graceland
Elvis

Once, his way of shaking his left leg evoked screams. His lips, his eyes, his sideburns were sexual organs.

Now a soft ball of flab, Elvis Presley, dethroned king of rock 'n' roll, lies in bed, his glance floating between six television screens. The TVs, suspended from the ceiling, are each tuned to a different channel. Between sleep and dreams, always more asleep than awake, Elvis fires unloaded pistols, click, click, at the images he doesn't like. The suet ball of his body covers a soul made of Codeine, Morphine, Valium, Seconal, Placidyl, Quaalude, Nembutal, Valmid, Demerol, Elavil, Aventyl, Carbrital, Sinutab, and Amytal.

(197 and 409)

1978: San Salvador

Romero

The archbishop offers her a chair. Marianela prefers to talk standing up. She always comes for others; but this time Marianela comes for herself. Marianela García Vilas, attorney for the tortured and disappeared of El Salvador, does not come this time to ask the archbishop's solidarity with one of the victims of D'Aubuisson, Captain Torch, who burns your body with a blowtorch, or of some other military horror specialist. Marianela doesn't come to ask help for anyone else's investigation or denunciation. This time she has something personal to say to him. As mildly as she can she tells him that the police have kidnapped her, bound, beaten, humiliated, stripped her—and that they raped her. She tells it without tears or agitation, with her usual calm, but Archbishop Arnulfo Romero has never before heard in Marianela's voice these vibrations of hatred, echoes of disgust, calls for vengeance. When Marianela finishes, the archbishop, astounded, falls silent too.

After a long silence, he begins to tell her that the Church does not hate or have enemies, that every infamy and every action against God forms part of a divine order, that criminals are also our brothers and must be prayed for, that one must forgive one's persecutors, one must accept pain, one must . . . Suddenly, Archbishop Romero stops.

He lowers his glance, buries his head in his hands. He shakes his head, denying it all, and says: *"No, I don't want to know."*

"I don't want to know," he says, and his voice cracks.

Archbishop Romero, who always gives advice and comfort, is weeping like a child without mother or home. Archbishop Romero, who always gives assurance, the tranquillizing assurance of a neutral God who knows all and embraces all—Archbishop Romero doubts.

Romero weeps and doubts and Marianela strokes his head.

(259 and 301)

1978: La Paz
Five Women

"What is the main enemy? The military dictatorship? The Bolivian bourgeoisie? Imperialism? No, compañeros. I want to tell you just this: Our main enemy is fear. We have it inside us."

This is what Domitila said at the Catavi tin mine, and then she came to the capital with four other women and more than twenty kids. On Christmas Day they started their hunger strike. No one believed in them. Some thought it a ridiculous joke: *"So five women are going to overthrow the dictatorship?"*

The priest Luis Espinal is the first to join them. In no time there are fifteen hundred people starving themselves all over Bolivia. The five women, accustomed to hunger since they were born, call water *chicken* or *turkey* and salt *pork chop*, and feed on laughter. Meanwhile the hunger strikers multiply—three thousand, ten thousand—until the Bolivians who have stopped eating and working can no longer be counted, and twenty-three days after the start of the hunger strike the people invade the streets, and now nothing can be done to stop them.

The five women have overthrown the military dictatorship.

(1)

1978: Managua
"The Pigsty"

is what Nicaraguans call the National Palace. On the first floor of this pretentious Parthenon senators spout off. On the second, deputies.

One midday in August, a handful of guerrillas led by Edén Pastora and Dora María Téllez attack the Pigsty and in three minutes capture all of Somoza's legislators. To get them released, Somoza has but to free Sandinista prisoners. People line the airport road to cheer them.

This is turning out to be a year of continuous war. Somoza started it with the murder of the journalist Pedro Joaquín Chamorro. Infuriated people promptly incinerate several of the dictator's businesses. Flames consume the prosperous Plasmaféresis, Inc., which exports Nicaraguan blood to the United States. The people swear that they won't rest until the vampire himself is buried in some place darker than the night, with a stake impaling his heart.

(10 and 460)

Tachito Somoza's Pearl of Wisdom

I am a businessman, but humble.

(434)

1978: Panama City
Torrijos

General Omar Torrijos says he does not want to enter history. He only wants to enter the Canal Zone, stolen by the United States at the turn of the century. Thus he wanders the world from country to country, government to government, platform to platform. When accused of serving Moscow or Havana, Torrijos laughs. Every people, he says, swallows its own aspirins for its own headache. If it comes to that, he says, he gets along better with the Castristas than with the castrati.

Finally the canal's fences fall. The United States, pressured by the world, signs a treaty that restores to Panama, by degrees, the canal and the prohibited zone that encloses it.

"It's better this way," says Torrijos, relieved. They've saved him the disagreeable task of blowing up the canal and all its installations.

(154)

1979: Madrid
Intruders Disturb the Quiet Ingestion of the Body of God

In a big church in Madrid, a special Mass celebrates the anniversary of Argentine independence. Diplomats, business executives, and military men have been invited by General Leandro Anaya, ambassador of the dictatorship which is so busy across the sea protecting the Argentine heritage of fatherland, faith, and other proprieties.

Through the stained-glass windows rich lights illumine the faces and fashions of the ladies and gentlemen. On Sundays like this, God is worthy of confidence. Very occasionally a timid cough decorates the silence, as the priest performs the rite: imperturbable silence of eternity, eternity of the Lord's elect.

The moment of communion comes. Ringed by bodyguards, the Argentine ambassador approaches the altar. He kneels, closes his eyes, opens his mouth. Instantly the flutter of white handkerchiefs unfurling, covering the heads of the women who walk up the aisles, all the aisles. The mothers of the Plaza de Mayo advance softly, cottony rustle, until they surround the bodyguards who surround the ambassador. Then they stare at him. Simply stare. The ambassador opens his eyes, looks at all these women looking at him without blinking, and swallows his saliva, while the priest's hand remains paralyzed in midair, the Host between his fingers.

The whole church is filled with these women. Suddenly there are no longer saints or merchants in this temple, nothing more than a multitude of uninvited women: black dresses, white handkerchiefs, all silent, all on their feet.

(173)

1979: New York
Banker Rockefeller Congratulates Dictator Videla

His Excellency Jorge Rafael Videla
President of Argentina
Buenos Aires, Argentina

Dear Mr. President,
I am very grateful to you for taking time to receive me during my recent visit to Argentina. Not having been there for seven years, it was encouraging to see what progress your government has made during the past three years, both in controlling terrorism and strengthening the economy. I congratulate you on what you have achieved and wish you every success for the future . . .
With warm good wishes,

Sincerely,

David Rockefeller

(384)

1979: Siuna

Portrait of a Nicaraguan Worker

José Villarreina, married, three children. Works for the North American company Rosario Mines, which seventy years ago overthrew President Zelaya. Since 1952, Villarreina has been scraping gold from the excavations at Siuna; even so, his lungs are not yet entirely rotted out.

At 1:30 P.M. on July 3, 1979, Villarreina looks out from one of the mineshafts and a mineral-loaded cart tears off his head. Thirty-five minutes later, the company notifies the dead man that in accordance with articles 18, 115, and 119 of the Labor Code, he is discharged for nonfulfillment of his contract.

(362)

1979: In All Nicaragua

The Earth Buckles

and shakes worse than in all the earthquakes put together. Airplanes fly over immense stretches of jungle dropping napalm, and bomb cities crisscrossed with barricades and trenches. The Sandinistas take over León, Masaya, Jinotega, Chinandega, Estelí, Carazo, Jinotepe . . .

While Somoza awaits a sixty-five-million-dollar loan, approved by the International Monetary Fund, in Nicaragua they fight tree by tree, house by house. With masks or handkerchiefs covering their faces, the youths attack with rifles or machetes, sticks or stones; even a toy gun serves to make an impression.

In Masaya, which in the language of the Indians means *city that burns*, the fighters, adept in pyrotechnics, turn drainpipes into mortars and invent a fuseless contact bomb which explodes on striking. Old women weave between the bullets carrying large bags full of bombs, which they hand around like loaves of bread.

(10, 238, 239, and 320)

1979: In All Nicaragua
Get It Together, Everyone,

don't lose it, the big one is here, the shit has hit the fan, hell has broken loose, we're at fever heat, fighting with nothing but a home-made arsenal against tanks, armored cars, and planes, so everyone get into it, from here on no one ducks out, it's our war, the real thing, if you don't die killing you'll die dying, shoulder to shoulder makes us bolder, all together now, the people is us.

(10, 238, and 239)

From the Datebook of Tachito Somoza

1979
Thursday, July 12,
Love

1979: Managua
"Tourism must be stimulated,"

orders the dictator while Managua's eastern barrios burn, set ablaze by the air force.

From his bunker, great steel and cement uterus, Somoza rules. Here nothing penetrates, not the thunder of bombs, not the screams of people, nothing to ruffle the perfect silence. Here one sees nothing, smells nothing. In this bunker Somoza has lived for some time, right in the center of Managua but about as far from Nicaragua as you can get; and in this bunker, he now sits down with Fausto Amador.

Fausto Amador is the father of Carlos Fonseca Amador. The son, founder of the Sandinista Front, understood patriotism; the father, administrator general for the richest man in Central America, understands patrimony.

Surrounded by mirrors and plastic flowers, seated before a computer, Somoza, with Fausto Amador's help, organizes the liquidation of his businesses, which means the total pillage of Nicaragua.

Afterward, Somoza says on the telephone: *"I'm not going and they're not throwing me out."*

(10, 320, and 460)

1979: Managua
Somoza's Grandson

They're throwing him out and he's going. At dawn, Somoza boards a plane for Miami. In these final days the United States abandons him, but he does not abandon the United States: *"In my heart, I will always be part of this great nation."*

Somoza takes with him the gold ingots of the Central Bank, eight brightly colored parrots, and the coffins of his father and brother. He also takes the living body of the crown prince.

Anastasio Somoza Portocarrero, grandson of the founder of the dynasty, is a corpulent military man who has learned the arts of command and good government in the United States. In Nicaragua, he founded, and until today directed, the Basic Infantry Training School, a juvenile army group specializing in interrogations of prisoners—and famous for its skill. Armed with pincers and spoons, these lads can tear out fingernails without breaking the roots and eyes without injuring the lids.

The Somoza clan goes into exile as Augusto César Sandino strolls through Nicaragua beneath a rain of flowers, a half century after they shot him. This country has gone mad; lead floats, cork sinks, the dead escape from the cemetery, and women from the kitchen.

(10, 322, and 460)

1979: Granada
The Comandantes

Behind them, an abyss. Ahead and to either side, an armed people on the attack. La Pólvora barracks in the city of Granada, last stronghold of the dictatorship, is falling.

When the colonel in command hears of Somoza's flight, he orders the machineguns silenced. The Sandinistas also stop firing.

Soon the iron gate of the barracks opens and the colonel appears, waving a white rag. *"Don't fire."*

The colonel crosses the street. *"I want to talk to the comandante."*

A kerchief covering one of the faces drops. *"I'm the comandante,"* says Mónica Baltodano, one of the Sandinista women who lead troops.

"What?"

Through the mouth of the colonel, this haughty macho, speaks the military institution, defeated but dignified. Virility of the pants, honor of the uniform. *"I don't surrender to a woman!"* roars the colonel.

And he surrenders.

1979: In All Nicaragua
Birth

The Nicaragua newly born in the rubble is only a few hours old, fresh new greenery among the looted ruins of war; and the singing light of the first day of Creation fills the air that smells of fire.

1979: Paris
Darcy

The Sorbonne confers the title of Doctor Honoris Causa on Darcy Ribeiro. He accepts, he says, on the merit of his failures.

Darcy has failed as an anthropologist, because the Indians of Brazil are still being annihilated. He has failed as rector of the university because the reality he wanted it to transform proved obdurate. He has failed as Minister of Education in a country where illiteracy never stops multiplying. He has failed as a member of a government that tried and failed either to make agrarian reform or to control the cannibalistic habits of foreign capital. He has failed as a writer who dreamed of forbidding history to repeat itself.

These are his failures. These are his dignities.

(376)

1979: Santiago de Chile

Stubborn Faith

General Pinochet stamps his signature on a decree that imposes private property on the Mapuche Indians. The government offers funds, fencing, and seeds to those who agree to parcel out their communities with good grace. If not, the government warns, they'll accept without any grace.

Pinochet is not the first to believe that greed is part of human nature and that God wants it that way. Long ago, the conquistador Pedro de Valdivia had tried to break up the indigenous communities of Chile. Since then, by fire and sword everything has been seized from the Indians, everything: land, language, religion, customs. But the Indians, hemmed in, trapped in poverty, exhausted by so much war and so much swindling, persist in believing that the world is a shared home.

1979: Chajul

Another Kind of Political Education in Guatemala

Patrocinio Menchú, Maya-Quiché Indian, born in the village of Chimel, had, along with his parents, defended the lands of his harassed community. From his parents he learned to walk the heights without slipping, to greet the sun according to ancient custom, to clear and fertilize the ground, and to stake his life on it.

Now, he is one of the prisoners that the army trucks have brought to the village of Chajul for the people to see. Rigoberta, his sister, recognizes him, although his face is swollen from beatings and he bleeds from his eyes, his tongueless mouth, and his nail-less fingers.

Five hundred soldiers—Indians too, Indians of other regions—stand guard over the ceremony. Herded into a circle, the whole population of Chajul is forced to watch. Rigoberta has to watch, while within her, as in everyone, a silent, moist curse blooms. The captain displays the nude bodies, flayed, mutilated, still alive, and says that these are Cubans who have come to stir up trouble in Guatemala. Showing off the details of the punishments that each one earned, the captain yells:

"Have a good look at what's in store for guerrillas!"
Then he soaks the prisoners with gasoline and sets fire to them.
Patrocinio Menchú was still tender corn. It was only sixteen years
ago that he was planted.

(72)

The Mayas Plant Each Child That Is Born

High up in the mountains, the Indians of Guatemala bury the umbilical cord while presenting the child to Grandpa Volcano, Mother
Earth, Father Sun, Grandma Moon, all the powerful grandparents,
and asking them to protect the newly born from danger and error.

*Before the rain that irrigates us and before the wind that bears
us witness, we, who are part of you, plant this new child, this new
compañero, in this place . . .*

1980: La Paz

The Cococracy

General Luis García Meza, author of the 189th coup d'état in a century
and a half of Bolivia's history, announces that he will establish a free
economy, as in Chile, and make sure all extremists disappear, as in
Argentina.

With García Meza, the cocaine traffickers take over the state.
His brand-new Interior Minister, Colonel Luis Arce Gómez, divides
his time and energy between drug smuggling and heading up the
Bolivian Section of the World Anticommunist League. He will not
rest, he says, never rest, *until the cancer of Marxism is extirpated.*

The military government raises the curtain by assassinating Marcelo Quiroga Santa Cruz, enemy of Gulf Oil and its forty thieves,
implacable foe of hidden filth.

(157 and 257)

1980: Santa Ana de Yacuma

Portrait of a Modern Businessman

He fires from the hip, both bullets and bribes. At his waist he carries a golden pistol, in his mouth a golden smile. His bodyguards use machineguns with telescopic sights. He has twelve missile-armed combat planes and thirty cargo planes that take off early each morning from the Bolivian jungle loaded with cocaine paste. Roberto Suárez, cousin and colleague of the new Interior Minister, exports a ton a month.

"*My philosophy,*" he says, "*is to do good.*"

He claims that the money he has given to the Bolivian military would suffice to pay the country's external debt.

Like a good Latin American businessman, Suárez sends his winnings to Switzerland, where they find refuge in banking secrecy. But in Santa Ana de Yacuma, the town where he was born, he has paved the main street, restored the church, and given sewing machines to widows and orphans; and when he turns up there he bets thousands of dollars on a roll of the dice or a cockfight.

Suárez is the most important Bolivian capitalist in a huge multinational enterprise. In his hands, the price of a coca leaf is multiplied by ten as it changes into paste and leaves the country. Later, as it becomes powder and reaches the nose that inhales it, its price soars two hundred times. Like any raw material from a poor country, coca lines the pockets of intermediaries, and above all intermediaries in the rich country that consumes it transformed into cocaine, the white goddess.

(157, 257, and 439)

The White Goddess

is the most expensive of the divinities. She costs five times as much as gold. In the United States, ten million devotees yearn and burn, ready to kill, and kill themselves for her. Every year they throw thirty billion dollars at the foot of her shining altar of pure snow. In the long run she will annihilate them; from the start she steals their souls; but in exchange she offers to make them, by her good grace, supermen for a moment.

(257 and 372)

1980: Santa Marta
Marijuana

Out of each dollar of dreams that a U.S. marijuana smoker buys, barely one cent reaches the hands of the Colombian campesinos who grow it. The other ninety-nine cents go to the traffickers, who in Colombia have fifteen hundred airports, five hundred airplanes, and a hundred ships.

On the outskirts of Medellín or Santa Marta, the drug mafiosi live in ostentatious mansions. In front they like to display on granite pedestals the small planes they used in their first operation. They rock their children in gold cradles, give golden fingernails to their lovers, and on ring finger or necktie wear diamonds as discreet as headlights.

The mafiosi habitually fumigate their forces. Four years ago they machinegunned Lucho Barranquilla, most popular of the traffickers, on a street corner in the city of Santa Marta. The murderers sent to the funeral a floral wreath in the form of a heart and took up a collection to erect a statue of the departed in the main plaza.

(95 and 406)

1980: Santa Marta
Saint Agatón

Lucho Barranquilla was widely mourned. The children who played in his amusement park wept for him, as did the widows and orphans he protected, and the cops who ate from his hand. In fact, the whole city of Santa Marta, which lived thanks to his loans and donations, wept. And Saint Agatón wept for him, too.

Saint Agatón is the patron saint of drunkards. On Carnival Sunday, drunks from the whole Colombian coast descend on the village of Mamatoco, on Santa Marta's outskirts. There they take Saint Agatón out of his church and parade him, singing dirty songs and spraying him with firewater, just the way he likes.

But what the drunks are parading is only a white-bearded impostor brought from Spain. The true Saint Agatón, who had an Indian face and a straw hat, was kidnapped half a century ago by a temperance priest who fled with the saint under his surplice. God punished that priest with leprosy and crossed the eyes of the sacristan who accompanied him, but left the real Saint Agatón hidden in the remote village of Sucre.

A committee has gone to Sucre in recent days to plead with him to return: *"Since you left,"* they tell him, *"there's no more miracles or fun."*

Saint Agatón refuses. He says he won't go back to Santa Marta, because there they killed his friend Lucho Barranquilla.

1980: Guatemala City
Newsreel

It was General Romeo Lucas García, president of Guatemala, who gave the order to set fire to the Spanish embassy with its occupants inside. This statement comes from Elías Barahona, official spokesman for the Ministry of the Interior, who calls a press conference after seeking asylum in Panama.

According to Barahona, General Lucas García is personally responsible for the deaths of the thirty-nine persons roasted alive by the police bombs. Among the victims were twenty-seven Indian leaders who had peacefully occupied the embassy to denounce the massacres in the Quiché region.

Barahona also states that General Lucas García commands the paramilitary and parapolice bands known as the Squadrons of Death, and helps draw up the lists of opponents condemned to disappear.

The former press secretary of the Interior Ministry claims that in Guatemala a "Program of Pacification and Eradication of Communism" is being carried out, based on a four-hundred-and-twenty-page document drawn up by specialists in the United States on the basis of their experience in the Vietnam war.

In the first half of 1980 in Guatemala, twenty-seven university professors, thirteen journalists, and seventy campesino leaders, mainly Indians, have been murdered. The repression has had a special intensity for Indian communities in the Quiché region, where large oil deposits have recently been discovered.

(450)

1980: Uspantán
Rigoberta

She is a Maya-Quiché Indian, born in the village of Chimel, who has been picking coffee and cotton on the coastal plantations since she learned to walk. In the cotton fields she saw two of her brothers die—Nicolás and Felipe, the youngest—and also her best friend, still only half grown. All fell victim to pesticide spraying.

Last year in the village of Chajul, Rigoberta Menchú saw how the army burned alive her brother Patrocinio. Soon afterward, her father suffered the same fate in the Spanish embassy. Now, in Uspantán, the soldiers have killed her mother, very gradually, cutting her to pieces bit by bit after dressing her up in guerrilla's clothing.

Of the community of Chimel, where Rigoberta was born, no one remains alive.

Rigoberta, who is a Christian, has been taught that true Christians forgive their persecutors and pray for the souls of their executioners. When they strike you on one cheek, she was taught, the true Christian offers the other.

"I no longer have a cheek to offer," says Rigoberta.

(72)

1980: San Salvador
The Offering

Until a couple of years ago, he only got along well with God. Now he speaks with and for everyone. Each child of the people tormented by the powerful is a child of God crucified; and in the people God is renewed after each crime the powerful commit. Now Monseñor Romero, archbishop of El Salvador, world-breaker, world-revealer, bears no resemblance to the babbling shepherd of souls whom the powerful used to applaud. Now ordinary people interrupt with ovations his sermons denouncing state terrorism.

Yesterday, Sunday, the archbishop exhorted the police and soldiers to disobey the order to kill their campesino brothers. In the name of Christ, Romero told the Salvadoran people: *Arise and go.*

Today, Monday, the murderer arrives at the church escorted by two police patrols. He enters and waits, hidden behind a pillar. Romero is celebrating Mass. When he opens his arms and offers the bread and the wine, body and blood of the people, the murderer pulls the trigger.

(259 and 301)

1980: Montevideo
A People Who Say No

The dictatorship of Uruguay calls a plebiscite and loses.

This people forced into silence seemed dumb; but when it opens its mouth, it says no. The silence of these years has been so deafening that the military mistook it for resignation. They never expected such a response. They asked only for the sake of asking, like a chef who orders his chickens to say with what sauce they prefer to be eaten.

1980: In All Nicaragua
On Its Way

The Sandinista revolution doesn't shoot anybody; but of Somoza's army not a brass band remains. The rifles pass into everybody's hands, while the banner of agrarian reform is unfurled over desolate fields.

An army of volunteers, whose weapons are pencils and vaccines, invades its own country. Revolution, revelation, of those who believe and create; not infallible gods of majestic stride, but ordinary people, for centuries forced into obedience and trained for impotence. Now, even when they trip, they keep on walking. They go in search of bread and the word: This land, which opened its mouth, is eager to eat and speak.

1980: Asunción
Stroessner

Tachito Somoza, dethroned, exiled, is blown to pieces on a street corner in Asunción.

"*Who did it?*" ask the journalists in Managua.

*"Fuenteovejuna,"** replies comandante Tomás Borge.

Tachito had found refuge in the capital of Paraguay, the only city in the world where there was still a bronze bust of his father, Tacho Somoza, and where a street was still named "Generalisimo Franco."

Paraguay, or the little that is left of Paraguay after so much war and plunder, belongs to General Alfredo Stroessner. Every five years this veteran colleague of Somoza and Franco holds elections to confirm his power. So that people can vote, he suspends for twenty-four hours Paraguay's eternal state of siege.

Stroessner believes himself invulnerable because he loves no one. The State is him. Every day, at precisely 6:00 P.M., he phones the president of the Central Bank and asks him:

"How much did we make today?"

1980: In All Nicaragua
Discovering

Riding horseback, rowing, walking, the brigadistas of the literacy campaigns penetrate the most hidden corners of Nicaragua. By lamplight they teach the handling of a pencil to those who don't know, so that they'll never again be fooled by people who think they're so smart.

While they teach, the brigadistas share what little food they have, stoop down to weed and harvest crops, skin their hands chopping wood, and spend the night on the floor slapping at mosquitos. They discover wild honey in the trees, and in the people legends, verses, lost wisdom; bit by bit they get to know the secret languages of the herbs that enliven flavors, cure pains, and heal snake bites. Teaching, the brigadistas learn the marvel and malevolence of this country, their country, inhabited by survivors; in Nicaragua, anyone who doesn't die of hunger, disease, or a bullet, dies of laughter.

(11)

---

* The allusion is to the play *Fuenteovejuna* by the Spanish playwright Lope de Vega (1562–1635), in which all the people of the town of that name claim collective responsibility for the death of a tyrant. The most famous passage in the play reads: "Who killed the Comendador? Fuenteovejuna, señor."

1980: New York

The Statue of Liberty Seems
Pitted with Smallpox

because of the poisonous gases so many factories throw into the sky, and which rain and snow bring back to earth. One hundred and seventy lakes have been murdered by this acid rain in New York State alone, but the director of the Federal Office of Management and Budget says it's not worth bothering about. After all, those lakes are only four percent of the state total.

The world is a racetrack. Nature, an obstacle. The deadly breath of the smokestacks has left four thousand lakes without fish or plants in Ontario, Canada.

"We'd better ask God to start over," says a fisherman.

1980: New York

Lennon

A shirt hung out on a roof flaps its arms. The wind complains. The roaring and screaming of city life is joined by the shriek of a siren rushing through the streets. On this dirty day in Manhattan, John Lennon, musical innovator, has been murdered.

He didn't want to win or kill. He didn't agree that the world should be a stock market or a barracks. Lennon was on the sidelines of the track. Singing or whistling with a distracted look, he watched the wheels of others turn in the perpetual vertigo that comes and goes between madhouse and slaughterhouse.

1981: Surahammar

Exile

What is the distance that separates a Bolivian mining camp from a city in Sweden? How many miles, how many centuries, how many worlds?

Domitila, one of the five women who overthrew a military dictatorship, has been sentenced to exile by another military dictatorship and has ended up, with her miner husband and her many children, in the snows of northern Europe.

From where there's too little anything to where there's too much everything, from lowest poverty to highest opulence. Eyes full of wonder in these faces of clay: Here in Sweden they throw in the garbage nearly new TVs, hardly used clothing and furniture, and refrigerators and dishwashers that work perfectly. To the junkyard goes last year's automobile.

Domitila is grateful for the support of the Swedes and admires them for their liberty, but the waste offends her and the loneliness troubles her. These poor rich folk live all alone before the television, drinking alone, eating alone, talking to themselves:

"Over there in Bolivia," says—recommends—Domitila, *"even if it's for a fight, we get together."*

(1)

1981: Celica Canton

"Bad Luck, Human Error, Bad Weather"

A plane crashes at the end of May, and so ends the life of Jaime Roldós, president of Ecuador. Some campesinos hear the explosion and see the plane in flames before it crashes.

Doctors are not permitted to examine the body. No autopsy is attempted. The black box never turns up; they say the plane had none. Tractors smooth over the scene of the disaster. Tapes from the Quito, Guayaquil, and Loja control towers are erased. Various witnesses die in accidents. The Air Force's report discounts in advance any crime.

Bad luck, human error, bad weather. But President Roldós was defending Ecuador's coveted oil, had restored relations with prohibited Cuba, and backed accursed revolutions in Nicaragua, El Salvador, Palestine.

Two months later another plane crashes, in Panama. *Bad luck, human error, bad weather.* Two campesinos who heard the plane explode in the air disappear. Omar Torrijos, guilty of rescuing the Panama Canal, knew he wasn't going to die in bed of old age.

Almost simultaneously, a helicopter crashes in Peru. *Bad luck, human error, bad weather.* This time the victim is the head of the

Peruvian army, General Rafael Hoyos Rubio, an old enemy of Standard Oil and other benevolent multinational corporations.

(154 and 175)

1982: South Georgia Islands
Portrait of a Brave Fellow

The mothers of the Plaza de Mayo called him *the Angel,* because of his pink baby face. He had spent some months working with them, always smiling, always ready to lend a hand, when, one evening, the soldiers pick up several of the movement's most active militants as they leave a meeting. These mothers disappear, like their sons and daughters, and nothing more is heard of them.

The kidnapped mothers have been fingered by *the Angel;* that is, Frigate Lieutenant Alfredo Astiz, member of Task Force 3-3-2 of the Navy's Mechanics School, who has a long and brilliant record in the torture chambers.

This spy and torturer, now a lieutenant on a warship, is the first to surrender to the English in the Malvinas war. He surrenders without firing a shot.

(107, 134, 143, and 388)

1982: Malvinas Islands
The Malvinas War,

patriotic war that for a moment united trampled and tramplers, ends with the victory of Great Britain's colonial army.

The Argentine generals and colonels who promised to shed their last drops of blood have not so much as cut a finger. Those who declared war haven't even put in a guest appearance. So that the Argentine flag might fly over these ice cubes, a just cause in unjust hands, the high command sent to the slaughterhouse youngsters roped into compulsory service, who died more of cold than of bullets.

Their pulses do not flicker. With firm hands, these rapers of bound women, hangmen of disarmed workers, sign the surrender.

(185)

1982: *The Roads of La Mancha*
Master Globetrotter

completes his first half century of life far from where he was born. In a Castilian village, in front of one of the windmills that challenged Don Quixote, Javier Villafañe, patriarch of America's puppeteers, celebrates the birthday of his favorite son. To be worthy of this great date, Javier decides to marry a pretty gypsy he has just met; and Master Globetrotter presides over the ceremony and banquet with his characteristic melancholy dignity.

They've gone through life together, these two, puppeteering along the roads of the world, sweetness and mischief, Master Globetrotter and the pilgrim Javier. Whenever Master Globetrotter gets sick, a victim of worms or moths, Javier heals his wounds with infinite patience and afterward watches over his sleep.

At the start of each performance, before an expectant crowd of children, the two tremble as if at their first show.

1982: *Stockholm*
Novelist García Márquez Receives the Nobel Prize and Speaks of our Lands Condemned to One Hundred Years of Solitude

I dare to think that it is this outsized reality, and not just its literary expression, that has deserved the attention of the Swedish Academy of Letters. A reality not of paper, but one that lives within us and determines each instant of our countless daily deaths, and that nourishes a source of insatiable creativity full of sorrow and beauty, of which this roving and nostalgic Colombian is but one cipher more, singled out by fortune. Poets and beggars, musicians and prophets, warriors and scoundrels, all creatures of that unbridled reality, we have had to ask but little of our imagination, for our crucial problem has been a lack of conventional means to render our lives believable. This, my friends, is the crux of our solitude . . .

The interpretation of our reality through patterns not our own serves only to make us ever more unknown, ever less free, ever more solitary . . .

No: the immeasurable violence and pain of our history are the result of age-old inequities and untold bitterness, and not a conspiracy plotted three thousand leagues from our homes. But many European leaders and thinkers have thought so, this with the childishness of old-timers who have forgotten the fruitful excesses of their youth, as if it were impossible to find another destiny than to live at the mercy of the two great masters of the world. This, friends, is the very scale of our solitude . . .

(189)

1983: Saint George's
The Reconquest of the Island of Grenada

Tiny Grenada, hardly visible speck of green in the immensity of the Caribbean, suffers a spectacular invasion of Marines. President Ronald Reagan sends them to murder socialism, but the Marines kill a corpse. Some days earlier, certain native military men, greedy for power, had already assassinated socialism, in the name of socialism.

Behind the Marines lands North American secretary of state George Shultz. At a press conference he says: *"At first sight I realized that this island could be a splendid real estate prospect."*

1983: La Bermuda
Marianela

Every morning at dawn, they lined up, these relatives, friends, and lovers of the disappeared of El Salvador. They came looking for or offering news; they had no other place to ask about the lost or bear witness. The door of the Human Rights Commission was always open; or one could simply step through the hole the last bomb had opened in its wall.

Since the guerrilla movement started growing in the countryside, the army has no longer bothered to use prisons. The Commission denounced them before the world: *July: fifteen children under fourteen who had been detained charged with terrorism are found decapitated. August: thirteen thousand five hundred civilians murdered or disappeared so far this year . . .*

Of the Commission's workers, Magdalena Enríquez, the one who laughed most, was the first to fall. Soldiers dumped her flayed body on the beach. Then came the turn of Ramón Valladares, found riddled with bullets in the roadside mud. Only Marianela García Vilas remained: *"The bad weed never dies,"* she said.

They kill her near the village of La Bermuda in the burned lands of Cuscatlán. She was walking with her camera and tape recorder collecting proof that the army fires white phosphorus at rebellious campesinos.

(259)

1983: Santiago de Chile
Ten Years after the Reconquest of Chile

"You have the right to import a camel," says the Minister of Finance. From the TV screen the minister exhorts Chileans to make use of free trade. In Chile anyone can decorate his home with an authentic African crocodile, and democracy consists of choosing between Chivas Regal and Johnnie Walker Black Label.

Everything is imported: brooms, birdcage swings, corn, water for the whiskey. Baguette loaves come by air from Paris. The economic system, imported from the United States, obliges Chileans to scratch at the entrails of their mountains for copper, and nothing more. Not a pin can they manufacture, because South Korean pins come cheaper. Any creative act is a crime against the laws of the market—that is, the laws of fate.

From the United States come television programs, cars, machineguns, and plastic flowers. In the upper-class neighborhoods of Santiago, one cannot move without bumping into Japanese computers, German videocassettes, Dutch TVs, Swiss chocolates, English marmalade, Danish hams, clothing from Taiwan, French perfumes, Spanish tuna, Italian oil . . .

He who does not consume does not exist. Everyone else is simply used and discarded, although they pay the bills for this credit-card fiesta.

The unemployed scavenge through refuse. Everywhere one sees signs that say: *No openings. Do not insist.*

The foreign debt and the suicide rate have increased six-fold.

(169 and 231)

1983: A Ravine Between Cabildo and Petorca

Television

The Escárates had nothing—until Armando brought that box on his mule.

Armando Escárate had been away a whole year, working at sea as a cook for fishermen, and also in the town of La Ligua, doing odd jobs and eating leftovers, toiling night and day until he could put together enough money to pay for it.

When Armando got off his mule and opened the box, the family was struck dumb with fright. No one had ever seen the like of it in these regions of the Chilean cordillera. From afar people came, as if on pilgrimage, to examine the full-color Sony that ran off a truck battery.

The Escárates had nothing. They still have nothing, and continue to sleep huddled together, barely getting by on the cheese they make, the wool they spin, and the flocks of goats they graze for the boss of the hacienda. But the television rises like a totem in the middle of their mud shanty roofed with reeds. From the screen Coca-Cola offers them the sparkle of life, and Sprite, bubbles of youth; Marlboro cigarettes give them virility; Cadbury candies, human communication; Visa credit cards, wealth; Dior perfumes and Cardin shirts, distinction; Cinzano vermouth, social status; the Martini, passionate love. Nestlé powdered milk provides them with eternal vigor, and the Renault automobile with a new way to live.

(230)

1983: Buenos Aires

The Granny Detectives

While the military dictatorship disintegrates in Argentina, the Plaza de Mayo grandmothers go looking for their lost grandchildren. These children, imprisoned with their parents or born in concentration camps, have been distributed as war booty, and more than one has for parents his own parents' murderers. The grannies investigate on the basis of whatever they can dig up—photos, stray data, a birthmark, someone who saw something—and so, beating out a path with native shrewdness and umbrella blows, they have recovered a few children.

Tamara Arze, who disappeared at one-and-a-half, did not end up in military hands. She is in a suburban barrio, in the home of the good folk who picked her up where she was dumped. At the mother's appeal, the grannies undertook the search for her. They had only a few leads, but after a long, complicated sweep, they have located her. Every morning Tamara sells kerosene from a horse-drawn cart, but she doesn't complain of her fate. At first she doesn't even want to hear about her real mother. Very gradually the grannies explain to her that she is the daughter of Rosa, a Bolivian worker who never abandoned her. That one night her mother was seized at the factory gate, in Buenos Aires . . .

(317)

1983: Lima

Tamara Flies Twice

Rosa was tortured—under the supervision of a doctor who indicated when to stop—and raped, and shot at with blank cartridges. She spent eight years in prison, without trial or explanation, and only last year was expelled from Argentina. Now, in Lima airport, she waits while her daughter Tamara flies over the Andes toward her.

Accompanying Tamara on the flight are two of the grannies who found her.

She devours every bit of food she is served on the plane, not leaving a crumb of bread or a grain of sugar.

In Lima, Rosa and Tamara discover each other. They look in the mirror together. They are identical: same eyes, same mouth, same marks in the same places.

When night comes, Rosa bathes her daughter. Putting her to bed, she smells a milky, sweetish smell on her; and so she bathes her again. And again. But however much soap she uses, there is no way to wash off the smell. It's an odd smell . . . And suddenly Rosa remembers. This is the smell of little babies when they finish nursing: Tamara is ten, and tonight she smells like a newly born infant.

(317)

1983: Buenos Aires

What If the Desert Were Ocean and the Earth Were Sky?

The mothers and grandmothers of the Plaza de Mayo are frightening. For what would happen if they tired of circling in front of the Pink House and began signing government decrees? And if the beggars on the cathedral steps grabbed the archbishop's tunic and biretta and began preaching sermons from the pulpit? And if honest circus clowns began giving orders in the barracks and courses in the universities? And if they did? And if?

(317)

1983: Plateau of Petitions

The Mexican Theater of Dreams

As they do every year, the Zapotec Indians come to the Plateau of Petitions.

On one side is the sea, on the other, peaks and precipices.

Here dreams are turned loose. A kneeling man gets up and goes into the wood, an invisible bride on his arm. Someone moves like a languid jellyfish, navigating in an aerial ship. One makes drawings in the wind and another rides by with slow majesty, astride a tree branch. Pebbles become grains of corn, and acorns, hen's eggs. Old people become children, and children, giants; the leaf of a tree becomes a mirror that imparts a handsome face to anyone looking at it.

The spell is broken should anyone dare not be serious about this dress rehearsal of life.

(418)

1983: Tuma River

Realization

In Nicaragua, bullets whiz back and forth between dignity and scorn; and the war extinguishes many lives.

This is one of the battalions fighting the invaders. These volunteers have come from the poorest barrios of Managua to the far plains of the Tuma River.

Whenever there is a quiet moment, Beto, *the prof*, spreads the contagion of letters. The contagion occurs when some militiaman asks him to write a letter for him. Beto does it, and then: *"This is the last one I'll write for you. I'm offering you something better."*

Sebastián Fuertes, iron soldier from El Maldito barrio, a middle-aged man of many wars and women, is one of those who came up and was sentenced to alphabetization. For some days he has been breaking pencils and tearing up sheets of paper in the respites from shooting, and standing up to a lot of heavy teasing. And when May First arrives, his comrades elect him to make the speech.

The meeting is held in a paddock full of dung and ticks. Sebastián gets up on a box, takes from his pocket a folded paper, and reads the first words ever born from his hands. He reads from a distance, stretching out his arm, because his sight is little help and he has no glasses.

"Brothers of Battalion 8221! . . ."

1983: Managua

Defiance

Plumes of smoke rise from the mouths of volcanos and the barrels of guns. The campesino goes to war on a burro, with a parrot on his shoulder. God must have been a primitive painter the day he dreamed up this land of gentle speech, condemned to die and to kill by the United States, which trains and pays the contras. From Honduras, the Somocistas attack it; from Costa Rica, Edén Pastora betrays it.

And now, here comes the Pope of Rome. The Pope scolds those priests who love Nicaragua more than heaven, and abruptly silences those who ask him to pray for the souls of murdered patriots. After quarreling with the Catholic multitude gathered in the plaza, he takes off in a fury from this bedeviled land.

1983: Mérida

The People Set God on His Feet,

and the people know that to stand up in the world, God needs their help.

Every year, the child Jesus is born in Mérida and elsewhere in Venezuela. Choristers sing to the strains of violins, mandolins, and guitars, while the godparents gather up in a big cloth the child lying in the manger—delicate task, serious business—and take him for a walk.

The godparents walk the child through the streets. The kings and shepherds follow, and the crowd throws flowers and kisses. After such a warm welcome into the world, the godparents put Jesus back in the manger where Mary and Joseph are waiting for him.

Then, in the name of the community, the godparents stand him up for the first time, and make sure he remains upright between his parents. Finally the rosary is sung and all present get a little cake of the old-fashioned kind with twelve egg yolks, and some sweet mistela wine.

(463)

1983: Managua

Newsreel

In a Managua barrio, a woman has given birth to a hen, according to the Nicaraguan daily *La Prensa*. Sources close to the ecclesiastical hierarchy do not deny that this extraordinary event may be a sign of God's anger. The behavior of the crowd before the Pope may have exhausted the Divine Patience, these sources believe.

Back in 1981, two miracles with equally broad repercussions occurred in Nicaragua. The Virgin of Cuapa made a spectacular appearance that year in the fields of Chontales. Barefoot, crowned with stars, and enveloped in a glowing aura that blinded witnesses, the Virgin made declarations to a sacristan named Bernardo. The Mother of God expressed her support for President Reagan's policies against atheistic, Communist-inspired Sandinismo.

Shortly afterward, the Virgin of the Conception sweated and wept copiously for several days in a Managua house. The archbishop, Monseñor Obando, appeared before his altar and exhorted the faithful to pray for the forgiveness of the Most Pure. The Virgin of the Conception's emanations stopped only when the police discovered that the owners of the plaster image were submerging it in water and shutting it in a refrigerator at night so that it would perspire when exposed to the intense local heat, before the crowd of pilgrims.

1984: The Vatican
The Holy Office of the Inquisition

now bears the more discreet name of the Congregation for the Doctrine of the Faith. It no longer burns heretics alive, although it might like to. Its chief headache these days comes from America. In the name of the Holy Father, the inquisitors summon Latin American theologians Leonardo Boff and Gustavo Gutiérrez, and the Vatican sharply reprimands them for lacking respect for the Church of Fear.

The Church of Fear, opulent multinational enterprise, devotee of pain and death, is anxious to nail on a cross any son of a carpenter of the breed that now circulates within America's coasts inciting fishermen and defying empires.

1984: London
Gold and Frankincense

Top officials of the United States, Japan, West Germany, England, France, Italy, and Canada, forgather at Lancaster House to congratulate the organization that guarantees the freedom of money. The seven powers of the capitalist world unanimously applaud *the work of the International Monetary Fund in the developing countries.*

The congratulations do not mention the executioners, torturers, inquisitors, jailers, and informers who are the functionaries of the Fund in these *developing countries.*

A Circular Symphony for Poor Countries, in Six Successive Movements

So that labor may be increasingly obedient and cheap, the poor countries need legions of executioners, torturers, inquisitors, jailers, and informers.

To feed and arm these legions, the poor countries need loans from the rich countries.

To pay the interest on these loans, the poor countries need more loans.

To pay the interest on the loans on top of loans, the poor countries need to increase their exports.

To increase their exports, products condemned to perpetually collapsing prices, the poor countries need to lower production costs.

To lower production costs, the poor countries need increasingly obedient and cheap labor.

To make labor increasingly obedient and cheap, the poor countries need legions of executioners, torturers, inquisitors . . .

1984: Washington

1984

The U.S. State Department decides to suppress the word *murder* in its reports on violations of human rights in Latin America and other regions. Instead of *murder*, one must say: *illegal or arbitrary deprivation of life.*

For some time now, the CIA has avoided the word *murder* in its manuals on practical terrorism. When the CIA murders an enemy or has him murdered, it *neutralizes* him.

The State Department calls any war forces it lands south of its borders *peace-keeping forces*; and the killers who fight to restore its business interests in Nicaragua *freedom fighters*.

(94)

1984: Washington

We Are All Hostages

Nicaragua and other insolent countries still act as if unaware that history has been ordered not to budge, under pain of total destruction of the world.

"We will not tolerate . . ." warns President Reagan.

Above the clouds hover the nuclear bombers. Farther up, the military satellites. Beneath the earth and beneath the sea, the missiles. The Earth still rotates because the great powers permit it to do so. A plutonium bomb the size of an orange would suffice to explode the entire planet, and a good-size discharge of radiation could turn it into a desert populated by cockroaches.

President Reagan says Saint Luke (14:31) advises increasing military funding to confront the Communist hordes. The economy is militarized; weapons shoot money to buy weapons to shoot money. They manufacture arms, hamburgers, and fear. There is no better business than the sale of fear. The president announces, jubilantly, the militarization of the stars.

(430)

1984: São Paulo

Twenty Years after the Reconquest of Brazil

The last president of the military dictatorship, General Figueiredo, leaves the government to civilians.

When they ask him what he would do if he were a worker earning the minimum wage, General Figueiredo replies: *"I would put a bullet through my head."*

Brazil suffers a famished prosperity. Among countries selling food to the world, it stands in fourth place; among countries suffering hunger in the world, sixth place. Now Brazil exports arms and automobiles as well as coffee, and produces more steel than France; but Brazilians are shorter and weigh less than they did twenty years ago.

Millions of homeless children wander the streets of cities like São Paulo, hunting for food. Buildings are turning into fortresses, doormen into armed guards. Every citizen is either an assailant or assailed.

(371)

1984: Guatemala City
Thirty Years after the Reconquest of Guatemala,

the Bank of the Army is the country's most important, after the Bank of America. Generals take turns in power, overthrowing each other, transforming dictatorship into dictatorship; but all apply the same policy of land seizure against the Indians guilty of inhabiting areas rich in oil, nickel, or whatever else turns out to be of value.

These are no longer the days of United Fruit, but rather of Getty Oil, Texaco, and the International Nickel Company. The generals wipe out many Indian communities wholesale and expel even more from their lands. Multitudes of hungry Indians, stripped of everything, wander the mountains. They come from horror, but they are not going to horror. They walk slowly, guided by the ancient certainty that someday greed and arrogance will be punished. That's what the old people of corn assure the children of corn in the stories they tell them when night falls.

(367 and 450)

1984: Rio de Janeiro
Mishaps of Collective Memory in Latin America

Public accountant João David dos Santos jumped for joy when he managed to collect his many overdue accounts. Only payment in kind, but something. For lack of funds, a social science research center paid him its whole library of nine thousand books and over five thousand magazines and pamphlets devoted to contemporary Brazilian history. It contained very valuable material on the peasant leagues of the Northeast and the Getulio Vargas administration, among other subjects.

Then accountant dos Santos put the library up for sale. He offered it to cultural organizations, historical institutes, and various ministries. No one had the money. He tried universities, state and private, one after another. No takers. He left the library on loan at one university for a few months, until they started demanding rent. Then he tried private citizens. No one showed the slightest interest. The nation's history is an enigma, a lie, or a yawn.

The unhappy accountant dos Santos feels great relief when he finally succeeds in selling his library to the Tijuca Paper Factory, which turns all these books, magazines, and pamphlets into tinted toilet paper.

(371)

1984: Mexico City
Against Forgetting,

the only death that really kills, Carlos Quijano wrote what he wrote. This grouch and troublemaker was born in Montevideo as the century was born, and dies in exile, as Uruguay's military dictatorship is falling. He dies at work, preparing a new Mexican edition of his magazine *Marcha*.

Quijano celebrated contradictions. Heresy for others to him was a sign of life. He condemned imperialism, humiliator of nations and multitudes, and proclaimed that Latin America is destined to create a socialism worthy of the hopes of its prophets.

(356)

1984: Mexico City
The Resurrection of the Living

The Mexicans make a custom of eating death, a sugar or chocolate skeleton dripping with colored caramel. In addition to eating it, they sing it, dance it, drink it, and sleep it. Sometimes, to mock power and money, the people dress death in a monocle and frock coat, epaulettes and medals, but they prefer it stripped naked, racy, a bit drunk, their companion on festive outings.

Day of the Living, this Day of the Dead should be called, although on reflection it's all the same, because whatever comes goes and whatever goes comes, and in the last analysis the beginning of what begins is always the end of what ends.

"My grandfather is so tiny because he was born after me," says a child who knows what he's talking about.

1984: Estelí
Believing

They preside over childbirth. Giving life and light is their profession. With practiced hands they straighten the child if it's coming out wrong, and communicate strength and peace to the mother.

Today, the midwives of the Estelí villages and mountains close to Nicaragua's border are having a party to celebrate something that truly deserves joy: For a year now not one new baby in this region has died of tetanus. The midwives no longer cut umbilical cords with a machete, or burn them with tallow, or tie them off without disinfectant; and pregnant women get vaccines that protect the child living inside. Now no one here believes that vaccines are Russian witches' brews meant to turn Christians into Communists; and no one, or almost no one, believes that a newborn can die from the fixed stare of a drunken man or a menstruating woman.

This region, this war zone, suffers continuous harassment by the invaders.

"Here, we are in the alligator's mouth."

Many mothers go off to fight. The ones who stay share their breasts.

1984: Havana
Miguel at Seventy-Nine

Since the dawn of the century, this man has gone through hell and died several times over. Now, from exile, he still energetically accompanies his people in their war.

The dawn light always finds him up, shaved and conspiring. He could just as easily keep turning in the revolving door of memory;

but he doesn't know how to be deaf when the voices of these new times and the roads he still hasn't traveled call out to him.

And so at seventy-nine every day is a new birth for Miguel Mármol, old master of the art of constant rebirth.

1984: Paris

The Echoes Go Searching for the Voice

While writing words that loved people, Julio Cortázar was making his own journey, a journey backward through the tunnel of time. He was traveling from the end to the beginning, from discouragement to enthusiasm, from indifference to passion, from solitariness to solidarity. At almost seventy, he was a child of all ages at once.

A bird that flew toward the egg, Cortázar went forward by going back, year after year, day after day, toward the embrace of lovers who make the love that makes them. And now he dies, now he enters the earth, like a man who, entering a woman, returns to the place he comes from.

1984: Punta Santa Elena

The Eternal Embrace

They were found only recently in the wasteland that once was Zumpa beach in Ecuador. And here they are, in full sunlight, for anyone who wants to see: a man and a woman lying in embrace, sleeping lovers, out of eternity.

Excavating an Indian cemetery, an archaeologist came upon this pair of skeletons bound together by love. It was eight thousand years ago that the lovers of Zumpa committed the irreverence of dying without separating themselves, and anyone who approaches can see that death does not cause them the slightest concern.

Their splendid beauty is surprising, considering that they are such ugly bones in such an ugly desert, pure dryness and grayness; and more surprising is their modesty. These lovers, sleeping in the wind, seem not to have grasped that they have more mystery and grandeur than the pyramids of Teotihuacán or the sanctuary of Machu Picchu or the waterfalls of Iguazú.

1984: Violeta Parra Community
The Stolen Name

The dictatorship of General Pinochet changes the names of twenty bone-poor communities, tin and cardboard houses, on the outskirts of Santiago de Chile. In the rebaptism, the Violeta Parra community gets the name of some military hero. But its inhabitants refuse to bear this unchosen name. They are Violeta Parra or nothing.

A while back they had decided in unanimous assembly to name themselves after the campesina singer with the raspy voice who in her songs of struggle knew how to celebrate Chile's mysteries.

Violeta was sinful and saucy, given to guitar-strumming and long talks and falling in love, and with all her dancing and clowning around she kept burning the empanadas. *Thanks to life, which has given me so much,* she sang in her last song; and a turbulent love affair sent her off to her death.

(334 and 440)

1984: Tepic
The Found Name

In the mountains of Nayarit in Mexico, there was a community that had no name. For centuries this community of Huichol Indians had been looking for a name. Carlos González found one by sheer accident.

This Huichol had come to the city of Tepic to buy seeds and visit relatives. Crossing a garbage dump, he picked up a book thrown into the rubbish. It was years ago that Carlos had learned to read the Castilian language, and he could still just about manage it. Sitting in the shade of a projecting roof, he began to decipher the pages. The book spoke of a country with a strange name, which Carlos couldn't place but which had to be far from Mexico, and told a story of recent occurrence.

On the way home, walking up the mountain, Carlos continued reading. He couldn't tear himself away from this story of horror and bravery. The central character of the book was a man who had kept his word. Arriving at the village, Carlos announced euphorically: "*At last we have a name!*"

And he read the book aloud to everyone. This halting recital took him almost a week. Afterward, the hundred and fifty families voted. All in favor. Dancing and singing they performed the baptism.

So finally they have a name for themselves. This community bears the name of a worthy man who did not doubt at the moment of choice between treachery and death.

"I'm going to Salvador Allende," the wayfarers say now.

(466)

1984: Bluefields

Flying

Deep root, lofty trunk, dense foliage: from the center of the world rises a thornless tree, one of those trees that know how to give themselves to the birds. Around the tree whirl dancing couples, navel to navel, undulating to a music that wakens stones and sets fire to ice. As they dance, they dress and undress the tree with streaming ribbons of every color. On this tormented, continuously invaded, continuously bombarded coast of Nicaragua, the Maypole fiesta is celebrated as usual.

The tree of life knows that, whatever happens, the warm music spinning around it will never stop. However much death may come, however much blood may flow, the music will dance men and women as long as the air breathes them and the land plows and loves them.

1986: Montevideo

A Letter

Cedric Belfrage
Apartado Postal 630
Cuernavaca, Morelos
Mexico

My Dear Cedric:
Here goes the last volume of Memory of Fire. *As you'll see, it ends in 1984. Why not before, or after, I don't know. Perhaps because that was the last year of my exile, the end of a cycle, the end of a century;*

or perhaps because the book and I know that the last page is also the first.

Forgive me if it came out too long. Writing it was a joy for my hand; and now I feel more than ever proud of having been born in America, in this shit, in this marvel, during the century of the wind.

No more now, because I don't want to bury the sacred in palaver.

Abrazos,

Eduardo

(End of the third volume of
Memory of Fire.)

The Sources

1. Acebey, David. *Aquí también Domitila*. La Paz: n.p., 1984.
2. Adams, Willi Paul. *Los Estados Unidos de América*. Madrid: Siglo XXI, 1979.
3. Aguiar, Cláudio. *Caldeirão*. Rio de Janeiro: José Olympio, 1982.
4. Aguilar Camín, Héctor. *Saldos de la revolución. Cultura y política de México, 1910–1980*. Mexico City: Nueva Imagen, 1982.
5. Aguiló, Federico. *Significado socio-antropológico de las coplas al Cristo de Santa Vera Cruz*. Paper presented at the second Conference of Bolivian Studies, Cochabamba, 1984.
6. Agudelo, William. *El asalto a San Carlos. Testimonios de Solentiname*. Managua: Asoc. para el Desarrollo de Solentiname, 1982.
7. Alape, Arturo. *El bogotazo. Memorias del olvido*. Bogotá: Pluma, 1983.
8. ———. *La Paz, la violencia: testigos de excepción*. Bogotá: Planeta, 1985.
9. Alegría, Claribel, and D. J. Flakoll. *Cenizas de Izalco*. Barcelona; Seix Barral, 1966.
10. ———. *Nicaragua: la revolución sandinista. Una crónica política, 1855–1979*. Mexico: Era, 1982.
11. Alemán Ocampo, Carlos. *Y también enséñenles a leer*. Managua: Nueva Nicaragua, 1984.
12. Alfaro, Eloy, *Narraciones históricas*. (Preface by Malcolm D. Deas.) Quito: Editora Nacional, 1983.
13. Alfaro, Hugo. *Navegar es necesario*. Montevideo: Banda Oriental, 1985.
14. Ali, Muhammad. *The Greatest: My Own Story*. New York: Random House, 1975.
15. Allen, Frederick Lewis. *Apenas ayer. Historia informal de la decada del 20*. Buenos Aires: EUDEBA, 1964.
16. Almaraz Paz, Sergio. *Requiem para una república*. La Paz: Universidad, 1969.
17. ———. *El poder y la caída*. La Paz and Cochabamba: Amigos del Libro, 1969.
18. Almeida Bosque, Juan. *Contra el agua y el viento*. Havana: Casa de las Américas, 1985.
19. Amado, Jorge. *Los viejos marineros*. Barcelona: Seix Barral, 1983.
20. Amorim, Enrique. *El Quiroga que yo conocí*. Montevideo: Arca, 1983.
21. Anderson, Thomas. *El Salvador. Los sucesos políticos de 1932*. San José de Costa Rica: EDUCA, 1982.
22. Andrade, Joaquim Pedro de. *Garrincha, alegria do povo*. (Film produced by Barreto, Nogueira, and Richers.) Rio de Janeiro, 1963.

23. Andrade, Mário de. *Macunaíma, o herói sem nenhum caráter.* Belo Horizonte and Brasília: Itatiaia, 1984.
24. Andrade, Roberto. *Vida y muerte de Eloy Alfaro.* Quito: El Conejo, 1985.
25. Andreu, Jean. "Borges, escritor comprometido," in *Texto crítico,* No. 13, Veracruz, April–June 1979.
26. Antezana, Luis E. *Proceso y sentencia de la reforma agraria en Bolivia.* La Paz: Puerta del Sol, 1979.
27. Arenales, Angélica. *Siqueiros.* Mexico City: Bellas Artes, 1947.
28. Arévalo Martínez, Rafael. *Ecce Pericles. La tiranía de Manuel Estrada Cabrera en Guatemala.* San José de Costa Rica: EDUCA, 1983.
29. Arguedas, Alcides. *Pueblo enfermo.* La Paz: Juventud, 1985.
30. Arguedas, José María. *El zorro de arriba y el zorro de abajo.* Buenos Aires: Losada, 1971.
31. ———. *Formación de una cultura nacional indoamericana.* Mexico City: Siglo XXI, 1975.
32. Aricó, José (ed.). *Mariátegui y los orígenes del marxismo latinoamericano.* Mexico City: Pasado y Presente, 1980.
33. Azuela, Mariano. *Los de abajo.* Mexico City: FCE, 1960.
34. Baptista Gumucio, Mariano. *Historia contemporánea de Bolivia, 1930–1978.* La Paz: Gisbert, 1978.
35. Barrán, José P., and Benjamín Nahum. *Batlle, los estancieros y el Imperio Británico. Las primeras reformas, 1911–1913.* Montevideo: Banda Oriental, 1983.
36. Barreto, Lima. *Os bruzundangas.* São Paulo: Ática, 1985.
37. Barrett, Rafael. *El dolor paraguayo.* (Preface by Augusto Roa Bastos.) Caracas: Ayacucho, 1978.
38. Bayer, Osvaldo. *Los vengadores de la Patagonia trágica.* Buenos Aires: Galerna, 1972, 1974; and Wuppertal: Hammer, 1977.
39. Beals, Carleton. *Banana Gold.* Managua: Nueva Nicaragua, 1983.
40. ———. *Porfirio Díaz.* Mexico City: Domés, 1982.
41. Belfrage, Cedric. *The American Inquisition, 1945–1960.* Indianapolis: Bobbs-Merrill, 1973.
42. Bell, John Patrick. *Guerra civil en Costa Rica. Los sucesos políticos de 1948.* San José de Costa Rica: EDUCA, 1981.
43. Beloch, Israel, and Alzira Alves de Abreu. *Dicionário histórico-biográfico brasileiro, 1930–1983.* Rio de Janeiro: Fundação Getúlio Vargas, 1984.
44. Benítez, Fernando. *Lázaro Cárdenas y la revolución mexicana. El porfirismo.* Mexico City: FCE, 1977.
45. ———. *Lázaro Cárdenas y la revolución mexicana. El cardenismo.* Mexico City: FCE, 1980.
46. ———. *Los indios de México* (Vol. 3). Mexico City: Era, 1979.

47. ———. *La ciudad de México, 1325–1982.* Barcelona and Mexico City: Salvat, 1981, 1982.
48. Benítez, Fernando, *et al. Juan Rulfo, homenaje nacional.* Mexico City: Bellas Artes/SEP, 1980.
49. Benvenuto, Ofelia Machado de. *Delmira Agustini.* Montevideo: Ministerio de Instrucción Pública, 1944.
50. Bernays, Edward. *Biography of an Idea.* New York: Simon and Schuster, 1965.
51. Berry, Mary Frances, and John W. Blassingame. *Long Memory: The Black Experience in America.* New York and Oxford: Oxford University Press, 1982.
52. Bezerra, João. *Como dei cabo de Lampião.* Recife: Massangana, 1983.
53. Bingham, Hiram. *Machu Picchu, la ciudad perdida de los incas.* Madrid: Rodas, 1972.
54. Bliss, Michael. *The Discovery of Insulin.* Toronto: McClelland and Stewart, 1982.
55. Bodard, Lucien. *Masacre de indios en el Amazonas.* Caracas: Tiempo Nuevo, 1970.
56. Bolaños, Pío. *Génesis de la intervención norteamericana en Nicaragua.* Managua: Nueva Nicaragua, 1984.
57. Bonfil Batalla, Guillermo. *El universo del amate.* Mexico City: Museo de Culturas Populares, 1982.
58. Borge, Tomás. *Carlos, el amanecer ya no es una tentación.* Havana: Casa de las Américas, 1980.
59. Borges, Jorge Luis. *Obras completas, 1923–1972.* Buenos Aires: Emecé, 1974.
60. Bosch, Juan. *Trujillo: causas de una tiranía sin ejemplo.* Caracas: Las Novedades, 1959.
61. ———. "Crisis de la democracia de América en la República Dominicana," in *Panoramas,* No. 14, supplement, Mexico City, 1964.
62. ———. *La revolución de abril.* Santo Domingo: Alfa y Omega, 1981.
63. ———. *Clases sociales en la República Dominicana.* Santo Domingo: PLD, 1982.
64. Bravo-Elizondo, Pedro. "La gran huelga del salitre en 1907," in *Araucaria,* No. 33, Madrid, 1986.
65. Branford, Sue, and Oriel Glock. *The Last Frontier, Fighting Over Land in the Amazon.* London: Zed, 1985.
66. Brecht, Bertolt. *Diario de trabajo.* Buenos Aires: Nueva Visión, 1977.
67. Buarque de Holanda, Sérgio. *Visão do paraíso.* São Paulo: Universidad, 1969.
68. Buitrago, Alejandra. *Conversando con los gamines.* (Unpublished.)
69. Bullrich, Francisco, *et al. América Latina en su arquitectura.* Mexico City: Siglo XXI, 1983.

70. Buñuel, Luis. *Mi último suspiro (memorias)*. Barcelona: Plaza y Janés, 1982.
71. ———. *Los olvidados*. Mexico City: Era, 1980.
72. Burgos, Elisabeth. *Me llamo Rigoberta Menchú y así me nació la conciencia*. Barcelona: Argos-Vergara, 1983.
73. Cabezas, Omar. *La montaña es algo más que una inmensa estepa verde*. Managua: Nueva Nicaragua, 1982.
74. Cabral, Sergio. *As escolas de samba: o quê, quem, como, quando e porquê*. Rio de Janeiro: Fontana, 1974.
75. ———. *Pixinguinha. Vida e obra*. Rio de Janeiro: Lidador, 1980.
76. Caputo, Alfredo. *Educación moral y cívica*. Montevideo: Casa del Estudiante, 1978. See also textbooks by Dora Noblía and Graciela Márquez, and by Sofía Corchs and Alex Pereyra Formoso.
77. Cardenal, Ernesto. *Antología*. Managua: Nueva Nicaragua, 1984.
78. Cárdenas, Lázaro. *Ideario político*. Mexico City: Era, 1976.
79. Cardona Pena, Alfredo. *El monstruo en el laberinto. Conversaciones con Diego Rivera*. Mexico City: Diana, 1980.
80. Cardoza y Aragón, Luis. *La nube y el reloj. Pintura mexicana contemporánea*. Mexico City, UNAM, 1940.
81. ———. *La revolución guatemalteca*. Mexico City: Cuadernos Americanos, 1955.
82. ———. *Diego Rivera. Los frescos en la Secretaría de Educación Pública*. Mexico City: SEP, 1980.
83. ———. *Orozco*. Mexico City: FCE, 1983.
84. Carías, Marco Virgilio, and Daniel Slutzky. *La guerra inútil. Análisis socio-económico del conflicto entre Honduras y El Salvador*. San José de Costa Rica: EDUCA, 1971.
85. Carpentier, Alejo. *Tientos y diferencias*. Montevideo: Arca, 1967.
86. ———. *La música en Cuba*. Havana: Letras Cubanas, 1979.
87. Carr, Raymond. *Puerto Rico: A Colonial Experiment*. New York: Vintage, 1984.
88. Casaus, Víctor. *Girón en la memoria*. Havana: Casa de las Américas. 1970.
89. Cassá, Roberto. *Capitalismo y dictadura*. Santo Domingo: Universidad, 1982.
90. Castro, Fidel. *La revolución cubana, 1953–1962*. Mexico City: Era, 1972.
91. ———. *Hoy somos un pueblo entero*. Mexico City: Siglo XXI, 1973.
92. Castro, Josué de. *Geografia da fome*. Rio de Janeiro: O Cruzeiro, 1946.
93. Cepeda Samudio, Álvaro. *La casa grande*. Buenos Aires: Jorge Álvarez, 1967.
94. Central Intelligence Agency. *Manuales de sabotaje y guerra psicológica*

para derrocar al gobierno sandinista. (Preface by Philip Agee.) Madrid: Fundamentos, 1985.

95. Cervantes Angulo, José. *La noche de las luciérnagas.* Bogotá: Plaza y Janés, 1980.
96. Céspedes, Augusto. *Sangre de mestizos. Relatos de la guerra del Chaco.* La Paz: Juventud, 1983.
97. ———. *El presidente colgado.* La Paz: Juventud, 1985.
98. "Cien años de lucha." Various authors, special edition of *Cuba*, Havana, October 1968.
99. Clark, Ronald William. *Edison: The Man Who Made the Future.* New York: Putnam, 1977.
100. Clase, Pablo. *Rubi. La vida de Porfirio Rubirosa.* Santo Domingo: Cosmos, 1979.
101. Crassweller, Robert D. *Trujillo. La tragica aventura del poder personal.* Barcelona: Bruguera, 1968.
102. Crawley, Eduardo. *Dictators Never Die: A Portrait of Nicaragua and the Somozas.* London: Hurst, 1979.
103. Colombres, Adolfo. *Seres sobrenaturales de la cultura popular argentina.* Buenos Aires: Del Sol, 1984.
104. Coluccio, Félix. *Diccionario folklórico argentino.* Buenos Aires: n.p., 1948.
105. Collier, James Lincoln. *Louis Armstrong: An American Genius.* New York: Oxford University Press, 1983.
106. Comisión Argentina por los Derechos Humanos. *Argentina: proceso al genocidio.* Madrid: Querejeta, 1977.
107. Comisión Nacional sobre la Desaparición de Personas. *Nunca más.* Buenos Aires: EUDEBA, 1984.
108. Committee on Foreign Relations, U.S. Senate. *Briefing on the Cuban Situation.* Washington, D.C., May 2, 1961.
109. Committee to Study Governmental Operations with Respect to Intelligence Activities, U.S. Senate. *Alleged Assassination Plots Involving Foreign Leaders: An Interim Report.* Washington, D.C., November 20, 1975.
110. Condarco Morales, Ramiro. *Zárate, el temible Willka. Historia de la rebelión indígena de 1899.* La Paz: n.p., 1982.
111. Condori Mamani, Gregorio. *De nosotros, los runas.* (Testimonies collected by Ricardo Valderrama and Carmen Escalante.) Madrid: Alfaguara, 1983.
112. Constantine, Mildred. *Tina Modotti. Una vida frágil.* Mexico City: FCE, 1979.
113. Cooke, Alistair. *America.* New York: Knopf, 1977.
114. Cordero Velásquez, Luis. *Gómez y las fuerzas vivas.* Caracas: Lumego, 1985.

115. Corrêa, Marcos Sá. *1964 visto e comentado pela Casa Branca*. Porto Alegre: L y PM, 1977.
116. Corretger, Juan Antonio. *Albizu Campos*. Montevideo: El Siglo Ilustrado, 1969.
117. Cueva, Gabriela de la. *Memorias de una caraqueña de antes del diluvio*. San Sebastián: n.p., 1982.
118. Cummins, Lejeune. *Don Quijote en burro*. Managua: Nueva Nicaragua, 1983.
119. Cunha, Euclides da. "A margem da história," in *Obra completa*. Rio de Janeiro: Aguilar, 1966.
120. Chandler, Billy Jaynes. *Lampião, o rei dos cangaceiros*. Rio de Janeiro: Paz e Terra, 1980.
121. Chaplin, Charles. *My Autobiography*. New York: Simon and Schuster, 1964.
122. Christensen, Eleanor Ingalls. *The Art of Haiti*. Philadelphia: Art Alliance, 1975.
123. Chumbita, Hugo. *Bairoletto. Prontuario y leyenda*. Buenos Aires: Marlona, 1974.
124. Daher, José Miguel. "Méndez: el Partido Demócrata de EE. UU. es socio de la sedición," in *La Mañana*, Montevideo, October 9, 1976.
125. Dalton, Roque. *Las historias prohibidas del Pulgarcito*. Mexico City: Siglo XXI, 1974.
126. ———. *Miguel Mármol. Los sucesos de 1932 en El Salvador*. Havana: Casa de las Américas, 1983.
127. ———. *Poesía*. (Mario Benedetti, ed.) Havana: Casa de las Américas, 1980.
128. Dardis, Tom. *Keaton: The Man Who Wouldn't Lie Down*. New York: Scribners, 1979.
129. Darío, Rubén. *Poesía*. (Preface by Angel Rama.) Caracas: Ayacucho, 1977.
130. Davies, Marion. *The Times We Had: Life With William Randolph Hearst*. Indianapolis and New York: Bobbs–Merrill, 1975.
131. Delgado Aparaín, Mario. "Mire que sos loco, Obdulio," in *Jaque*, Montevideo, January 25, 1985.
132. Deutscher, Isaac. *The Prophet Outcast: Trotsky, 1929–1940*. London: Oxford University Press, 1963.
133. Della Cava, Ralph. *Milagre em Joaseiro*. Rio de Janeiro: Paz e Terra, 1977.
134. *Diario de Juicio, El*. (Court record of trial of heads of Argentine dictatorship.) Buenos Aires: Perfil, 1985.
135. *El Nacional* and *Ultimas Noticias*, Caracas, August 28–29, 1977.
136. Dias, José Humberto. "Benjamin Abrahão, o mascate que filmou Lam-

pião," in *Cadernos de Pesquisa*, No. 1, Rio de Janeiro, Embrafilme, September 1984.
137. *Documentos de la CIA. Cuba acusa.* Havana: Ministerio de Cultura, 1981.
138. *Documentos secretos de la I.T.T.* Santiago de Chile: Quimantú, 1972.
139. Dorfman, Ariel, and Armand Mattelart. *Para leer al Pato Donald.* Mexico City: Siglo XXI, 1978.
140. Dower, John. *War Without Mercy: Race and Power in the Pacific War.* New York: Pantheon, 1986.
141. Dreifuss, René Armand. *1964: A conquista do Estado. Ação politica, poder e golpe de classe.* Petrópolis: Vozes, 1981.
142. Drot, Jean-Marie. *Journal de voyage chez les peintres de la Fête et du vaudou en Haiti.* Geneva: Skira, 1974.
143. Duhalde, Eduardo Luis. *El estado terrorista argentino.* Buenos Aires: El Caballito, 1983.
144. Dumont, Alberto Santos. *O que eu vi, o que nós veremos.* Rio de Janeiro: Tribunal de Contas, 1983.
145. Duncan, Isadora. *My Life.* New York: Liveright, 1955.
146. Durst, Rogério. *Madame Satã: com o diabo no corpo.* São Paulo: Brasiliense, 1985.
147. Eco, Umberto. *Apocalíptis e integrados ante la cultura de masas.* Barcelona: Lumen, 1968.
148. Edison, Thomas Alva. *Diary.* Old Greenwich: Chatham, 1971.
149. Edwards, Audrey, and Gary Wohl. *Muhammad Ali. The People's Champ.* Boston and Toronto: Little Brown, 1977.
150. Einstein, Albert. *Notas autobiográficas.* Madrid: Alianza, 1984.
151. Eisenstein, S. M. *¡Que viva México!.* (Preface by José de la Colina.) Mexico City: Era, 1971.
152. Elgrably, Jordan. "A través del fuego. Entrevista con James Baldwin," in *Quimera*, No. 41, Barcelona, 1984.
153. Enzensberger, Hans Magnus. *Política y delito.* Barcelona: Seix Barral, 1968.
154. Escobar Bethancourt, Rómulo. *Torrijos: ¡colonia americana, no!* Bogotá: Valencia, 1981.
155. Faingold, Raquel Zimerman de. *Memorias de una familia inmigrante.* (Unpublished.)
156. Fairbank, John K. *The United States and China.* Cambridge: Harvard University Press, 1958.
157. Fajardo Sainz, Humberto. *La herencia de la coca. Pasado y presente de la cocaína.* La Paz: Universo, 1984.
158. Falcão, Edgard de Cerqueira. *A incompreensão de uma época.* São Paulo: Tribunais, 1971.

159. Fals Borda, Orlando. *Historia doble de la Costa. Resistencia en el San Jorge.* Bogotá: Valencia, 1984.
160. ———. *Historia doble de la Costa. Retorno a la tierra.* Bogotá: Valencia, 1986.
161. Faría Castro, Haroldo and Flavia de. "Los mil y un sombreros de la cultura boliviana," in *Geomundo*, Vol. 8, No. 6, Santiago de Chile, June 1984.
162. Fast, Howard. *The Passion of Sacco and Vanzetti: A New England Legend.* Westport, Conn.: Greenwood, 1972.
163. Faulkner, William. *Absalom, Absalom.* New York: Modern Library, 1951.
164. Federación Universitaria de Córdoba. *La reforma universitaria.* Buenos Aires: FUBA, 1959.
165. Feinstein, Elaine. *Bessie Smith, Empress of the Blues.* New York: Viking, 1985.
166. Folino, Norberto. *Barceló, Ruggierito y el populismo oligárquico.* Buenos Aires: Falbo, 1966.
167. Foner, Philip S. *The Case of Joe Hill.* New York: International Publications, 1965.
168. Ford, Henry (with Samuel Crowther). *My Life and Work.* New York: Doubleday, 1926.
169. Foxley, A. *Experimentos neoliberales en América Latina.* Santiago de Chile: CIEPLAN, 1982.
170. Freyre, Gilberto. *Casa grande e senzala.* Rio de Janeiro: José Olympio, 1966.
171. Fróes, Leonardo. *A casa de flor.* Rio de Janeiro: Funarte, 1978.
172. Frontaura Argandoña, Manuel. *La revolución boliviana.* La Paz and Cochabama: Amigos del Libro, 1974.
173. Gabetta, Carlos. *Todos somos subversivos.* Buenos Aires: Bruguera, 1983.
174. Gaitán, Jorge Eliécer. *1928. La masacre de las bananeras.* Bogotá: Los Comuneros, n.d.
175. Galarza Zavala, Jaime. *Quiénes mataron a Roldós.* Quito: Solitierra, 1982.
176. Galasso, Norberto, *et al. La década infame.* Buenos Aires: Carlos Pérez, 1969.
177. Galíndez, Jesús. *La era de Trujillo.* Buenos Aires: Sudamericana, 1962.
178. Gálvez, Manuel. *Vida de Hipólito Yrigoyen.* Buenos Aires: Tor, 1951.
179. Gálvez, William. *Camilo, señor de la vanguardia.* Havana: Ciencias Sociales, 1979.
180. Gandarillas, Arturo G. "Detrás de linderos del odio: laimes y jucumanis," in *Hoy*, La Paz, October 16, 1973.

181. Garcés, Joan. *El estado y los problemas tácticos en el gobierno de Allende.* Mexico City: Siglo XXI, 1974.
182. García, F. Chris. *Chicano Politics: Readings.* New York: n.p., 1973.
183. García Canclini, Néstor. *Las culturas populares en el capitalismo.* Havana: Casa de las Américas, 1982.
184. García Lupo, Rogelio. "Mil trescientos dientes de Gardel," in *Marcha,* No. 1004, Montevideo, April 8, 1960.
185. ————. *Diplomacia secreta y rendición incondicional.* Buenos Aires: Legasa, 1983.
186. García Márquez, Gabriel. *La hojarasca.* Buenos Aires: Sudamericana, 1969.
187. ————. *Cien años de soledad.* Buenos Aires: Sudamericana, 1967.
188. ————. "Algo más sobre literatura y realidad," in *El País,* Madrid, July 1, 1981.
189. ————. "La soledad de la América Latina" (Nobel Prize acceptance speech), in *Casa,* No. 137, Havana, March–April 1983.
190. Garmendia, Hermann. *María Lionza, ángel y demonio.* Caracas: Seleven, 1980.
191. Garrido, Atilio. "Obdulio Varela. Su vida, su gloria y su leyenda," in *El Diario,* "Estrellas deportivas" supplement, Montevideo, September 20, 1977.
192. Gallegos Lara, Joaquín. *Las cruces sobre el agua.* Quito: El Conejo, 1985.
193. Gil, Pío. *El Cabito.* Caracas: Biblioteca de autores y temas tachirenses, 1971.
194. Gilly, Adolfo. *La revolución interrumpida.* Mexico City: El Caballito, 1971.
195. Gilman, Charlotte Perkins. *Herland.* (Preface by Ann J. Lane.) New York: Pantheon, 1979.
196. ————. *The Yellow Wallpaper.* New York: Feminist Press, 1973.
197. Goldman, Albert. *Elvis.* New York: McGraw-Hill, 1981.
198. Gómez Yera, Sara. "La rumba," in *Cuba,* Havana, December 1964.
199. González, José Luis. *El país de cuatro pisos y otros ensayos.* San Juan de Puerto Rico: Huracán, 1980.
200. González, Luis. *Pueblos en vilo.* Mexico City: FCE, 1984.
201. ————. *Historia de la Revolución Mexicana, 1934–1940: Los días del presidente Cárdenas.* Mexico City: Colegio de México, 1981.
202. González Bermejo, Ernesto. "Interview with Atahualpa Yupanqui," in *Crisis,* No. 29, Buenos Aires, September 1975.
203. ————. "¿Qué pasa hoy en el Perú?," in *Crisis,* No. 36, Buenos Aires, April 1976.
204. ————. *Las manos en el fuego.* Montevideo: Banda Oriental, 1985.

205. Granados, Pedro. *Carpas de México. Leyendas, anécdotas e historia del teatro popular.* Mexico City: Universo, 1984.
206. Grigulevich, José. *Pancho Villa.* Havana: Casa de las Américas, n.d.
207. Grupo, Areíto. *Contra viento y marea.* Havana: Casa de las Américas, 1978.
208. Guerra, Ramiro. *La expansión territorial de los Estados Unidos.* Havana: Ciencias Sociales, 1975.
209. Guevara, Ernesto Che. *Pasajes de la guerra revolucionaria.* Havana: Arte y Literatura, 1975.
210. ———. "Camilo, imagen del pueblo," in *Granma,* Havana, October 25, 1967.
211. ———. *El socialismo y el hombre nuevo.* Mexico City: Siglo XXI, 1977.
212. ———. *El diario del Che en Bolivia.* Bilbao: Zalla, 1968.
213. ———. *Escritos y discursos.* Havana: Ciencias Sociales, 1977.
214. Guiles, Fred Lawrence. *Norma Jean.* New York: McGaw-Hill, 1969.
215. Guillén, Nicolás. "Un olivo en la colina," in *Hoy,* Havana, April 24, 1960.
216. Guzmán, Martín Luis. *El águila y la serpiente.* Mexico City: Cía. General de Ediciones, 1977.
217. Guzmán Campos, Germán (with Orlando Fals Borda and Eduardo Umaña Luna). *La violencia en Colombia.* Bogotá: Valencia, 1980.
218. Hardwick, Richard. *Charles Richard Drew: Pioneer in Blood Research.* New York: Scribners, 1967.
219. Hellman, Lillian. *Scoundrel Time.* Boston: Little Brown, 1976.
220. Hemingway, Ernest. *Enviado especial.* Barcelona, Planeta, 1968.
221. Henault, Mirta. *Alicia Moreau de Justo.* Buenos Aires: Centro Editor, 1983.
222. Heras León, Eduardo. Interview with Miguel Mármol. (Unpublished.)
223. Hermann, Hamlet. *Francis Caamāno.* Santo Domingo: Alfa y Omega, 1983.
224. Herrera, Hayden. *Frida. A Biography of Frida Kahlo.* New York: Harper and Row, 1983.
225. Hervia Cosculluela, Manuel. *Pasaporte 11.333. Ocho años con la CIA.* Havana: Ciencias Sociales, 1978.
226. Hidrovo Velasquez, Horacio. *Un hombre y un río.* Portoviejo: Gregorio: 1982.
227. Hobsbawm, Eric J. *Primitive Rebels.* New York: Norton, 1965.
228. Hoffman, Banesh. *Einstein.* Barcelona: Salvat, 1984.
229. Huezo, Francisco. *Últimos días de Rubén Darío.* Managua: Renacimiento, 1925.
230. Huneeus, Pablo. *La cultura huachaca o el aporte de la televisión.* Santiago de Chile: Nueva Generación, 1981.

231. ———. *Lo comido y lo bailado.* . . . Santiago de Chile: Nueva Generación, 1984.

232. Hurt, Henry. *Reasonable Doubt: An Investigation into the Assassination of John F. Kennedy.* New York: Holt, Rinehart, and Winston, 1986.

233. Huxley, Francis. *The Invisibiles.* London: Hart-Davis, 1966.

234. Ianni, Octavio. *El Estado capitalista en la época de Cárdenas.* Mexico City: Era, 1985.

235. Informes sobre la violación de derechos humanos en el Uruguay, realizados por Amnesty International, la Comisión de Derechos Humanos y el Comité de Derechos Humanos de las Naciones Unidas y La Comisión Interamericana de Derechos Humanos de la OEA. [Accounts of the violation of human rights in Uruguay. Collected by Amnesty International; the Committee on Human Rights of the United Nations; and the Inter-American Commission on Human Rights of the OAS.]

236. Instituto de Edustios del Sandinismo. *Ni vamos a poder caminar de tantas flores.* (Testimonies of Sandino's soldiers; unpublished).

237. ———. *El sandinismo. Documentos básicos.* Managua: Nueva Nicaragua, 1983.

238. ———. *La insurrección popular sandinista en Masaya.* Managua: Nueva Nicaragua, 1982.

239. ———. *¡Y se armó la runga!* Managua: Nueva Nicaragua, 1982.

240. Jaramillo-Levi, Enrique, *et al. Una explosión en América: el canal de Panamá.* Mexico City: Siglo XXI, 1976.

241. Jenks, Leland H. *Nuestra colonia de Cuba.* Buenos Aires: Palestra, 1961.

242. Johnson, James Weldon. *Along This Way.* New York: Viking, 1933.

243. Jonas Bodenheimer, Susanne. *La ideología socialdemócrata en Costa Rica.* San José de Costa Rica: EDUCA, 1984.

244. Julião, Francisco, and Angélica Rodríguez. Testimony of Gregoria Zúñiga in "Los últimos soldados de Zapata," in *Crisis,* No. 21, Buenos Aires, January 1975.

245. Katz, Friedrich. *La servidumbre agraria en México en la época porfiriana.* Mexico City: Era, 1982.

246. ———. *La guerra secreta en México.* Mexico City: Era, 1983.

247. Kerr, Elizabeth M. *William Faulkner's Gothic Domain.* Port Washington, New York: Kennikat, 1979.

248. Klare, Michael T., and Nancy Stein. *Armas y poder en América Latina.* Mexico City: Era, 1978.

249. Kobal, John. *Rita Hayworth: The Time, the Place, and the Woman.* Norton, 1978.

250. Krehm, William. *Democracia y tiranías en el Caribe.* Buenos Aires: Palestra, 1959.

251. Labourt, José. *Sana, sana, culito de rana.* . . . Santo Domingo: Taller, 1979.
252. Landaburu, Jon, and Roberto Pineda. "Cuentos del diluvio de fuego," in *Maguaré*, No. 1, Bogotá, Universidad Nacional, June 1981.
253. Landes, Ruth. *A cidade das mulheres.* Rio de Janeiro: Civilização Brasileira, 1967.
254. Lane, Mark, and Dick Gregory. *Code Name Zorro: The Murder of Martin Luther King.* Englewood Cliffs, N.J.: Prentice-Hall, 1977.
255. Lapassade, Georges, and Marco Aurélio Luz. *O segredo da macumba.* Rio de Janeiro: Paz e Terra, 1972.
256. Larco, Juan. *et al. Recopilación de textos sobre José María Arguedas.* Havana: Casa de las Américas, 1976.
257. Latin America Bureau. *Narcotráfico y política.* Madrid: IEPALA, 1982.
258. Lauer, Mirko. *Crítica de la artesanía. Plástica y sociedad en los Andes peruanos.* Lima: DESCO, 1982.
259. La Valle, Raniero, and Linda Bimbi. *Marianella e i suoi fratelli. Una storia latinoamericana.* Milan: Feltrinelli, 1983.
260. Lavretski, I., and Adolfo Gilly. *Francisco Villa.* Mexico City: Macehual, 1978.
261. Levy, Alan. *Ezra Pound: The Voice of Silence.* Sag Harbor, N.Y.: Permanent, 1983.
262. Lichello, Robert. *Pioneer in Blood Plasma: Dr. Charles R. Drew.* New York: Messner, 1968.
263. Lima, Lourenço Moreira. *A coluna Prestes (marchas e combates).* São Paulo: Alfa-Omega, 1979.
264. Loetscher, Hugo. *El descubrimiento de Suiza por los indios.* Cochabamba: Amigos del Libro, 1983.
265. Loor, Wilfrido. *Eloy Alfaro.* Quito: n.p., 1982.
266. López, Oscar Luis. *La radio en Cuba.* Havana: Letras Cubanas, 1981.
267. López, Santos. *Memorias de un soldado.* Managua: FER, 1974.
268. López Virgil, José Ignacio. *Radio Pío XII: una mina de coraje.* Quito: Aler/Pío XII, 1984.
269. Lowenthal, Abraham F. *The Dominican Intervention.* Cambridge: Harvard University Press, 1972.
270. Luna, Félix. *Atahualpa Yupanqui.* Madrid: Júcar, 1974.
271. Machado, Carlos. *Historia de los orientales.* Montevideo: Banda Oriental, 1985.
272. Magalhães Júnior, R. *Rui. O homem e o mito.* Rio de Janeiro: Civilização Brasileira, 1964.
273. Maggiolo, Oscar J. "Política de desarrollo científico y tecnológico de América Latina," in *Gaceta de la Universidad*, Montevideo, March–April 1968.
274. Mailer, Norman. *Marilyn.* New York: Grossett and Dunlap, 1973.

275. Maldonado-Denis, Manuel. *Puerto Rico: mito y realidad*. San Juan de Puerto Rico: Antillana, 1969.
276. Manchester, William. *The Glory and the Dream: A Narrative History of America*. Boston: Little Brown, 1972.
277. Mariátegui, José Carlos. *Obras*. Havana: Casa de las Américas, 1982.
278. Marín, Germán. *Una historia fantástica y calculada: la CIA en el país de los chilenos*. Mexico City: Siglo XXI, 1976.
279. Mário Filho. *O negro no futebol brasileiro*. Rio de Janeiro: Civilização Brasileira, 1964.
280. Mariz, Vasco. *Heitor Villa-Lobos, compositor brasileiro*. Rio de Janeiro: Zahar, 1983.
281. Martin, John Bartlow. *El destino dominicano. La crisis dominicana desde la caída de Trujillo hasta la guerra civil*. Santo Domingo: Editora Santo Domingo, 1975.
282. Martínez, Thomas M. "Advertising and Racism: The Case of the Mexican-American," in *El Grito*, Summer 1969.
283. Martínez Assad, Carlos. *El laboratorio de la revolución: el Tabasco garridista*. Mexico City: Siglo XXI, 1979.
284. Martínez Moreno, Carlos. "Color del 900," in *Capítulo oriental*. Montevideo: CEDAL, 1968.
285. Matos, Cláudia. *Acertei no milhar. Samba e malandragem no tempo de Getúlio*. Rio de Janeiro: Paz e Terra, 1982.
286. Matos Díaz, Eduardo. *Anecdotario de una tiranía*. Santo Domingo: Taller, 1976.
287. Mattelart, Armand. *La cultura como empresa multinacional*. Mexico City: Era, 1974.
288. May, Stacy, and Galo Plaza. *United States Business Performance Abroad: The Case Study of United Fruit Company in Latin America*. Washington, D.C.: National Planning, 1958.
289. Medina Castro, Manuel. *Estados Unidos y América Latina, siglo XIX*. Havana: Casa de las Américas, 1968.
290. Mella, Julio Antonio. *Escritos revolucionarios*. Mexico City: Siglo XXI, 1978.
291. Mende, Tibor. *La Chine et son ombre*. Paris: Seuil, 1960.
292. Méndez Capote, Renée. *Memorias de una cubanita que nació con el siglo*. Santa Clara (de Cuba): Universidad, 1963.
293. Mendoza, Vincente T. *El corrido mexicano*. Mexico City: FCE, 1976.
294. Mera, Juan León. *Cantares del pueblo ecuatoriano*. Quito: Banco Central, n.d.
295. Métraux, Alfred. *Haiti. La terre, les hommes et les dieux*. Neuchâtel: La Baconnière, 1957.
296. Meyer, Eugenia. Interview with Juan Olivera López. (Unpublished.)

297. Meyer, Jean. *La cristiada. La guerra de los cristeros.* Mexico City: Siglo XXI, 1973.
298. Molina, Gabriel. *Diario de Girón.* Havana: Política, 1983.
299. Monsiváis, Carlos. *Días de guardar.* Mexico City: Era, 1970.
300. ———. *Amor perdido.* Mexico City: Era, 1977.
301. Mora, Arnoldo. *Monseñor Romero.* San José de Costa Rica: EDUCA, 1981.
302. Morais, Fernando. *Olga.* São Paulo: Alfa-Omega, 1985.
303. Morel, Edmar. *A revolta da chibata.* Rio de Janeiro: Graal, 1979.
304. Morison, Samuel E., and Henry S. Commager. *A Concise History of the American Republic.* New York: Oxford University Press, 1977.
305. Moussinac, Léon. *Sergei Michailovitch Eisenstein.* Paris: Seghers, 1964.
306. Mota, Carlos Guilherme. *Ideologia da cultura brasileira, 1933–1974.* São Paulo: Ática, 1980.
307. Maurão Filho, Olympio. *Memórias: a verdade de um revolucionário.* Porto Alegre: L y PM, 1978.
308. Murúa, Dámaso. *En Brasil crece un almendro.* Mexico City: El Caballito, 1984.
309. ———. *40 cuentos del Güilo Mentiras.* Mexico City: Crea, 1984.
310. Nalé Roxlo, Conrado, and Mabel Mármol. *Genio y figura de Alfonsina Storni.* Buenos Aires: EUDEBA, 1966.
311. Navarro, Marysa. *Evita.* Buenos Aires: Corregidor, 1981.
312. Nepomuceno, Eric. *Hemingway: Madrid no era una fiesta.* Madrid: Altalena, 1978.
313. Neruda, Pablo. *Confieso que he vivido.* Barcelona: Seix Barral, 1974.
314. ———. *Obras completas.* Buenos Aires: Losada, 1973.
315. Niemeyer, Oscar. Texts, drawings, and photos in a special edition of *Módulo,* Rio de Janeiro, June 1983.
316. Nimuendajú, Curt. *Mapa etno-histórico.* Rio de Janeiro: Fundaçao Nacional Pró-Memória, 1981.
317. Nosiglia, Julio E. *Botín de guerra.* Buenos Aires: Tierra Fértil, 1985.
318. Novo, Salvador. *Cocina mexicana. Historia gastronómica de la ciudad de México.* Mexico City: Porrúa, 1979.
319. Núñez Jiménez, Antonio. *Wifredo Lam.* Havana: Letras Cubanas, 1982.
320. Núñez Téllez, Carlos. *Un pueblo en armas.* Managua: FSLN, 1980.
321. O'Connor, Harvey. *La crisis mundial del petróleo.* Buenos Aires: Platina, 1963.
322. Olmo, Rosa del. *Los chigüines de Somoza.* Caracas: Ateneo, 1980.
323. Orozco, José Clemente. *Autobiografía.* Mexico: Era, 1979.
324. Ortiz, Fernando. *Los bailes y el teatro de los negros en el folklore de Cuba.* Havana: Letras Cubanas, 1981.
325. Ortiz Echagüe, Fernando. "Sobre la importancia de la vaca argentina

en París." Originally published in 1930; republished by Rogelio García Lupo in *Crisis*," No. 29, Buenos Aires, September 1975.

326. Ortiz Letelier, Fernando. *El movimiento obrero en Chile. Antecedentes 1891–1919*. Madrid: Michay, 1985.

327. Page, Joseph A. *Perón*. Buenos Aires: Vergara, 1984.

328. Paleari, Antonio. *Diccionario mágico jujeño*. San Salvador de Jujuy: Pachamama, 1982.

329. Paliza, Héctor. "Los burros fusilados," in *Presagio*, Culiacán, Sinaloa, No. 10, April 1978.

330. Paoli, Francisco J., and Enrique Montalvo. *El socialismo olvidado de Yucatán*. Mexico City: Siglo XXI, 1980.

331. Paramio, Ludolfo. *Mito e ideología*. Madrid: Corazón, 1971.

332. Pareja Diezcanseco, Alfredo. *Ecuador. La república de 1830 a nuestros días*. Quito: Universidad, 1979.

333. Pareja y Paz Soldán, José. *Juan Vicente Gómez. Un fenómeno telúrico*. Caracas: Ávila Gráfica, 1951.

334. Parra, Violeta. *Violeta del pueblo*. (Javier Martínez Reverte, ed.) Madrid: Visor, 1983.

335. Pasley, F. D. *Al Capone*. (Preface by Andrew Sinclair.) Madrid: Alianza, 1970.

336. Payeras, Mario. *Los días de la selva*. Havana: Casa de las Américas, 1981.

337. Peña Bravo, Raúl. *Hecos y dichos del general Barrientos*. La Paz: n.p., 1982.

338. Pérez, Ponciana (known as Chana la Vieja). Public testimony in *Cuba*, Havana, May–June 1970.

339. Pérez Valle, Eduardo. *El martirio del héroe. La muerte de Sandino*. Managua: Banco Central, 1980.

340. Perlman, Janice, E. *O mito da marginalidade. Favelas e política no Rio de Janeiro*. Rio de Janeiro: Paz e Terra, 1981.

341. Perón, Juan Domingo. *Tres revoluciones militares*. Buenos Aires: Síntesis, 1974.

342. Pineda, Virginia Gutiérriz de, *et al. El gamín*. Bogotá: UNICEF/Instituto Colombiano de Bienestar Familiar, 1978.

343. Pinto, L. A. Costa. *Lutas de famílias no Brasil*. São Paulo: Editora Nacional, 1949.

344. Pocaterra, José Rafael. *Memorias de un venezolano de la decadencia*. Caracas: Monte Ávila, 1979.

345. Politzer, Patricia. *Miedo en Chile*. (Testimonies of Moy de Tohá and others.) Santiago de Chile: CESOC, 1985.

346. Pollak-Eltz, Angelina. "María Lionza, mito y culto venezolano," in *Montalbán*, No. 2, Caracas, UCAB, 1973.

347. Poniatowska, Elena. *La noche de Tlatelolco*. Mexico City: Era, 1984.

348. Portela, Fernando, and Cláudio Bojunga. *Lampião. O cangaceiro e o outro*. São Paulo: Traço, 1982.
349. Pound, Ezra, *Selected Cantos*. New York: New Directions, 1970.
350. Powers, Thomas. *The Man Who Kept the Secrets: Richard Helms and the CIA*. New York: Knopf, 1979.
351. Presidency of the Republic of Haiti. Law of April 29, 1969. Palais National, Port-au-Prince.
352. Queiroz, María Isaura Pereira de. *Os cangaceiros*. São Paulo: Duas Cidades, 1977.
353. ———. *História do cangaço*. São Paulo: Global, 1982.
354. Querejazu Calvo, Roberto, *Masamaclay. Historia política, diplomática y militar de la guerra del Chaco*. Cochabamba and La Paz: Amigos del Libro, 1981.
355. Quijano, Aníbal. *Introducción a Mariátegui*. Mexico City: Era, 1982.
356. Quijano, Carlos. Various articles from *Cuadernos de Marcha*, Mexico City and Montevideo: CEUAL, 1984–85.
357. Quiroga, Horacio. *Selección de cuentos*. (Preface by Emir Rodríguez Monegal.) Montevideo: Ministerio de Instrucción Pública, 1966.
358. ———. *Sobre literatura*. (Preface by Roberto Ibáñez.) Montevideo: Arca, 1970.
359. Quiroz Otero, Ciro. *Vallenato. Hombre y canto*. Bogotá: Icaro, 1983.
360. Rama, Ángel. *Las máscaras democráticas del modernismo*. Montevideo: Fundación Ángel Rama, 1985.
361. Ramírez, Sergio, ed. *Augusto C. Sandino. El pensamiento vivo*. Managua: Nueva Nicaragua, 1984.
362. ———. *Estás en Nicaragua*. Barcelona: Muchnik, 1985.
363. Ramírez, Pedro Felipe. *La vida maravillosa del Siervo de Dios*. Caracas: n.p., 1985.
364. Ramos, Graciliano. *Memórias do cárcere*. Rio de Janeiro: José Olympio, 1954.
365. Ramos, Jorge Abelardo. *Revolución y contrarevolución en la Argentina*. Buenos Aires: Plus Ultra, 1976.
366. Rangel, Domingo Alberto. *Gómez, el amo del poder*. Caracas: Vadell, 1980.
367. Recinos, Adrián, trans. *Popol Vuh. Las antiguas historias del Quiché*. Mexico City: FCE, 1976.
368. Reed, John. *Insurgent Mexico*. New York: Simon and Schuster, 1969.
369. Rendón, Armando B. *Chicano manifesto*. New York: Macmillan, 1971.
370. Rengifo, Antonio. "Esbozo biográfico de Ezequiel Urviola y Rivero," in *Los movimientos campesinos en el Perú, 1879–1965*. Lima: Delva, 1977.
371. *Retrato do Brasil*. (Various authors.) São Paulo: Tres, 1984.
372. See 445a.

373. Revueltas, José. *México 68: Juventud y revolución.* Mexico City, Era, 1978.
374. Ribeiro, Berta G. "O mapa etno-histórico de Curt Nimuendajú," in *Revista de Antropologia,* Vol. XXV, São Paulo: Universidad, 1982.
375. Ribeiro, Darcy. *Os índios e a civilização.* Petrópolis: Vozes, 1982.
376. ————. Reception Speech on the Occasion of Receiving Doctorate honoris causa at the University of Paris VII, May 3, 1979; in *Módulo,* Rio de Janeiro, 1979.
377. ————. *Ensaios insólitos.* Porto Alegre: L y PM, 1979.
378. ————. *Aos trancos e barrancos. Como o Brasil deu no que deu.* Rio de Janeiro: Guanabara, 1986.
379. Rivera, Jorge B. "Discépolo," in *Cuadernos de Crisis,* No. 3, Buenos Aires, December 1973.
380. Roa Bastos, Augusto. *Hijo de hombre.* Buenos Aires: Losada, 1960.
381. Robeson, Paul. *Paul Robeson Speaks.* (Edited and with preface by Philip S. Foner.) Secaucus: Citadel, 1978.
382. Robinson, David. *Buster Keaton.* Bloomington: University of Indiana Press, 1970.
383. ————. *Chaplin: His Life and Art.* London: Collins, 1985.
384. Rockefeller, David. Letter to Gen. Jorge Rafael Videla, in *El Periodista,* No. 71, Buenos Aires, January 17–23, 1986.
385. Rodman, Selden. *Renaissance in Haiti: Popular Painters in the Black Republic.* New York: Pellegrini and Cudahy, 1948.
386. Rodó, José Enrique. *Ariel.* Madrid: Espasa-Calpe, 1971.
387. Rodríguez, Antonio. *A History of Mexican Mural Painting.* London: Thames and Hudson, 1969.
388. Rodríguez, Carlos. "Astiz el ángel exterminador," in *Madres de Plaza de Mayo,* No. 2, Buenos Aires, January 1985.
389. Rodríguez Monegal, Emir. *Sexo y poesía en el 900.* Montevideo: Alfa, 1969.
390. ————. *El desterrado. Vida y obra de Horacio Quiroga.* Buenos Aires: Losada, 1968.
391. Roeder, Ralph. *Hacia el México moderno: Porfirio Díaz.* Mexico City: FCE, 1973.
392. Rojas, Marta. *El que debe vivir.* Havana: Casa de las Américas, 1978.
393. Román, José. *Maldito país.* Managua: El pez y la serpiente, 1983.
394. Rosencof, Mauricio. Statement to Mercedes Ramírez and Laura Oreggioni, in *Asamblea,* No. 38, Montevideo, April 1985.
395. Rovere, Richard H. *Senator Joe McCarthy.* New York: Harcourt Brace Jovanovich, 1959.
396. Rowles, James. *El conflicto Honduras–El Salvador y el orden jurídico internacional.* San José de Costa Rica: EDUCA, 1980.

397. Rozitchner, León. *Moral burguesa y revolución*. Buenos Aires: Procyón, 1963.
398. Ruffinelli, Jorge. *El otro México. México en la obra de Traven, Lawrence y Lowry*. Mexico City: Nueva Imagen, 1978.
399. Rugama, Leonel. *La tierra es un satélite de la luna*. Managua: Nueva Nicaragua, 1983.
400. Rulfo, Juan. *Pedro Páramo* and *El llano en llamas*. Barcelona: Planeta, 1982.
401. Saia, Luiz Henrique. *Carmen Miranda*. São Paulo: Brasiliense, 1984.
402. Salamanca, Daniel. *Documentos para una historia de la guerra del Chaco*. La Paz: Don Bosco, 1951.
403. Salazar, Ruben. Articles in *Los Angeles Times*, February–August 1970.
404. Salazar Valiente, Mario. "El Salvador: crisis, dictadura, lucha, 1920–1980," in *América Latina: historia de medio siglo*. Mexico City: Siglo XXI, 1981.
405. Salvatierra, Sofonías. *Sandino o la tragedia de un pueblo*. Madrid: Talleres Europa, 1934.
406. Samper Pizano, Ernesto, *et al. Legalización de la marihuana*. Bogotá: Tercer Mundo, 1980.
407. Sampson, Anthony. *The Sovereign State of ITT*. Greenwich, Conn., Fawcett, 1974.
408. Sánchez, Gonzalo, and Donny Meertens. *Bandoleros, gamonales y campesinos. El caso de la violencia en Colombia*. Bogotá: El Áncora, 1983.
409. Sante, Luc. "Relic," in *The New York Review of Books*, Vol. 28, No. 20, New York, December 17, 1981.
410. Saume Barrios, Jesús. *Silleta de cuero*. Caracas: n.p., 1985.
411. Schaden, Egon. "Curt Nimuendajú. Quarenta anos a servico do índio brasileiro e ao estudo de suas culturas," in *Problemas brasileiros*, São Paulo, December 1973.
412. Scalabrini Ortiz, Raúl. *El hombre que está solo y espera*. Buenos Aires: Plus Ultra, 1964.
413. Schinca, Milton. *Boulevard Sarandí. Anécdotas, gentes, sucesos, del pasado montevideano*. Montevideo: Banda Oriental, 1979.
414. Schifter, Jacobo. *La fase oculta de la guerra civil en Costa Rica*. San José de Costa Rica: EDUCA, 1981.
415. Schlesinger, Arthur M. *The Thousand Days: John F. Kennedy in the White House*. Boston: Houghton Mifflin, 1965.
416. Schlesinger, Stephen, and Stephen Kinzer. *Bitter Fruit: The Untold Story of the American Coup in Guatemala*. New York: Anchor, 1983.
417. Sebreli, Juan José. *Eva Perón: ¿aventurera o militante?*. Buenos Aires: Siglo Veinte, 1966.

418. Séjourné, Laurette. *Supervivencias de un mundo mágico*. Mexico: FCE, 1953.

419. Selser, Gregorio. *El pequeño ejército loco*. Managua: Nueva Nicaragua, 1983.

420. ———. *El guatemalazo*. Buenos Aires: Iguazú, 1961.

421. ———. *¡Aquí, Santo Domingo! La tercera guerra sucia*. Buenos Aires: Palestra, 1966.

422. ———. "A veinte años del Moncada," in *Cuadernos de Marcha*, No. 72, Montevideo, July 1973.

423. ———. *El rapto de Panamá*. San José de Costa Rica: EDUCA, 1982.

424. Senna, Orlando. *Alberto Santos Dumont*. São Paulo: Brasiliense, 1984.

425. Serpa, Phocíón. *Oswaldo Cruz. El Pasteur del Brasil, vencedor de la fiebre amarilla*. Buenos Aires: Claridad, 1945.

426. Silva, Clara. *Genio y figura de Delmira Agustini*. Buenos Aires: EU-DEBA, 1968.

427. Silva, José Dias da. *Brasil, país ocupado*. Rio de Janeiro: Record, 1963.

428. Silva, Marília T. Barboza da, and Arthur L. de Oliveira Filho. *Cartola. Os tempos idos*. Rio de Janeiro: Funarte, 1983.

429. Silveira, Cid. *Café: um drama na economia nacional*. Rio de Janeiro: Civilização Brasileira, 1962.

430. Slosser, Bob. *Reagan Inside Out*. New York: World Books, 1984.

431. Smith, Earl E. T. *El cuarto piso. Relato sobre la revolución comunista de Castro*. Mexico City: Diana, 1963.

432. Sodré, Nelson Werneck. *Oscar Niemeyer*. Rio de Janeiro: Graal, 1978.

433. ———. *História militar do Brasil*. Rio de Janeiro: Civilização Brasileira, 1965.

434. Somoza Debayle, Anastasio. *Filosofía social*. (Armando Luna Sulva, ed.) Managua: Presidencia de la República, 1976.

435. Sorensen, Theodore C. *Kennedy*. New York: Harper and Row, 1965.

436. Souza, Tárik de. *O som nosso de cada dia*. Porto Alegre: L y PM, 1983.

437. Stock, Noel. *Poet in Exile: Ezra Pound*. New York: Barnes and Noble, 1964.

438. Stone, Samuel. *La dinastía de los conquistadores. La crisis del poder en la Costa Rica contemporánea*. San José de Costa Rica: EDUCA, 1982.

439. Suárez, Roberto. Statements to *El Diario* and *Hoy*, La Paz, July 3, 1983.

440. Subercaseau, Bernardo (with Patricia Stambuk and Jaime Londoño). *Violeta Parra: Gracias a la vida. Testimonios*. Buenos Aires: Galerna, 1985.

441. Taibo, Paco Ignacio II, and Roberto Vizcaíno. *El socialismo en un solo puerto, Acapulco, 1919–1923*. Mexico City: Extemporáneos, 1983.

442. Teitelboim, Volodia. *Neruda*. Madrid: Michay, 1984.

443. Tello, Antonio, and Gonzalo Otero Pizarro. *Valentino, La seducción manipulada.* Barcelona: Bruguera, 1978.
444. Tibol, Raquel. *Frida Kahlo. Crónica, testimonio y aproximaciones.* Mexico City: Cultura Popular, 1977.
445. *Time Capsule, 1927: A History of the Year Condensed from the Pages of Time.* New York: Time-Life, 1928.
445a. *Time.* "High on Cocaine: A $30 Billion U.S. Habit," July 6, 1981.
446. Toqo. *Indiomanual.* Humahuaca: Instituto de Cultura Indígena, 1985.
447. Toriello, Guillermo. *La batalla de Guatemala.* Mexico City: Cuadernos Americanos, 1955.
448. Torres, Camilo. *Cristianismo y revolución.* Mexico City: Era, 1970.
449. Touraine, Alain. *Vida y muerte del Chile popular.* Mexico City: Siglo XXI, 1974.
450. Tribunal Permanente de los Pueblos. *El caso Guatemala.* Madrid: IEP-ALA, 1984.
451. Turner, John Kenneth. *Barbarous Mexico.* Austin: Univesity of Texas Press, 1969.
452. Universidad Nacional de Río Cuarto, Córdoba, Argentina. Resolution No. 0092 of February 22, 1977, signed by rector Eduardo José Pesoa; in *Soco Soco*, No. 2, Río Cuarto, April 1986.
453. Valcárcel, Luis E. *Machu Picchu.* Buenos Aires: EUDEBA, 1964.
454. Valle-Castillo, Julio. Introduction to Rubén Darío, *Prosas políticas.* Managua: Ministerio de Cultura, 1983.
455. Vásquez Díaz, Rubén. *Bolivia a la hora del Che.* Mexico City: Siglo XXI, 1968.
456. Vásquez Lucio, Oscar E. (Siulnas). *Historia del humor gráfico y escrito en la Argentina, 1801–1939.* Buenos Aires: EUDEBA, 1985.
457. Vélez, Julio, and A. Merino. *España en César Vallejo.* Madrid: Fundamentos, 1984.
458. Viezzer, Moema. *Si me permiten hablar: testimonio de Domitila, una mujer de las minas de Bolivia.* Mexico City: Siglo XXI, 1978.
459. Vignar, Maren. "Los ojos de los pájaros." In Maren and Marcelo Vignar, *Exilio y tortura.* (Unpublished.)
460. Waksman Schinca, Daniel, *et al. La batalla de Nicaragua.* Mexico City: Bruguera, 1980.
461. Walsh, Rodolfo. Letter to the Military Junta, in *Operación masacre.* Buenos Aires: De la Flor, 1984.
462. Weinstein, Barbara. *The Amazon Rubber Boom, 1850–1920.* Stanford: Stanford University Press, 1983.
463. Wettstein, Germán. "La tradición de la Paradura del Niño," in *Geomundo* (special edition on Venezuela), Panama City: 1983.
464. White, Judith. *Historia de una ignominia: La United Fruit Company en Colombia.* Bogotá: Presencia, 1978.

465. Wise, David, and Thomas B. Ross. *The Invisible Government*. New York: Random House, 1964.
466. Witker, Alejandro. *Salvador Allende, 1908–1973. Prócer de la liberación nacional*. Mexico City: UNAM, 1980.
467. Woll, Allen L. *The Latin Image in American Film*. Los Angeles: UCLA Press, 1977.
468. Womack, John, Jr. *Zapata and the Mexican Revolution*. New York: Knopf, 1968.
469. Wyden, Peter. *Bay of Pigs: The Untold Story*. New York: Simon and Schuster, 1980.
470. Ycaza, Patricio. *Historia del movimiento obrero ecuatoriano*. Quito: Cedime, 1984.
471. Ydígoras Fuentes, Miguel (with Mario Rosenthal). *My War with Communism*. Englewood Cliffs, N.J.: Prentice-Hall, 1963.
472. Yupanqui, Atahualpa. *Aires indios*. Buenos Aires: Siglo Veinte, 1985.
473. Zavaleta Mercado, René. *El desarrollo de la conciencia nacional*. Montevideo: Diálogo, 1967.
474. ———. "Consideraciones generales sobre la historia de Bolivia, 1932–1971." In *América Latina: historia de medio siglo*, (various authors). Mexico City: Siglo XXI, 1982.
475. ———. "El estupor de los siglos," in *Quimera* No. 1, Cochabamba, September 1985.

About the Author

The author was born in Montevideo, Uruguay, in 1940. His full name is Eduardo Hughes Galeano. He entered journalism as a political caricaturist for the socialist weekly *El Sol*, signing himself "Gius," the nearest approximation to the Spanish pronunciation of his paternal surname. Later he was an editor of the weekly *Marcha*, and he edited the daily *Epoca* and various Montevideo weeklies. In 1973 he went into exile in Argentina, where he founded and edited the magazine *Crisis*. He lived in Spain from 1976 to 1984, but has now returned to Uruguay.

Among his books, *Open Veins of Latin America* (1971), *Days and Nights of Love and War* (1978), and the first two volumes of this trilogy: *Genesis* (1982) and *Faces and Masks* (1984), have been published in English, and both *Days and Nights* and *The Song of Ourselves* (a novel, 1975) have won the Cuban Casa de las Américas prizes.

About the Translator

Born in London in 1904, Cedric Belfrage came to the U.S. in 1925 and began writing about movies in Hollywood. He was a co-founder of the *National Guardian* in 1948 and its editor until 1955, when a brush with McCarthy led to his deportation. He has written ten books and novels, published in this country, including *Away from It All*, *Abide with Me*, *My Master Columbus*, and *The American Inquisition, 1945–1960*. He lives with his wife, Mary, in Cuernavaca, Mexico.